Lead Like Julius Caesar

Paul Vanderbroeck

Lead Like Julius Caesar

Timeless Leadership Lessons from History's Most Influential Leader

Paul Vanderbroeck
Geneva, Switzerland

ISBN 978-3-031-83223-9   ISBN 978-3-031-83224-6   (eBook)
https://doi.org/10.1007/978-3-031-83224-6

© The Editor(s) (if applicable) and The Author(s), under exclusive license to Springer Nature Switzerland AG 2025

This work is subject to copyright. All rights are solely and exclusively licensed by the Publisher, whether the whole or part of the material is concerned, specifically the rights of translation, reprinting, reuse of illustrations, recitation, broadcasting, reproduction on microfilms or in any other physical way, and transmission or information storage and retrieval, electronic adaptation, computer software, or by similar or dissimilar methodology now known or hereafter developed.

The use of general descriptive names, registered names, trademarks, service marks, etc. in this publication does not imply, even in the absence of a specific statement, that such names are exempt from the relevant protective laws and regulations and therefore free for general use.

The publisher, the authors and the editors are safe to assume that the advice and information in this book are believed to be true and accurate at the date of publication. Neither the publisher nor the authors or the editors give a warranty, expressed or implied, with respect to the material contained herein or for any errors or omissions that may have been made. The publisher remains neutral with regard to jurisdictional claims in published maps and institutional affiliations.

This Springer imprint is published by the registered company Springer Nature Switzerland AG
The registered company address is: Gewerbestrasse 11, 6330 Cham, Switzerland

If disposing of this product, please recycle the paper.

To my family

Preface

With my publisher, Dr Prashanth Mahagaonkar, I have been thinking about the right title for this book. We have been particularly mulling over whether to call Julius Caesar the 'most influential' or 'one of the most influential' leaders of history. Finally, I chose the former and let me tell you why.

Certainly, there have been leaders who conquered more territory or established a state or an organisation that lasted longer than the Roman Empire. Others have constructed more impressive buildings and founded a greater number of cities. Furthermore, Caesar is not the only leader who has inspired playwrights and other artists. We also know of great leaders who, unlike Caesar, had an uneventful end to their careers and managed a smooth transition of power to their successors. Yet what makes Julius Caesar stand out is the accumulation of his achievements and the legacy he left as a consequence. Indeed, as far as I can tell, he is the only one whose name became eponymic for the title of top leader: Caesar for the Roman Emperor, Kaiser for the senior monarch in the German-speaking world and Czar in Russia (plus the current quaint usage of 'czar' in the US government). Because of Julius Caesar, the concept of dictator received its modern pejorative meaning of illegitimate autocrat, even if that is not what he had intended, as will be revealed later in this book. Caesar's influence becomes tangible in the archetypes he created and the 'firsts' that are attributed to him. Crossing the Rubicon—referring to the moment when he started the civil war that propelled him to sole ruler of Rome—has become the mother of all points of no return. Caesar's dictum at that event—'let the die be cast'—is the archetype of risk-taking. 'I came, I saw, I conquered' is the archetype of the victory speech. Caesar and Cleopatra formed the archetypical power couple. Caesar initiated the first triumvirate, the mother of all political coalitions. Finally, on the Ides of March 44 BC, he left us with the mother of all political assassinations and the archetype of treacherous backstabbing. To be sure, history has produced leaders who have written letters, memos, diaries and pieces of literature. Yet Caesar wrote his *Commentaries on the Gallic War* in the saddle while it was all happening, making him the first to engage in embedded journalism. In short, Julius Caesar was a giant.

Caesar has been the object of my attention several times during my career. He was one of the individuals I researched for my PhD on the interaction between leaders and followers during Caesar's lifetime. He is central to my 2012 article, which compares the crisis of the Roman Republic with the financial crisis of 2008. Then, in 2014, he figures as Cleopatra's manager in *Leadership Strategies for Women,* my book on four historic queens. I also had the opportunity to discuss him at length with master's students during my Leadership Made in Italy course at LUISS Business School in Rome. As I have learned more about leadership, my view of him has changed over time, allowing me to see him as a more multidimensional person than I had originally thought, which deserves a study of its own.

My publisher and I thus landed on *Lead Like Julius Caesar* as the title, and this book brings together my competencies both as a historian and as a leadership expert. As the former, I can access and interpret the historical data we have at our disposal. As a leadership expert, I can evaluate Julius Caesar as I usually do in my leadership consulting and executive coaching practice. Finally, the motivation for my research is to discover what really works for leaders to make them successful in their careers and in exercising their leadership. This is also what drives me in my professional practice as a leadership expert and educator. I'm interested in identifying what gets practical results, and this book provides answers to just that.

This book would have been difficult to achieve without the generous help and support I have received from the individuals mentioned here. First of all, I am greatly indebted to Oriane Kets de Vries, Managing Director of KDVI, and to Dr Maria Brown, Head of Research and Education at MRG® for permitting me to use their respective instruments experientially. However, it is important to note that this should not be interpreted in any way as an endorsement or a recommendation on their part for using KDVI's and MRG®'s instruments as I have done in this book.

Numerous coaching colleagues—expert in using KDVI's GELM—have given me helpful and generous feedback on applying this instrument to Julius Caesar's behaviour, without limiting themselves to this aspect, for which I owe them my sincere thanks: Coen Aalders, Alicia Cheak, Peter Boback, Fabiana Diaz-Gufler, Claire Finch, Dr Elizabeth Florent Treacy, Hanneke Frese,

Margot Schumacher, Martine Vandenpoel and Christina von Wackerbath. Maria Brown kindly gave me access to MRG°'s research material, and she and her colleagues at MRG° provided helpful feedback, for which I am grateful.

I am honoured and most obliged that Professor Robert Morstein-Marx from the University of California, Santa Barbara, read the manuscript draft. As an historian myself, I consider Professor Morstein-Marx as Julius Caesar's foremost contemporary biographer, and his comments, feedback and corrections have given me confidence that at least this book's historical aspect is sound. Thank you, Bob, your input has been most precious. I am indebted to Professor Martin Gutmann from the Lucerne University of Applied Sciences and Arts, with whom I share an interest in the history of leadership, for his encouragement and for sharing his knowledge on the theory and methodology of bringing history and leadership studies together.

Four leaders from different generations and professions—Elizabeth Armstrong, Joëlle Comé, Jack Horsburgh and Arjan Overwater—graciously read the manuscript. Their comments and suggestions have been immensely helpful. My wife Joëlle and my children Magdalena and Joseph have encouraged me greatly and consistently to pursue this project, and I am glad they did. Joseph's feedback, notably on how to use illustrations, demonstrates well that his talent matches his ambition to become a teacher. Finally, here's a shout-out to the numerous members of my network who have helped me choose the title and the cover of this book.

To conclude this preface, I would like to emphasise that if there are any errors or inaccuracies in this book, they are my own and I bear full responsibility.

Geneva, Switzerland Paul Vanderbroeck
Rome, Italy
December 2024

Competing Interests The author has no competing interests to declare that are relevant to the content of this manuscript.

Endorsements

'This book stands out because it systematically analyses Caesar's behavior, career and personality through the lens of modern leadership theories. As a result, its conclusions are more profound and insightful than you usually get from a biography of a successful leader. A must-read for both junior and senior leaders who are looking for an inspiring benchmark.'
 —Jean-François Manzoni, *Professor of Leadership & Organizational Development and former President, IMD International, Lausanne, Switzerland*

'This book about the making of Julius Caesar is an enlightening exploration into leadership development. The lesson for our times is that leaders are made as much from their low points as their "highs". That they learn as much from failure as from success, and harness the lessons to master the next challenge. You'll never read history quite the same again…'
 —Avivah Wittenberg-Cox, *CEO, 20-first, London, UK*

'It is a brilliant idea to teach leadership through the life of probably the most famous leader in history—Julius Caesar. Paul Vanderbroeck pulls this off with the insights of a leadership expert combined with the eye for detail of a historian.'
 —Alex Hungate, *President & COO, Grab Holdings Inc., Singapore*

'Lead Like Julius Caesar: Timeless Leadership Lessons from History's Most Influential Leader masterfully bridges the ancient and modern worlds, delivering a fresh take on Caesar's legendary life and leadership. By blending rich historical context with contemporary leadership models and frameworks, this book offers a rare dual perspective that brings to life Caesar's behavioural complexities that led to his extraordinary triumphs and contributed to his ultimate downfall. With its engaging narrative and

actionable insights, this is a must-read for those seeking to learn from the past to lead more collaboratively and effectively in today's dynamic world.'
—Rev. Dr. Susan Goldsworthy OLY, *Affiliate Professor, Leadership, Communications & Organizational Change, IMD International, Lausanne, Switzerland*

'Paul Vanderbroeck's comprehensive exploration of Julius Caesar's leadership is an exceptional fusion of history and leadership theory. By delving into Caesar's remarkable journey—from his turbulent early years to his pinnacle as a powerful leader—this book offers a profound and actionable case study for leaders at all stages of their careers. Through rigorous application of proven leadership models, Paul dissects Caesar's strengths, vulnerabilities, and transformative decisions. Readers are invited not to imitate but to learn from Caesar's successes and missteps, applying these insights to their own leadership challenges. The book is particularly valuable for its nuanced exploration of how Caesar's leadership evolved across distinct phases, from ambitious young strategist to a leader navigating the complexities of absolute power. By combining academic depth with practical application, this book transcends a mere historical narrative. It serves as a strategic guide for leaders, offering tools to reflect, adapt, and grow. Whether you are a seasoned executive or an aspiring leader, this engaging and insightful read promises to sharpen your understanding of leadership dynamics and inspire your personal development.

A must-read for mastering the art of leadership.'
—Artur Umerkaev. *Director Life Sciences, Capgemini, Switzerland*

'Self-to-prototype comparisons are a powerful tool for deciding whether to become a leader or what kind of a leader to be. This book is a fascinating self-development tool that invites the reader to use Caesar not as an example of effective or ineffective leadership, but rather an opportunity to look at oneself as an emerging, established, or evolving leader.'
—Prof. Konstantin Korotov, PhD, *Professor of Organizational Development, Founder of the ESMT Coaching Colloquia, ESMT Berlin, Germany.*

Contents

1 **Mapping a Leadership Biography: Set-Up and Approach**   1
    1.1 Why This Book and Why Julius Caesar?   1
    1.2 The Context of a Leader: Rome in the First Century BC   3
    1.3 Methods and Theories: Evaluating a Leader and a Leader's Career   10
       1.3.1 Leadership Behaviour: The Global Executive Leadership Mirror   11
       1.3.2 Leadership Career: The Leadership Pipeline   14
       1.3.3 Leadership Personality: The Individual Directions Inventory™   16
       1.3.4 History, Leadership and Organisational Behaviour   16
    1.4 What Is in this Book and What Is Not   18
    Bibliography   19

2 **The Making of a Leader: Caesar's Early Life and Education**   23
    2.1 Caesar's Youth and Early Life Experiences   24
    2.2 Career Beginnings   31
    2.3 Expectations and First Achievements   33
    2.4 Leadership Behaviours   38
       2.4.1 Leading Self   39
       2.4.2 Leading Stakeholders and Networks   40

	2.5	Career Development: The Identification of a High Potential	41
	2.6	What Aspiring Leaders Can Learn from the Dawn of Caesar's Career	44
		Bibliography	46
3	**Rising Above the Fray: From High Potential to Leader**		**47**
	3.1	Caesar's Life and Mid-Career	48
	3.2	Caesar's Mid-Career Achievements	54
		3.2.1 Performance in Different Roles	54
		3.2.2 Building a Leadership Organisation to Mobilise Followers	58
	3.3	Caesar's Mid-Career Leadership Behaviours	63
		3.3.1 Leading Self	63
		3.3.2 Leading Teams	66
		3.3.3 Leading Organisations	66
		3.3.4 Leading Stakeholders and Networks	68
	3.4	Caesar's Career Development	68
		3.4.1 Career Competition	68
		3.4.2 Leadership Brand and Reputation	76
		3.4.3 Leadership Pipeline	78
	3.5	What Leaders Can Learn from the Middle Stage of Caesar's Career	84
		Bibliography	86
4	**Proving His Mettle: The Conquest of Gaul**		**89**
	4.1	Life Abroad	90
	4.2	Caesar's Achievements in Gaul and in Rome	91
		4.2.1 Winning the War	92
		4.2.2 Winning the Peace	99
		4.2.3 Winning the Home Front	101
	4.3	Caesar's Leadership During the Gallic War	105
		4.3.1 Leading Self	106
		4.3.2 Leading Teams	107
		4.3.3 Leading the Organisation	111
		4.3.4 Leading Stakeholders and Networks	112

	4.4	Caesar's Career Development During the Gallic War	113
	4.5	What Leaders Can Learn from Caesar's Assignment in Gaul	118
	Bibliography		120
5	**No Turning Back: How Followers Can Push a Leader into Crossing the Rubicon**		**123**
	5.1	Caesar's Challenges and Achievements in the Civil War	124
		5.1.1 Preventing a Civil War	124
		5.1.2 Winning the Civil War	129
	5.2	Caesar's Leadership During the Civil War	137
		5.2.1 Leading Self	137
		5.2.2 Leading Teams	138
		5.2.3 Leading Organisations	140
		5.2.4 Leading Stakeholders and Networks	143
	5.3	Caesar's Career Development During the Civil War	143
	5.4	What Leaders Can Learn from Caesar as a Military Leader During the Civil War	145
	Bibliography		148
6	**Alone at the Top: Chairman and CEO**		**151**
	6.1	The Final Stretch to the Top	153
	6.2	Caesar's Vision and Achievements	159
		6.2.1 Establishing Order in Italy: Winning the Peace	159
		6.2.2 Establishing Peace in the Provinces: Safeguarding the Empire's Security and Stability	165
		6.2.3 Establishing Prosperity in the Empire: Creating a Sustainable Future	167
	6.3	Caesar's Leadership Behaviours at the Top	168
		6.3.1 Leading Self	168
		6.3.2 Leading Teams	172
		6.3.3 Leading the Organisation	179
		6.3.4 Leading Stakeholders and Networks	180
	6.4	The End of a Career	181
	6.5	What Top Leaders Can Learn from the Final Chapter of Caesar's Career	185
	Bibliography		187

7	**Becoming a Leader: Caesar's Leadership Development**		189
	7.1 Leading Self		190
		7.1.1 Emotional Intelligence	190
		7.1.2 Being Exemplary	191
		7.1.3 Tenacity and Courage	191
	7.2 Leading Teams		191
		7.2.1 Coaching and Feedback	191
		7.2.2 Empowering	192
		7.2.3 Team Building	192
	7.3 Leading the Organisation		193
		7.3.1 Ability to Execute	193
		7.3.2 Change Orientation	193
		7.3.3 Energising	194
		7.3.4 Visioning	194
	7.4 Leading Stakeholders and Networks		195
		7.4.1 Clients and Stakeholders	195
		7.4.2 Networks and Alliances	195
	7.5 How Did Caesar's Leadership Develop over Time?		196
	Bibliography		197
8	**Being a Leader: Caesar's Leadership Personality**		199
	8.1 Affiliating		201
		8.1.1 Giving	201
		8.1.2 Receiving	202
		8.1.3 Belonging	202
		8.1.4 Expressing	202
	8.2 Attracting		203
		8.2.1 Gaining Stature	203
		8.2.2 Entertaining	203
	8.3 Perceiving		204
		8.3.1 Creating	204
		8.3.2 Interpreting	204
	8.4 Mastering		204
		8.4.1 Excelling	205
		8.4.2 Enduring	205
		8.4.3 Structuring	205
	8.5 Challenging		206
		8.5.1 Manoeuvring	206
		8.5.2 Winning	206
		8.5.3 Controlling	206

	8.6	Maintaining	207
		8.6.1 Stability	207
		8.6.2 Independence	207
		8.6.3 Irreproachability	207
	8.7	Caesar's Motivational Pattern	208
	Bibliography	211

9 Conclusion 213

About the Author

Paul Vanderbroeck, PhD is a Swiss-Dutch historian, leadership scholar, and executive coach. He has accompanied many leaders and high-potential individuals across the world in their leadership careers. Among his publications are two business books: *Leadership Strategies for Women* (Springer, 2014) and *The International Career Couple Handbook* (2021). He has co-created a theatre play on women leaders. He is married, father of two adult children and currently lives in Geneva.

Mail: paul@pvdb.ch

1

Mapping a Leadership Biography: Set-Up and Approach

As a reader, you have the option to read specific sections of this introductory chapter. If you are interested in understanding the historical context before diving into Caesar's life and career, Sect. 1.2 is your guide. Section 1.3 explains the leadership concepts that serve to evaluate Caesar's career and leadership. You can learn about them now or revisit them once you see them being applied in the subsequent chapters. For those with a particular interest in the theoretical underpinning of this book, Sect. 1.4 is indispensable. For a comprehensive understanding of this book's essence and structure, the first and the last sections are recommended.

1.1 Why This Book and Why Julius Caesar?

Writing about Julius Caesar, one of history's most compelling figures, presents a challenge and an opportunity. His name alone conjures images of military genius, political manoeuvring and both spectacular triumph and tragic downfall. But why is Caesar still relevant for a modern audience, particularly for today's leaders? Why does he deserve yet another biography, especially one aimed at leadership development? These are the questions this book aims to address and answer.

As a biographer, it is impossible not to form a connection with one's subject. Whether it is a fascination with the ruthless ambition of a figure like Stalin or the admiration that might be felt for Napoleon's monumental achievements, the biographer is inevitably drawn into the lives he or she chronicles. My connection to Caesar is no different. I hold a positive view of him, a man whose talent for leadership I find both captivating and instructive, as I am fascinated by all talented leaders and how they interact with their followers. But this book is not merely an expression of my admiration. By looking at Caesar's life and work through a modern lens, I attempt to understand the leadership of one of history's most successful and ultimately tragic figures.

The book you hold in your hands is unique because it profiles Julius Caesar and approaches him through the rigorous application of three well-recognised leadership, personality and career development models. Systematically comparing Caesar to the many leaders that lie at the basis of these models allows for a deeper understanding of Caesar's strengths and successes, as well as his weaknesses and failures. In addition, this approach helps identify explanations for behaviour from the perspective of motivational drivers and how that personality was forged by life and professional experiences as strongly as it was by professional development. Finally, by applying a model for career development in an organisational setting, we can understand the career path of an individual whose professional ambition was to reach the top of his organisation.

As someone who has spent years helping leaders maximise their potential, I have found that the key to effective leadership is leveraging strengths while acknowledging vulnerabilities. With all his brilliance and flaws, Caesar provides a perfect case study for this kind of reflection. His rise to power and, ultimately, his assassination—at the hands of those he trusted—illustrate how even the most talented leaders can falter if they fail to become aware of their own weaknesses.

Moreover, this book does not limit itself to Caesar's leadership in a particular period (e.g. 'the Gallic War') or during a specific event (e.g. 'the Battle of Pharsalus') but considers how it changed over time. In this way, it offers a comprehensive review of Caesar's leadership throughout his career, examining how his personal attributes, experiences, choices and professional context shaped his approach to leadership and, ultimately, his fate. As Yuval Noah Harari claims, history is the study of change.

This approach is valuable for today's leaders because it emphasises learning. By observing Caesar's behaviours and decisions and applying proven leadership models to interpret them, we can distil actionable insights. This is not a call to imitate Caesar—it is risky to generalise behaviour from a single case study with its unique features, context and events. Instead, this book invites readers to engage with Caesar's life as a benchmark, as one of many possible case studies of the complexities of leadership. By examining what drove his decisions, what behaviours led to his success and what missteps precipitated his downfall, readers are encouraged to reflect on their own leadership journeys. When working with groups of leaders, I have seen how effective comparing oneself to the successes, failures, vicissitudes and drivers of other leaders can be for learning. Benchmarking against Julius Caesar is of particular value because his is an imperfect success story, which makes him both an inspirational and a realistic case study.

This book's methodology is grounded in a practical approach to leadership development. The leadership models employed throughout this book are not merely theoretical; they have been tested and proven through years of application in the context of modern leadership development. By evaluating Caesar's career using these models, we go beyond mere biography and create a compelling case study in leadership behaviour and career development that resonates with the challenges of leadership today.

Therefore, this book allows leaders, both novice and accomplished, to develop personal scenarios for their professional future. By approaching Caesar's biography as a case study to analyse his career, personality and leadership competencies, one can discover one's own drivers and learn how to become an effective leader and develop a successful career. Leadership development professionals can use Caesar as a benchmark for the leaders they are supporting so as to be better equipped to foresee the potential outcomes of particular behaviours, understand how personality drives action and help construct a career strategy.

This introduction offers an overview of the context in which Caesar lived and worked; an explanation of the models employed to evaluate Caesar's behaviour, career and personality; an account of where this study fits in academic research and, at the end, a few words on how to read the book.

1.2   The Context of a Leader: Rome in the First Century BC

The context in which a leader develops and operates provides both challenges and opportunities. However, context should not be seen as unchangeable. My work with many leaders has confirmed the value of Situational Leadership theory, as espoused by Hershey and Blanchard. This theory demonstrates how leadership success depends on adapting one's behaviour to the situation, that is, one's context. Importantly, I have also observed the opposite: some exceptionally talented leaders can adapt the context to their behaviour, thus creating an entirely new context. This was what happened with Julius Caesar towards the end of his career, although he may not have fully realised it.

The different sub-contexts, in which Caesar developed and exercised his leadership as well as the important changes within these sub-contexts are explained. Of all of these, the organisational context is the most relevant for studying the interplay between leader and followers and between leader and stakeholders; this holds for leadership development in an organisational setting as well. This book analyses the career development of an individual whose professional ambition was to develop a formal leadership career at the highest levels, which by definition requires an organisational structure. In Caesar's case, that was the Roman Republic.

Spatial Context: Rome's emergence as the only superpower on both shores of the Mediterranean in the century before Caesar's birth (100 BC), after eliminating Carthage as its main competitor, was a significant contextual development. In that period, Roman territory had tripled; during Caesar's lifetime, the empire doubled in size yet again, effectively ruling the entire Mediterranean basin and a significant portion of Western Europe. Well before Caesar's birth, the Mediterranean had become busy with maritime traffic, and trade routes flourished. The Romans built a network of roads through Italy (Italia in Latin) that transported troops, goods and people rapidly across the peninsula and to and from its ports. They had also started expanding this network into the provinces.

According to Dionysius, a Greek author who relocated from Halicarnassus in Asia Minor to Rome in the First Century BC, the Roman empire's extraordinary greatness manifested itself above all in three things: its aqueducts, paved roads and drainage or sewer system. Indeed, the Roman Republic's capital was well on its way to becoming the largest urban centre in the Mediterranean world, its growth made possible by the expansion of the empire. The Tiber River and the highways Rome built connected the capital to the sea and the rest of Italy. Interestingly, the city, where Caesar grew up, lacked a protective wall since the Romans relied on their armed forces for protection. Rome had approximately 750,000 inhabitants, most of whom lived densely packed in high-rise apartment blocks in busy streets lined with shops and street-food stalls. The houses of the rich were built on the cooler hilltops, whilst the Roman Forum occupied the city's centre. The Forum had open spaces, temples and government buildings such as the Senate House. Pop-up theatres and arenas offered performances and gladiator combats. The one permanent entertainment structure was the massive Circus Maximus, used for chariot racing and live animal hunts.

Economic Context: The Roman economy was to a large extent based on agriculture, which depended on manual labour. As a pre-industrial economy, there was little opportunity to increase productivity. Furthermore, Rome,

Italy and the conquered territories functioned as a single market, which did stimulate growth through trade; pottery manufacture; and oil, wine and wool production. Raw materials and commodities—but also objects of art—were transported across the Mediterranean. Landownership was the primary source of wealth.

During the second and first centuries BC, however, the economy changed significantly—conquests brought great wealth to Rome in the forms of booty, foreign taxes, confiscated land and slaves. Its citizens drew substantial dividends, both direct and indirect, from the empire, mainly through three channels. First, annexed land and taxes went into the state treasury and were redistributed as plots of land for veterans, food subsidies and tax relief for the Roman people. Next, many private businesses created jobs by providing supplies and services to the Roman government and military and through corporate growth because of increased trade opportunities. Third, generals and provincial governors reinvested their revenues in the military, construction projects and putting on public games or spectacles, thus providing dividends to the 'shareholders' through generating jobs, town planning and providing entertainment. Rome's citizens, who had an active say in political decision-making, were acutely aware of their power and had a strong sense of ownership regarding the Roman empire. They were proud to belong to a winning organisation, or the 'Number One' empire.

Institutional Context: The Roman Republic was governed by a hierarchy of elected public officials (magistrates), an advisory council (the Senate) and popular assemblies. Only male citizens could hold public office, be a senator or vote in the popular assemblies. Magistrates included consuls, praetors, aediles, quaestors and tribunes of the plebs. Consuls held the highest office and were responsible for the state's general administration and military command. In contrast, the tribunes of the plebs, whose role was to balance the power distribution by representing the lower classes' interests, wielded significant influence through their veto rights. All Roman magistrates were subject to annuity (one-year tenure) and collegiality (sharing power with at least one colleague). In this way, the one kept the other in check; thus, no one could exercise the same authority for too long. The magistrates, including the tribunes of the plebs, were members of the Senate. Magistrates did not receive a salary. They were, however, allocated a small staff of civil servants and in the execution of their office they often had to contribute from their own private means.

The Senate was the most powerful institution, with lifelong membership reserved for those who had held public office. The Republic was oligarchic in practice, with the Senate controlling foreign affairs and finances and advising on legislation. However, the People had a significant voice in elections and legislation; hence, decisions were formally in the name of the Senate and People of Rome (SPQR). Rome's voting system in the popular assemblies was highly stratified and skewed towards the wealthy. The *comitia centuriata*, which was organised hierarchically by wealth and property, elected the highest officials with votes favouring the propertied classes. The *comitia tributa*, in contrast, was more representative of the citizenry and handled most legislation. Figure 1.1 gives an overview of the key institutions of the Roman Republic.

Another significant change that impacted Caesar's context was increased competition for the Roman government's top two positions (consul and praetor). Recently, the pool of citizens and therefore candidates for office had increased by granting citizenship to most inhabitants of Italy. This change was particularly relevant for those who had the time and money to travel to Rome and participate in politics. Some of these men saw their careers benefit from the number of senators doubling from 300 to 600 and the number of junior—though not senior—offices increasing. Consequently, the odds of any given senator winning the consulship, the highest position, rose from 1:150 each year to 1:300. This boost in competition led to a more dynamic political landscape, with more voices and perspectives being represented in the government.

Despite all this, the processes and procedures remained at the level of a city-state. Boundaries between roles and responsibilities sometimes blurred and therefore could have been clearer. This worked well when it was possible to oversee the organisation and when critical stakeholders could meet and

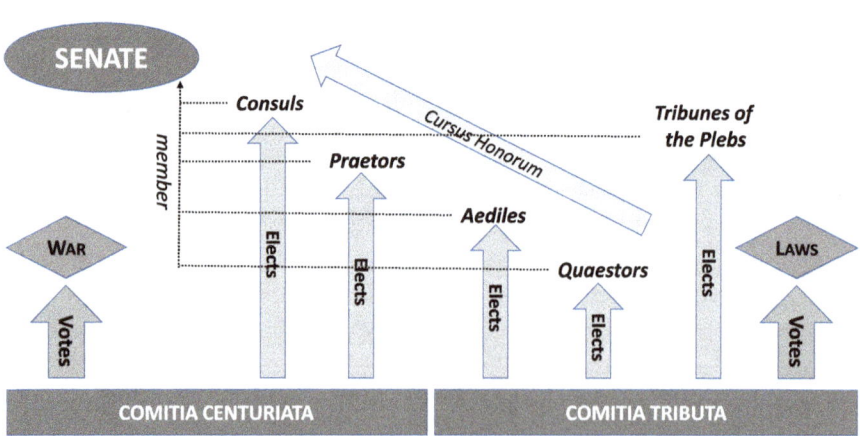

Fig. 1.1 Key institutions of the Roman Republic 100 BC. Author's own illustration

discuss issues. However, Rome's rapid territorial expansion created significant administrative and logistical challenges. Despite the empire's vast resources, its internal systems remained underdeveloped, leading to inefficiencies in governance and control. For instance, in 50 BC, Rome and the provinces were administered by about 60 magistrates. Unclear boundaries could not contain competition or resolve conflicts of interest; this weakness was exploited by individuals who wanted to leverage their own economic or political interests. This lack of oversight also extended to Roman's urban environment itself, where citizens suffered from poor living conditions, crime and economic disparity. Undermanaged, the state found it difficult to ensure an uninterrupted food supply or provide affordable housing in the growing city of Rome. Some politicians, starting with the Gracchi brothers in the 120 s BC, were effective at mobilising the citizen's discontent, encouraging protests and attending the popular assembly to vote in their favour.

Social Context: The Roman upper stratum was composed of two groups—senators and *equites*—which essentially belonged to one status group. Admittance into the equestrian order required having a minimum amount of property. Access to the senate was open to members of the equestrian order who had held a magistracy belonging to the *cursus honorum*. Among senators, the *nobiles* formed the top elite, the actual oligarchical nucleus. The nobles belonged to families that produced most of the higher magistrates. Interestingly and importantly, senators' social status and prestige were not bestowed by heredity. Thus, to remain part of the senatorial elite, families of the Roman upper class constantly had to prove themselves through election to the highest magistracies, military commands and by serving the Republic successfully. This resulted in permanent competition for the offices, which was further enhanced by the lucrative opportunities offered by a provincial assignment after having served in Rome.

Roman political life was therefore not just about policies and ideologies but was deeply intertwined with personal networks and friendships. These networks, strengthened through mutual services, social entertainment, marriages and kinship ties, were the backbone of political alliances. The nobles, advantaged in the elections due to their prestige and capacity to mobilise resources, often formed alliances based on these personal ties rather than around shared beliefs. Moreover, competition bred jealousy over social status, so the nobles tried to keep newcomers out. Entering into the elite became increasingly difficult for outsiders.

At the lowest stratum of society were the free citizens, of which only the men had the right to vote and participate in the popular assemblies. This demographic was highly economically differentiated, ranging from wealthy farmers, artisans and shopkeepers to day labourers. At the very bottom and without any rights at all were the slaves. Once freed, however, they were enfranchised.

During Caesar's life time, the Roman legionaries became a social group of their own. Caesar's uncle Marius transformed the Roman armed forces into a volunteer army, ultimately resulting in a professional military. Poor citizens joined to earn a living. Over time, soldiers' income depended increasingly on the share in the booty they received from their general and a plot of land after retirement. Agrarian laws regarding distributing land to veterans were a frequent point of contention between generals and their political opponents. Officers were often recruited from the Italian upper class, which, though having been recently enfranchised, was integrated into the Roman elite only with difficulty. As a result, officers settled for the best career available to them. Gradually, such developments shifted loyalties among the armed forces from the Roman state to the individual commander. Military leaders, therefore, could use their armies to gain political power, which several times resulted in civil war.

Political Context: Political parties, in the sense of an organised group of individuals whose concerted action is independent of the issues being discussed, did not exist. For particular political problems, ad hoc coalitions were formed between families and their supporters or between politicians and an interest group like veterans, tax farmers or city dwellers. Nevertheless, there was some continuity concerning the membership of political factions and their leaders, who built their influence on specific constituencies through distinct political methodologies. During the late Republic, two groupings were active. The first was called the *populares*, which, as its name indicates, sought the People's support through the popular assembly by serving their interests. This was often done by pushing, for instance, land distribution, grain subsidies or debt relief. The other was the *optimates*, comprising those who believed in the oligarchy's primacy and influenced the political process via the Senate. The conflict, which was also a vehicle for competition within the elite, between these two factions increasingly culminated in violence and civil strife.

The members of the Roman elite were no strangers to conflict, often resorting to lawsuits to settle political differences and feuds. The competitive nature of Roman politics, combined with the high financial stakes of election campaigns, fostered a culture of corruption. Politicians sought financial backing from private interests, such as merchants and government suppliers, in exchange for political favours. Once in office, these politicians were often compelled to repay their debts by allocating contracts and resources to their supporters, further entangling public governance with private interests.

Organisational Context: The Roman Republic knew one formal career system: the *cursus honorum* from quaestor to consul, interspaced with assignments in the provinces and the army. Initially, it was meritocratic; performance was crucial for getting elected to the next office in the hierarchy. Originally, the system was intended to create generalists to rule the state, and it had served the Republic well. This structure was an important reason why Rome survived and grew during its first 500 years.

This traditional generalist career path, oscillating between growing political responsibility in the *cursus honorum* and provincial assignments, remained the most prestigious. Furthermore, it is the one Julius Caesar followed. Yet, in the late Republic, competing for public office led to skyrocketing campaign costs, outpacing even the wealthiest senators' revenues. The growing opportunities for profit from Rome's military campaigns and resource-rich provinces drove candidates to spend heavily, hoping to recover their losses afterward. This resulted in a rivalry cycle and imperial expansion. Many senators and their family members invested in the companies that supplied the state and the army with services, thus creating a stake in Rome's conquests and provinces.

The increasing size and complexity of the Roman state also offered opportunities for professional differentiation, particularly for those who found the traditional career path challenging or less attractive. New career tracks thus evolved. For instance, young nobles and social newcomers from outside the city specialised as military officers or in the legal profession. At the top level were individuals who choose military careers, with occasional political participation, to acquire further military commands (e.g. Pompey, Caesar's ally and later adversary). Others focused on political careers based on bringing forward legislation and political reform while occasionally accepting a military assignment to enhance their chances of being elected to the next level of the magisterial hierarchy: For example Cato, Caesar's nemesis; Cicero, the thought leader and orator; and Clodius, the popular leader. Or consider someone like Crassus, the business tycoon who sometimes assumed political office to further his own business interests.

Social differentiation allowed leaders to mobilise various followers: the urban poor, urban middle class, rural citizens, soldiers, veterans, business owners, socially mobile newcomers, senators and nobles. Such men often had individual interests and therefore competed for resources. If anything, this reality made the exercise of leadership more complex.

Ideological Context: For most of the Republic, the balance of power among magistrates, the Senate and popular assemblies had been functioning well for all stakeholders. There was a consensus that this was the best system. However, the expansion, influx of wealth and undermanaged public administration placed great pressure on this equilibrium. Increasingly, it became clear that the succession of problems due to elite competition, political conflict, social differentiation and economic crises could only be resolved by reforming the entire system. As a result, consensus broke down and conforming to the elite's traditional norms and values decreased. The Roman upper class therefore became increasingly individualistic. Conventional ties of mutual solidarity between the elite and the lower classes weakened, and social groups started vying for their own interests, looking to whichever political leader would offer support.

Despite such individuals, ideas for reform were voiced, and some were even implemented. Social climbers, like Cicero and the author Sallust, unsurprisingly pleaded for more social diversity in the elite to make it easier for outsiders or successful freedmen in Rome to enter the Senate and attain public office. Clodius was well on his way to making the popular assembly the most powerful body in the institutional triangle of assembly, Senate and magistrates. His political career, and his life were cut short by a political opponent. Other, more conservative thinkers, like Cato the Younger, favoured strengthening the traditional oligarchy's power and influence by reinforcing the Senate's role. As we will see, Caesar believed in concentrating power in the executive branch, that is, the magistrates, for more effective decision-making and execution.

Caesar crossed the Rubicon in 49 BC, setting off a series of civil wars that battered the empire until his adoptive son, Octavian, later known as Augustus, appointed himself the first Roman emperor in 27 BC. Augustus brought peace and stability by imposing autocracy. He established the Principate, a system of government that preserved the Republic's outward forms but concentrated real power in the domain of a single ruler. This new system ended a century of chaos and civil war that had plagued Rome, ushering in the Pax Romana and the Roman Empire's long reign.

1.3 Methods and Theories: Evaluating a Leader and a Leader's Career

To learn from Julius Caesar, we must know and understand him first. This is why *Lead Like Julius Caesar* addresses the three core questions of leadership development practice:

1. What did Caesar do? How was this behaviour helpful or not helpful for his leadership effectiveness? How did his leadership competencies develop over time?

2. How did Caesar progress his career as a leader?
3. Why did Caesar do what he did? What were his motivations and how did his personality affect his behaviour?

Next, Caesar needs to be benchmarked against other leaders so that his personality, behaviour and career can be assessed. To this end, this book draws upon three instruments, which are all based on quality research and which I have found effective in my own practice as a leadership development professional: The Global Executive Leadership Mirror (GELM®), the Leadership Pipeline and the Individual Directions Inventory™ (IDI™). The following sections explain these instruments, what they entail and how they will be applied in this book.

1.3.1 Leadership Behaviour: The Global Executive Leadership Mirror

The GELM® is an instrument developed by business school professor Manfred Kets de Vries and the Kets De Vries Institute Ltd. (KDVI), a UK-based leadership development firm. The GELM is used for 360° evaluation and measures twelve specific leadership behaviours across four main levels: Self, Teams, Organisation and Networks. KDVI's research has demonstrated that these behaviours are particularly relevant for effective leadership.

360° evaluations come essentially in two forms: a questionnaire (sometimes with additional comments from respondents) like the GELM or through interviews. In both cases, both the leader being evaluated and his or her reports or colleagues are questioned about their perceptions of that leader's behaviour in the workplace. Perhaps surprisingly, we do in fact have quite a bit of data on Julius Caesar from individuals who worked with him, including the orator and politician Cicero and the historian Sallust, who also worked for Caesar as a provincial governor. Moreover, we have reports by contemporaries such as Nicolaus of Damascus. As for self-perception, Caesar himself, and his ghost writer Aulus Hirtius, wrote entire books on his behaviour. As such, both the volume of data and the quality resemble what one could obtain from a 360° report. Still, it should be noted that because the data were not systematically collected through a tailored set of questions to a selected group of respondents, an ex-post 360° evaluation would be taking the experiment too far.

Therefore, the GELM's twelve leadership behaviours will be used as a benchmark, against which Caesar's behaviours will be classified and evaluated throughout this book. Instead of the seven-point scale of the 360° questionnaire, a three-point scale will be used for evaluation: *Strength*, when the

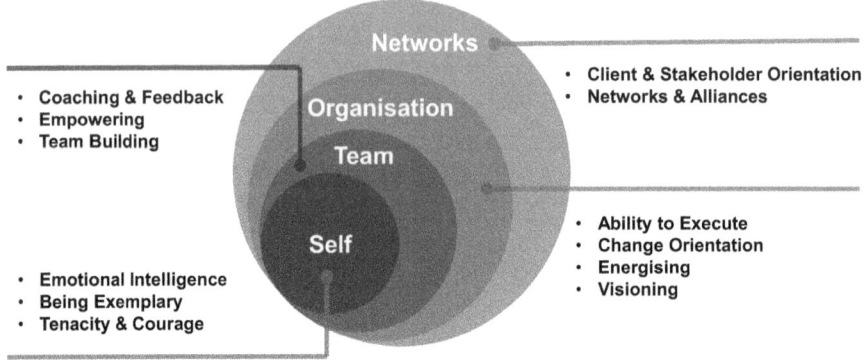

Fig. 1.2 The twelve key leadership behaviours. © KDVI. Reprinted with permission by KDVI

behaviour exceeds the requirement; *Competent* when the behaviour meets the requirement; *Needs Development* when the behaviour does not meet the requirement. This qualitative analysis will give insights into Caesar's strengths and development needs and how these developed over the different stages of his career. The definitions of the leadership behaviours that follow correspond to the Global Executive Leadership Mirror™ report with some alterations for clarity. Figure 1.2 gives an overview of the twelve leadership behaviours and the four organisational levels to which they apply.

1.3.1.1 Leading Self

Emotional Intelligence: The ability to identify, control and recognise emotions, both in oneself and, to an extent, in others. Leaders with high emotional intelligence possess strong levels of self-awareness and can recognise, understand and regulate their own emotions. In addition, they are skilful at interpreting others' emotional responses.

Being Exemplary: This means being loyal to one's own values and acting accordingly. Leaders with elevated levels of integrity are open and fair when dealing with others. In other words, what they do aligns with what they say. They accept responsibility for their actions and others consider them trustworthy.

Tenacity & Courage: Tenacity denotes the ability to work persistently towards a goal despite setbacks. Courage is having the capacity to overcome one's own fears and insecurities to achieve that goal. Leaders need both to see challenging tasks through to their completion.

1.3.1.2 Leading Teams

Coaching & Feedback: Coaching is the practice of investing in others' continuous learning and growth. Feedback involves establishing a dialogue about one's own and others' performance. Both involve recognising others' achievements and contributions.

Empowering: A leader's ability to delegate authority empowers others. Empowering leaders involve others in the decision-making process, thereby indicating their high expectations of and confidence in those they manage. Such leaders minimise secrecy and create an open and transparent environment. They tolerate mistakes and failures as part of the learning process.

Team Building: Team building brings together the right people equipped with the qualities needed to ensure the commitment and cooperation needed to attain established goals. As such, it also involves managing differences in personality and skills within a diverse group to resolve conflict constructively.

1.3.1.3 Leading the Organisation

Ability to Execute: Strong leaders go to great lengths to realise their vision. They know that vision without action is simply a hallucination. They are results-driven and know how to get things done. Furthermore, they establish structures and processes to ensure that their team remains focused, hits deadlines and achieves its goals.

Change Orientation: This means having the ability to manage oneself and others effectively through planned or unplanned, discontinuous organisational changes. Change-oriented leaders not only embrace change but also initiate and drive it. They are always looking for new ways of doing things better and they know how to cope with difficult and ambiguous situations.

Energising: Effective leadership includes having the skills to channel others' energy creatively whilst striving for common goals. Such leaders energise, inspire and motivate others to do their best to realise the organisation's vision. They are enthusiastic about what they do and can transfer this enthusiasm to others.

Visioning: Visioning comprises looking ahead to identify new opportunities for the business and creating a strategy for leveraging them. This behaviour requires an open, entrepreneurial mind and a willingness to challenge the status quo and look for innovative approaches to accomplishing tasks and reaching objectives.

1.3.1.4 Leading Networks

Client & Stakeholder Orientation: Having the requisite skillset to develop a relationship of trust and mutual respect with clients and other stakeholders, as well as to effectively meet their needs, defines this behavioural trait.

Networks & Alliances: Networks, both formal and informal, are created and used strategically to achieve organisational and personal goals. Leaders who are effective in networking will be better at sense-making and, therefore, defter in selecting the best course of action.

1.3.2 Leadership Career: The Leadership Pipeline

Ram Charan, Stephen Drotter and James Noel have developed a model, called the *Leadership Pipeline*, for leadership careers in large organisations. The model puts forth seven levels of leadership with six transitions in between. To reach the next career level, leaders must successfully manage these passages by mastering new skills and values along the way. The *Leadership Pipeline* therefore describes an ideal type of a corporate career system as well as an ideal type of a leader's career progression. Unlike the GELM and the IDI™, which are applied in an experiential way, the *Leadership Pipeline* will be used throughout this book for one of its intended purposes: to classify and evaluate a leader's—Julius Caesar's—professional progression according to the six career steps of the model. The explanations of these six passages that follow summarise the definitions in Charan, Drotter and Noel's book. Figure 1.3 shows the hierarchy of the six critical career passages in an organisation that constitute the leadership pipeline.

From Leading Self to Leading Others: The passage from individual contributor to letting others work for you entails learning to plan, delegate and appraise others' performance. Leaders who master this transition become convinced that such managerial work adds value and relinquish the idea that they are more effective on their own.

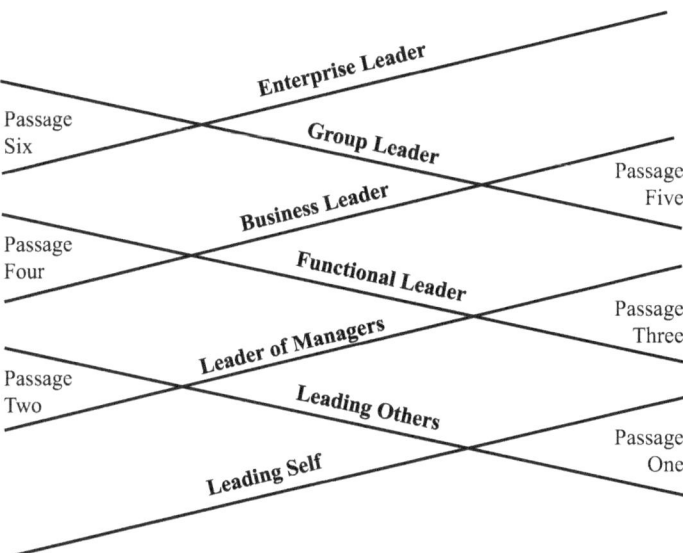

Fig. 1.3 Critical career passages in the leadership pipeline. Author's adaptation after Charan et al. (2001)

From Leading Others to Leading Leaders: Learning to build an effective team of managers requires recognising people's strengths that differ from one's own. Developing managers and allocating resources are thus key competencies to acquire. Successful leaders of leaders recognise that management is now their primary task.

From Leading Leaders to Functional Leader: Acquiring the capacity to cooperate with other functional leaders and compete for resources progresses leaders away from depending on their own areas of expertise. This passage requires developing strategic thinking to align the contribution of the function with the strategy of the organisation.

From Functional Leader to Business Leader: This denotes gaining knowledge about how to make decisions based on financial data. Leading a business usually comes with attaining greater autonomy whilst simultaneously having more responsibility for the bottom line. Therefore, it requires leaders to transition from having a product or service focus to cultivating a profit focus. It also entails learning to interact deftly with the external world of governments, customers and markets.

From Business Leader to Group Leader: Learning to lead a portfolio of businesses requires a shift towards coaching and developing the business leaders who report to the group leader. Whereas before being a leader was only about managing one's own business effectively, successful group leaders value their direct reports', that is other business leaders', accomplishments.

From Group Leader to Enterprise Leader: The final transition to the highest position demands learning to lead an entire corporation and manage shareholders, the supervisory board and the media. Leading the organisation as a whole means developing a vision, setting direction and steering the workforce to effective execution.

1.3.3 Leadership Personality: The Individual Directions Inventory™

The IDI™, developed by Management Research Group® (MRG®), the US-based publisher of psychometric assessments, will be used to understand Caesar's motivational pattern. Since Caesar's personality traits will be discussed in-depth in the final chapter, it makes the most sense to explain the instrument in that section of the book.

1.3.4 History, Leadership and Organisational Behaviour

Leadership is highly diverse; it depends on the individuals—the leader and the followers—involved and the different contexts in which it occurs. In this vein, historian Martin Gutmann argues that when reflecting on the value of the historical perspective for leadership studies, leadership is best considered in practice, for example, through a case study. Indeed, teaching leadership in business schools without case studies is unthinkable. A case study is, by definition, a piece of history. Even cases that describe ongoing situations cannot go without explicating what has happened.

I agree with management scholars Eisenhardt and Graebner's argument that generalising from multiple cases builds more robust theory than single-case research. The same applies to case studies that go further back in history, too. Gutmann's *Unseen Leader* and my *Leadership Strategies for Women* exemplify building theory from multiple historical case studies. For this reason, this single-case-study book refrains from generalising.

But is it then possible to learn well from just one case study of a single individual? On this note, I concur with Albert Madansky, a business professor, who warns about the pitfalls of engaging with one case study only. Indeed, it is difficult to say whether what happens in a single case study is a matter of coincidence, context or deliberate choice and action, whereas only the latter would be worth replicating by the learner in another situation. However, there are two helpful ways in which leaders or leadership development professionals can learn from a case study like Caesar's. The first is to be inspired by the example, which differs from replicating a behaviour or generalising. A case study can in fact present new ideas, as management scholar Nicolaj Siggelkow contends. Inspiration from a case study could mean starting to consider an aspect one had not considered before or the importance of which one may have underestimated. Business historian Nancy Koehn talks about how several CEOs felt inspired by her leadership biography of Abraham Lincoln. For example, reading Caesar's case study could inspire a leader to open him- or herself to feedback. Another way is by benchmarking the leader against other examples before concluding what behaviour is worth replicating, what is not and in which circumstances. This study therefore benchmarks Caesar against many leaders—who come from different yet comparable contexts—through three frameworks of behaviour, career and personality, respectively, which are all based on comparing multiple examples.

How far back should one go to make historical examples relevant and helpful in leadership learning? The distant past offers a unique alternative perspective. On the one hand, these examples are close enough to be recognisable: Caesar's biography provides insights into a leader in a free-market economy and a society with many similarities to the culture, thinking and values of the developed world. Moreover, because the Roman Republic's economy and organisation were less complex and changed more slowly than ours, the connection between cause and effect is easier to discern. On the other hand, the distance in time permits the luxury of learning from such examples without contemporary political bias and contextual noise. In this way, studying history can help us understand more comprehensively the implications of contemporary and future leaders' choices and actions.

The data we have on Julius Caesar, like that of many historical figures, are incomplete and, at least in part, subjective. However, this is not unique to historical figures; contemporary leaders, including those studied through interviews, also present a subjective picture. To understand what happened during Caesar's time, an approach that political science calls 'interpretive' is necessary. This method, as defined by Mark Bevir and Rod Rhodes, focuses on the meanings that shape actions and institutions and how they do so. I share their viewpoint that we can understand and explain actions adequately only by referencing the relevant actors' beliefs and desires. In the context of organisational behaviour, 'beliefs and desires' are generally considered under 'motivation'. This is why *Lead Like Julius Caesar* gives special attention to Caesar's motivational pattern and how it was determined by his personality.

This book also tries to explain how that personality was forged by his life and professional experiences as well as his professional development. Understanding the motivation of a leader from the past can help current and future leaders understand their own motivations and how these affect their leadership.

Hüseyin Leblebici, a business school professor, wrote an important paper on how history and social sciences could work together more productively despite their different research approaches. Leblebici raised the fundamental question:

> As social scientists and historians, do we have the right methodological tools to accurately report historical events, to understand the motivations and justifications of the historical agents in action, to explain theoretically both the agents' behavior as well as the events they are involved in; and, finally to provide an evaluation of these actions based on the moral or political sensibilities that the researchers render in understanding the rationalisation used by actors in question?

The solution that Leblebici suggested is to opt for transdisciplinary rather than interdisciplinary research. In the former, both disciplines leverage their unique contribution and approach to respond to questions that would otherwise be difficult to answer. Such research is particularly relevant for managerial and organisational issues that demand contemporary solutions and are informed by historical analyses. This book follows Leblebici's call for transdisciplinary research by using models from organisational behaviour and organisational psychology to understand a historical leader's career and leadership to inspire and teach today's leaders and leadership development professionals.

1.4   What Is in this Book and What Is Not

An entire library has been written about Julius Caesar, including works by Shakespeare and Napoleon. This book contains no new historical facts. Instead, I have followed the consensus of historians in the publications cited at the end or in general works of reference. For instance, we know for certain that Julius Caesar crossed the Rubicon in 49 BC, was assassinated on the Ides of March 44 BC and by whom. Why he crossed the Rubicon, however, is still being debated. In such cases of interpretation and inference, I sometimes follow a certain point of view and, in that case, mention whose interpretation I support (e.g. Morstein-Marx's opinion that the risk of being prosecuted in 49 for Caesar was slim). In other cases, I develop my own personal view (e.g. regarding the role of Caesar's followers in the decision to cross the Rubicon). In the interest of readability, I have generally refrained from references and self-referencing in the text or footnotes, except when the argument depends on a particular source or scholarly contribution.

The book is ordered chronologically. The following five chapters each describe and analyse an important phase in Caesar's career. Each starts with a chronological overview in the form of a *Leadership Timeline*, which depicts the most important gyrations, or ups and downs, of Caesar's life and career. I have found this instrument helpful in my executive coaching practice to visualise significant events and trends that have impacted a leader's development. The book concludes with two chapters: one that evaluates Caesar's leadership development throughout his career and another that analyses Caesar's personality and draws conclusions about his motivation. The dates in the book are BC, unless otherwise indicated.

Finally, researching, writing on and explicating history can sometimes be frustrating because one never fully grasps the complete picture. I find it difficult, for instance, to refrain from filling gaps with my imagination and instead to discipline myself to stick to the known facts. However, at the start of each chapter, I've allowed myself a brief indulgence: one scene emerging from my imagination, and always clearly marked by italics. The rest, I promise, has been done with academic rigour.

Bibliography

Greek and Roman Sources

Cicero, M.T., *On the Republic*.
Dionysius of Halicarnassus, *Roman Antiquities*.
Polybius, *The Histories*, Book VI.

Modern Works

Arena, V., & Prag, J. (Eds.). (2022). *A companion to the political culture of the Roman Republic*. Wiley.
Badian, E. (1983). *Publicans and sinners: Private Enterprise in the Service of the Roman Republic*. Cornell University Press.
Bevir, M., & Rhodes, R. A. W. (2003). *Interpreting British governance*. Routledge.
Bleicken, J. (2004). *Geschichte der römischen Republik*. R. Oldenbourg Verlag.

de Blois, L. (1987). *The Roman Army and politics in the first century B.C.* J.C. Gieben.
Charan, R., Drotter, S., & Noel, J. (2001). *The leadership pipeline. How to build the leadership powered company.* Jossey-Bass.
Crook, J. A., Lintott, A., & Rawson, E. (Eds.). (1994). *The Cambridge ancient history* (The last age of the Roman Republic, 146–43 B.C.) (Vol. IX, 2nd ed.). Cambridge University Press.
Eisenhardt, K. M., & Graebner, M. E. (2007). Theory building from cases: Opportunities and challenges. *Academy of Management Journal, 50*(1), 25–32.
Guillén, L., & Florent-Treacy, E. (2011). Emotional intelligence and leadership effectiveness: The mediating influence of collaborative behaviors. *INSEAD Working Papers Collection, 23*, 1–28.
Gutmann, M. (2020). Introduction: The value of the historical perspective for leadership studies. In M. Gutmann (Ed.), *Historians on leadership and strategy. Case studies from antiquity to modernity* (pp. 1–12). Springer Nature.
Gutmann, M. (2023). *The Unseen Leader.* How History Can Help Us Rethink Leadership. Cham: Springer Nature.
Harari, Y. N. (2024, March 11). *Disruption, democracy & the global order, panel discussion at the University of Cambridge.* Accessed October 18, 2024, from https://youtu.be/XmhLmZwc2es?si=ns8rlngFlmQgPf9k
Hersey, P., & Blanchard, K. H. (1977). *The Management of Organizational Behavior.* Prentice-Hall.
Hölkeskamp, K.-J. (Ed.). (2009). *Eine politische Kultur (in) der Krise? Die "letzte Generation" der römischen Republik.* De Gruyter.
Hölkeskamp, K.-J. (2010). *Reconstructing the Roman Republic: An ancient political culture and modern research.* Princeton University Press.
KDVI. (n.d.). https://kdvi.com/tools/
Kets de Vries, M. F. R., Vrignaud, P., & Florent-Treacy, E. (2004). The global leadership life inventory: Development and psychometric properties of a 360-degree feedback instrument. *International Journal of Human Resource Management, 15*, 475–492.
Koehn, N. (2018). The leadership journey of Abraham Lincoln. *McKinsey Quarterly, 2*, 77–87.
Leblebici, H. (2014). History and organization theory: Potential for a transdisciplinary convergence. In M. Bucheli & R. D. Wadhwani (Eds.), *Organizations in time: History, theory, methods.* Oxford University Press.
Madansky, A. (2008). Teaching history in business schools: An Outsider's view. *Academy of Management Learning & Education, 7*(4), 553–562.
Morstein-Marx, R. (2021). *Julius Caesar and the Roman People.* Cambridge: Cambridge University Press.
Nicolet, C. (Ed.). (1978). *Rome et la conquête du monde méditerranéen. 264–27 avant J.-C.* Presses Universitaires de France.
Siggelkow, N. (2007). Persuasion with case studies. *Academy of Management Journal, 50*(1), 20–24.

Rosenstein, N., & Morstein-Marx, R. (Eds.). (2006). *A companion to the Roman Republic*. Blackwell.
Vanderbroeck, P. (1988). *Antieke Beschaving. Cursusdl. 1: Leereenheden 1–10*. Kok; Stichting Open Theologisch Onderwijs.
Vanderbroeck, P. J. J. (1987). *Popular leadership and collective behavior ca. 80–50 BC*. J.C. Gieben.
Vanderbroeck, P. (2010, March). When in Rome…Lessons on executive pay from Ancient Rome. *Financial World*. pp. 33–34.
Vanderbroeck, P. (2012). Crises: Ancient and modern. Understanding an ancient Roman crisis can help us move beyond our own. *Management & Organizational History, 7*(2), 113–131.
Vanderbroeck, P. (2014). *Leadership Strategies for Women Lessons from Four Queens on Leadership and Career Development*. Berlin/Heidelberg: Springer.

2

The Making of a Leader: Caesar's Early Life and Education

> *…When they stormed aboard his ship, shouting and swaying swords, spears and sticks, he suddenly leaped forward—dagger in hand—pushing through the small group of personal slaves, who had formed a feeble protective ring around their master. 'Don't even think of it!', the ship's captain hissed, seeing the fire in the young man's eyes. For he knew that the pirates would not hurt his noble passenger. Alive he was worth much more…*
> (This quote is fictional and created by the author for illustrative purposes.)

Upbringing, early life experiences and significant encounters impact the development of a leadership career. They serve as obstacles to as well as springboards for leadership success. To understand this evolution, executive coaching often starts by asking the leader to analyse and reflect on their own biography. In this first chapter, therefore, we examine Caesar's life, career and origins while addressing questions such as, what was the influence of his family, upbringing, education and the context in which he grew up on the development of his personality and career? What were the key events and individuals that shaped his character and forged his ambition, values and view of the world? How did his formative years set him up for a career in leadership? What was the social and psychological platform that launched his career? What obstacles could have potentially prevented his later career success?

This chapter first provides a historical perspective through a factual overview of Caesar's life, career and achievements during the years 100 to 70 BC before enquiring into his leadership competencies and career development

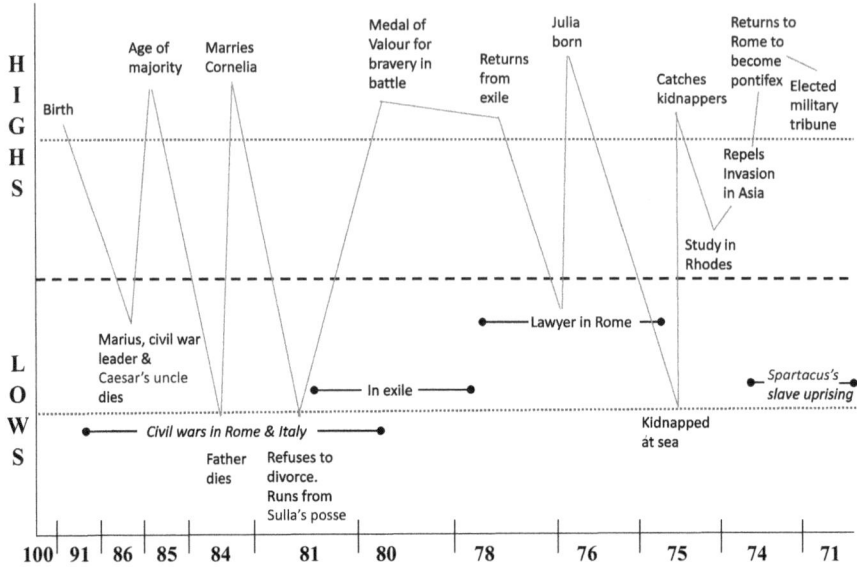

Fig. 2.1 Caesar's leadership timeline: Highs and Lows 100–71 BC. Author's own illustration

from a modern perspective. Figure 2.1 summarises the highs and lows of Caesar's life and career during this period.

2.1 Caesar's Youth and Early Life Experiences

Gaius Julius Caesar Jr. was born in July 100 BC. His father, Gaius Sr, belonged to the patrician (aristocratic) family of the Julii, who claimed that their origins could be traced to the foundation of Rome. Few patrician families existed, and everybody else—rich or poor—belonged to the plebeian class. Among these were nobles, who constituted a larger group of families than patricians. Nobles secured the highest offices in the Roman Republic through merit (political and military careers). Such a career also required certain wealth to be member of the Senate and to finance these unpaid careers. But many other affluent families did not achieve or aspire to political office. These individuals, for example Atticus, the best friend of Marcus Tullius Cicero (the politician and orator) were the *equites*, whose wealth was often generated from business. Merit in government positions or the military was essential to keeping one's status because social standing was not hereditary. Membership of the Senate required the election to at least one public office, yet recognition as a noble required having recent consuls in the family.

2 The Making of a Leader: Caesar's Early Life and Education

Underperforming in the competition for public office, Caesar's patrician family lost considerable wealth and social standing over the years compared with the nobles. Nevertheless, the career successes of Gaius Sr and Gaius Jr's uncle Sextus had recently rebooted the family's fortunes. To this, a strong network and wealth were added through the marriage of Gaius Sr to Aurelia, a member of a powerful family. Caesar's aunt was married to Gaius Marius, a military hero and political leader.

The first 20 years of Caesar's life were violent and turbulent. Between the ages of nine and thirteen, he witnessed the war of Rome against its allies in Italy. 'Divide and conquer', the principle that had allowed the Romans to rule over Italy, had been exhausted. The Italian peoples united and rebelled to demand the equality that they felt was their due after being loyally allied with Rome for centuries. This uprising compelled the Roman army to fight their former fellows-in-arms who had the same weapons and training. The conflict was bloody, with both sides committing atrocities such as starving prisoners of war and placing entire cities under siege. The Romans and their adversaries both decided to bury their dead on the battlefield rather than bring them home to hide the staggering losses that made it increasingly difficult to recruit new fighting men. The Romans had to mobilise all their resources to keep from being overwhelmed by the enemy. The rebellion started in Asculum, a prosperous town a little over 200 kilometres away from Rome on the Via Salaria, the ancient road built to transport salt to the city. The locals slaughtered all the Romans in the town—men, women, even children—and plundered their possessions. Two years later saw the Romans return with a siege, during which local commanders killed city dwellers who wanted to surrender. Caesar's uncle Sextus, a general, died during the battle to reconquer the city. The Romans won the war and their allies received Roman citizenship, but the entire affair could have been resolved without bloodshed.

When Caesar was eleven, the Roman empire was attacked in the East, but when he was fifteen, the army managed to repel the invasion. Between the ages of twelve and eighteen, Caesar saw up close the civil war waged by his uncle Gaius Marius and L. Cornelius Cinna against L. Cornelius Sulla, with fighting and executions happening near Caesar's home. Anarchy and rioting reigned in the streets for days, until one party had taken the upper hand. People knifed each other in the city centre, the heads of decapitated senators were displayed on the Forum, the houses of adversaries were broken into and plundered—their owners hunted down or betrayed by spies, while others committed suicide.

Sulla started the civil war in 88 BC by deploying his army to attack the capital—an event that had not occurred since several centuries. The city changed hands several times until Sulla, nicknamed *Felix* ('the lucky'), prevailed in 82 BC. He then went about establishing his power systematically through a reign of terror. He published lists of enemies and put a bounty on their heads, prompting a hunting and killing spree in Rome and throughout Italy. Many were killed in their homes, their hiding places or their beds. Thousands fell victim, many of whom were not on Sulla's lists but murdered for their wealth. Goods were confiscated and the children of the persecuted lost their citizen rights. M. Licinius Crassus, Caesar's future ally, became rich during this period by repossessing the riches of the proscribed.

Caesar and his whole generation never really lived through a peaceful period during the first decades of their lives. The fraternal conflicts of the allied and civil wars that swept over Rome and Italy like a tornado were traumatic experiences. Apart from causing violence and destruction, they split families, friendships, alliances and business ventures. They would create tensions in Roman politics and society for years to come. Such experiences, as understood from psychology, penetrate the collective consciousness. Some of Caesar's generation, unconsciously, will have considered civil strife to be the norm. Others will have been driven to prevent it from happening again.

Growing up as a young man in the upper classes meant a private education, with slaves and freedmen as teachers. Home schooling, sometimes together with children of friends and relatives, was the norm. The subjects were Latin and Greek, rhetoric and law. There were plenty of physical activities as well. From what we know about Caesar as an adult, he excelled in mental and physical education. As a boy, he rode his horse at full speed without using his hands. In his early years, Caesar shared his home with his elder sisters, Julia Maior and Julia Minor, until they married and left home when they were about fourteen years old. By then, Rome was a bustling and crowded capital city of about 750,000 inhabitants and growing. It was the capital of an empire in expansion, second only to Egypt's capital, Alexandria. Young Gaius Jr. saw a diversity of tradesmen and foreign envoys from all corners of the empire and beyond travel to the city. While visiting the port of Ostia, he would see ships that brought corn from overseas to feed the city dwellers and other goods.

The city where Caesar grew up (Fig. 2.2) was home to impassioned citizens voting in assemblies to elect their governments and pass laws. These citizens knew well of their power in society as shareholders in this mighty empire. Still, of course, their pride came with the knowledge that their prosperity depended on the dividends that the empire brought home. These people held their elite—including the young Caesar, born in the shadow of future greatness—responsible for the city's governance and the empire. Apart from these, politics was a public affair in Rome. Popular assemblies, often loud with

2 The Making of a Leader: Caesar's Early Life and Education

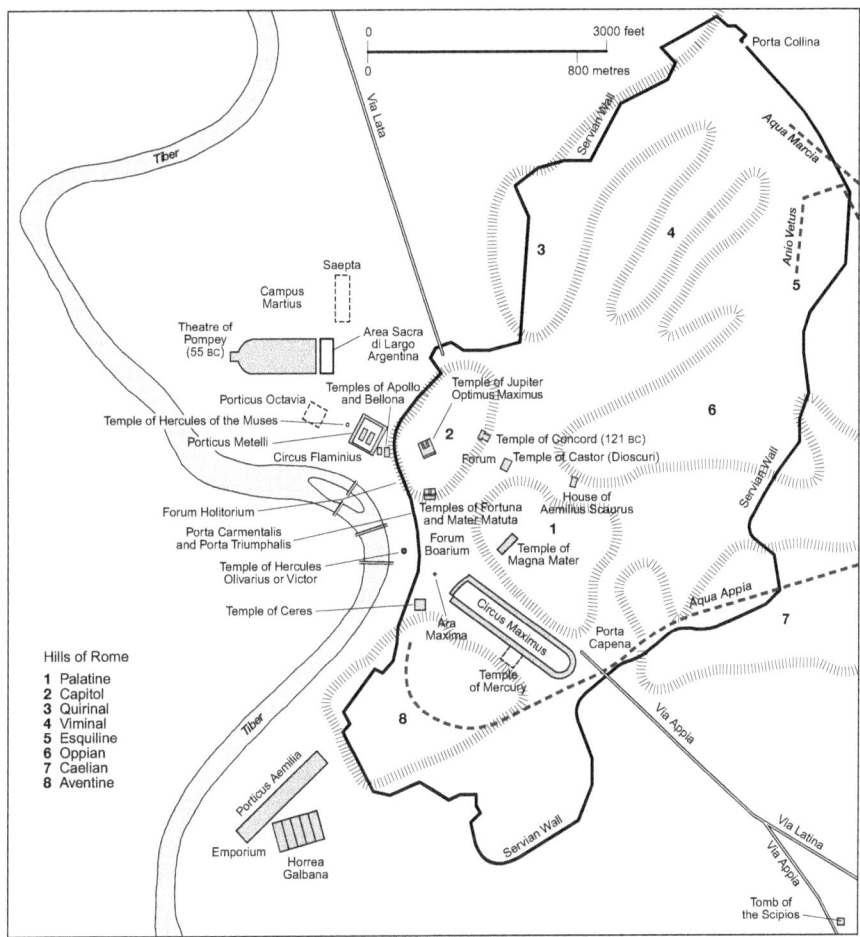

Fig. 2.2 The city of Rome during the time of Julius Caesar. From: *A Companion to the Roman Republic* © John Wiley & Sons 2007. Reprinted under license

emotions and debates, happened in the open. Frequently, orators held spontaneous speeches for all to hear. These developments and processes were witnessed by Caesar, who would come to know them well. When he was eight years old, Gaius Sr was praetor, the second highest office of the Republic—a busy job that brought numerous activities and visitors to the house of the Julii. The following year, Caesar's father spent a year abroad to govern the rich province of Asia (in modern Turkey). He will have brought gifts and stories for his son when he came back.

Not particularly wealthy, the Julii Caesares lived comfortably, albeit not in an upscale neighbourhood. Caesar's mother, Aurelia, who hailed from a much more prosperous and influential family, had to adjust her standard of living after moving in with Gaius Sr. From his home in the Suburra, Caesar witnessed up close the living conditions of the less privileged: a neighbourhood bustling round the clock, filled with shops, craftsmen, bars and street food restaurants; streets where free citizens, former slaves and slaves intermingled. A place, too, that could be dangerous at night. Gaius Jr. will have witnessed his father receiving his clients every morning, a colourful group of people that assembled in the courtyard to pay their respects and ask for support. The Roman practice of patronage meant that members of the elite, even the less wealthy ones, maintained a group of clients. These citizens, not necessarily the humblest or poorest, supported the patron in political matters and added to the patron's prestige. In return, the patron looked after their clients' interests. Patronage filled the gap in Rome's limited public services.

At the age of fifteen, a Roman youth was considered an adult. Now Caesar was allowed to wear a toga for the first time: the *toga virilis*, a plain white toga that symbolised adult manhood. A toga was the traditional dress of Roman men and said to resemble what Romulus, the founder of Rome, had worn. It was made of a single woollen cloth, several metres long. It was worn over a tunic and draped around the body and over the shoulders. It usually covered the left arm but not the right. A toga was not easy to put on and typically required the assistance of a slave to get it right. Moving around dressed in a toga also took some practice. Caesar paid attention to his clothing, which he tended to wear in a loose-fitting manner, contrary to the classic tight fit. He was tall and kept himself in shape. He groomed himself and paid particular attention to his hairdo. He seemed to dislike that he had little hair and was virtually bald throughout most of his life.

By now, the Roman upper class had accumulated considerable wealth through conquests, business and governing provinces. They developed new tastes inspired by what they had seen and imported from the richness of the East. The youth started to spend it on luxury goods, parties and entertainment. Some of the elderly deplored the fact that their offspring diverged from the traditional Roman values of restraint and discipline. It was around this time that the Roman elite started to develop a taste for orgies. Caesar shared this lifestyle in his twenties, but not in a way that caught the public eye or the rumour mill. Besides, contrary to others, he could already boast of several military accomplishments against foreign enemies (more on that below)—there is nothing more Roman than this.

However, reaching full adulthood in Rome took longer. Men of sufficient means became eligible for a magisterial career at age 30. Before this, the state expected them to pursue studies, do a traineeship and gain some work

2 The Making of a Leader: Caesar's Early Life and Education

experience. Once an adult, Caesar will have spent a year shadowing a politician and will have also been allowed to listen to Senate meetings. And, of course, he will have voted in assemblies and elections. On the political continuum, Caesar's family stood on the side of the *populares,* the political faction that used the People rather than the Senate as its power base. His uncle Marius, together with his father-in-law Cinna, were its leaders. They had lost the civil war against Sulla.

In 82 BC, the end of the civil war saw the Senate appoint Sulla dictator. The dictator, a Roman invention, was a crisis manager. It was the Roman version of declaring a state of emergency. It temporarily abolished the constitutional principle of always having at least one colleague to share power with. Dictators were customarily appointed for a renewable term of six months together with a deputy (*magister equitum*). They enjoyed full decision-making power without needing confirmation by the Senate or the People, and they were exempt from later prosecution for acts committed in office. Sulla's dictatorship created two precedents. Thus far, dictators had been instituted to deal with external threats. Now, for the first time, the dictator had a mandate to deal with internal matters: to restore order and reform the state. Sulla was the first dictator who contravened the customary time limit. He was nominated for an indefinite time period. He remained in power for two years until he retired.

Sulla was convinced that the Roman constitution bred excessive conflict and tension. He issued reforms to reinforce the oligarchy. The rights of the People were downgraded in favour of the Senate, which was doubled in size from 300 to 600 members. He reinforced the government by increasing the number of praetors and quaestors. Henceforth, a minimum ten-year tenure was necessary before one was afforded a second or third consulship. Finally, he reformed the law and the judiciary.

Sulla's reign directly affected Caesar during his teens. Shortly after Gaius Sr died, Caesar, then sixteen, was married to Cinna's daughter Cornelia. Being married to the daughter of one of Sulla's main enemies and being the nephew of the other put him in the middle of the political conflict. Once in power, Sulla unleashed a bloody purge of Marius' and Cinna's partisans. Neither Caesar nor his father were directly involved in the war, so both were spared persecution. Nevertheless, Sulla asked Caesar to prove his loyalty by divorcing the daughter of his defeated adversary. Caesar refused and had to flee Rome to escape Sulla's wrath. Sulla confiscated Cornelia's substantial dowry and the inheritance from his father, leaving Caesar without means. He was forced to hide in the wilderness like an outlaw, moving from hiding place to hiding place, with Sulla's posse in pursuit. Later, Caesar found passage on a ship bound for the eastern provinces, where he took refuge. Here he gained his first experience in government and military matters. He distinguished himself through his bravery. Finally, his mother and her family intervened on his behalf, persuading Sulla to pardon him. Still, Caesar remained in voluntary exile for several years until Sulla passed away. In 78 BC, Caesar returned home to commence his professional career.

On the personal side, Caesar enjoyed life throughout his existence, starting from his youth. In his late twenties, he spent large sums on his passions and hosting dinner parties. He was known primarily for his intimate relationships with women from the upper strata, also while being married. As we have seen above, formal marriages were, first of all, political and economic arrangements between families. Friendships and love relationships happened outside these boundaries, and women and men alike initiated such connections. There were many opportunities to meet. Rome's high society entertained itself through privately held dinners, parties and cultural performances in city homes and country estates. In his early twenties, Caesar met Nicomedes, King of Bithynia and an ally of Rome. Throughout his life, there have been rumours that they became lovers. Throughout his education, he regularly engaged in sports. When on the run from Sulla, he fell seriously ill, possibly from malaria, but he recovered. The different challenges over which he prevailed during this period show that he did not lack in physical and mental energy. When Caesar came into the world, Rome controlled the northern half of the Mediterranean basin (Fig. 2.3).

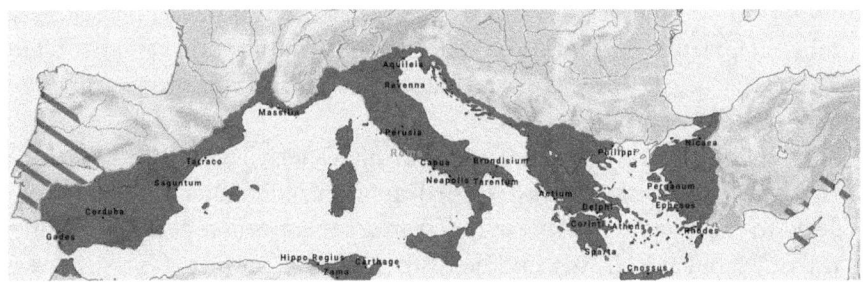

Fig. 2.3 Rome and its empire at the time of Caesar's birth in 100 BC. By Portasa Cristian—Own work, CC0 1.0 Universal—Creative Commons. https://commons.wikimedia.org/w/index.php?curid=148278853

2.2 Career Beginnings

For young nobles and patricians, the prominent and most prestigious careers lay in government, which encompassed service in the provinces and the army. A business career was not impossible, but it held a lower status. A law career was another option but best pursued after an initial magistracy to enter the Senate. In 78 BC, Caesar returned to Rome to practice law. Sulla's reign had been vastly unpopular, and the years following were replete with political conflict about abolishing his reforms. As a young lawyer, Caesar sued two senior senators on behalf of the Greeks. The two men, both partisans of Sulla, were accused of extortion while working as government officials in the province of Greece. Up against some of Rome's best solicitors as well as behind-the-scenes manoeuvring, Caesar lost both lawsuits. Nonetheless, it served as a breeding ground for forging a reputation as an excellent orator. With these two lawsuits he had rubbed the post-Sullan establishment the wrong way. Possibly at the behest of his family, he thought it better to again spend some time away, leaving Rome to pursue studies on the island of Rhodes. It looked as though he was eager to depart because he set sail in early winter, which came with adverse weather conditions that brought most seafaring to a halt. The journey from Rome to Rhodes via Greece would take about two weeks.

During his second foray abroad, Caesar embarked on two other military adventures, which he mastered with speed and intrepidness—experiences that served as building blocks for his career (Box 2.1).

Box 2.1 Kidnapped

The first transpired on his way to Rhodes. Passing through the Dodecanese islands, the island chain between the Cyclades and western Turkey, he had an unpleasant encounter to say the least. Near the island of Pharmacussa, with its sand-coloured rocks and a green landscape formed by shrubs, olive groves and vineyards, his ship was attacked by pirates. The pirates, lying in wait in the dark blue waters, will have spotted Caesar's ship from a lookout on the island. Launching their small, swift coast-going vessels, they rapidly overtook and surrounded their defenceless prey. On the route from Rome to Rhodes the ship, a merchantman, probably carried minimal cargo, apart from some passengers such as Caesar and his small band of aides. It would have been transporting mail, documents and coin with which to purchase goods in Rhodes, a large port of transfer. Late in the shipping season, the ship provided an opportunity for the brigands to round up this year's profits. Their main business was the slave trade and kidnapping. The crew of Caesar's ship, usually already slaves, would be sold to a new master on the slave market on the island of Delos. Finding a Roman on the ship was a bonus. Caesar and his attendants were taken to the pirates' home base on the coast and held for ransom.

> When the pirates told him how much the ransom was, Caesar—25 years old—exclaimed, 'You must be joking! Don't you know who I am? You must at least double that figure'. (Greek being the lingua franca in the Eastern Mediterranean, they could understand each other.) His captors happily obliged and sent off some of his companions to collect the money from cities in the Roman provinces nearby. It took them close to 40 days to get the ransom together and hand it over to the kidnappers. Although vexed, Caesar made the most of the situation. He bossed the pirates around, ordered them to keep quiet during his afternoon nap and used them as his audience to practice his oratory and poetry. He scolded them whenever they failed to appreciate the particular qualities of his work and called them illiterate barbarians, but he also played sports with them and participated in their exercises. The pirates found all of this rather funny and laughed at Caesar's promise that he would come back after his release and settle scores. Caesar would have the last laugh.
>
> The ransom was paid and Caesar was released in the port of Miletus. On the spur of the moment, he convinced the locals to man vessels with which to pursue the robbers. Arriving after dark, Caesar and his squadron found them lying at anchor at their base. Caught by surprise, the robbers put up little resistance. Several ships were sunk, and most of the raiders were arrested. The prisoners and their treasure were brought back to Miletus, and they were placed in custody. Caesar then travelled inland to the capital of the province to meet with the Roman governor, Marcus Juncus, to ask him to preside over the judgement of the criminals. Juncus, however, refused to give Caesar a straight answer. Apparently, he was considering making some money for himself by selling the pirates as slaves or holding them for ransom in return. Caesar would have none of it. He headed for the coast and, true to his promise, had his kidnappers crucified. Mercifully, he had them killed beforehand to save them an agonising death. He pocketed their treasure of loot and proceeded to Rhodes.

Another remarkable act characterised Caesar's time pursuing his studies. When King Mithridates invaded the Roman empire in Asia Minor, Caesar deferred his academic pursuits to travel to the southern mainland off Rhodes. Without holding official authority, he assembled local troops from various cities and prevented the enemy from marching south before eventually returning to his school.

The subsequent progression of Caesar's career owes itself to his mother's network, which facilitated his acceptance into the priesthood as pontifex. *Pontifices*, of which there were fifteen, were an ancient and prestigious position. Among other responsibilities, they regulated the Roman calendar. Caesar ceased his scholarly undertakings and returned home in 73 BC. Having learned his lesson, he travelled under cover in a small fishing boat to prevent himself from being prey to pirates.

The Rome and empire waiting for him were in dire straits: It was under attack in the East, the Mediterranean was unsafe due to piracy, civil war renegades occupied Spain, the slave revolt of Spartacus threatened Rome and food supply to the city was insecure. What's more, many senators with leadership experience had fallen victim to purges. As a result, political conflicts and competition for office resurfaced. Some politicians, notably Pompey and Crassus, despite having won honour, fame and wealth serving Sulla, were unwilling to render their careers dependent on the ruling group within the élite who had been installed by the dictator. They began to roll back Sullan reforms that had limited popular influence in legislation. These efforts were openly supported by Caesar, who also pleaded for amnesty for anti-Sullan exiles. Politically, therefore, he advocated the cause and the original ideas of his uncle Marius and his father-in-law Cinna.

Two years later, at 29 years old, he became a military tribune. It was an army officer rank, not a political or government function, but nevertheless awarded through election by the popular assembly in Rome. It was the first office Caesar attained in this manner, marking the initiation of his political adulthood and ushering him towards a political career that he could begin the following year at age 30. As a military tribune in 71 BC, he may have seen military action against Spartacus and his slave army. Since his return to Rome, Caesar had been living well above his means. He hosted generous parties and dinners, which helped him build a network. He made himself popular among his neighbours in the modest dwelling that was his family home. Outside the city, he had acquired an upscale country house. Living the high life made him a notorious public figure.

Accordingly, Caesar's career had rocky beginnings. Coming out winning at the age of 29 must have convinced him that luck was on his side. In any case, he showed remarkable self-confidence. He had also learned that courage, speed and daring paid off. As fate would have it, he had already spent more than 50% of the time that he had to live.

2.3 Expectations and First Achievements

Caesar's initial professional achievements and especially his upbringing lay the foundation for his leadership. We have previously seen his remarkable feats in the military, both in an official capacity and at his own initiative. As a lawyer, his first experiences were ineffective but laudable. His main achievement during his youth and early adulthood was meeting his family's expectations—an objective that he carried with him throughout his career.

The (extended) family of the Roman upper class was more than a group of individuals connected through blood relationships or affinity. It was also an enterprise meant to sustain and grow its members' wealth and social standing. Marriages were often arranged to construct business or political alliances. This did not exclude solid emotional bonds between spouses, siblings, parents and children. Ancestry and tradition were valued.

Caesar's family, despite having an excellent aristocratic pedigree, had declined in social status due to the lack of senior magistrates in the family in the past century. In terms of wealth, as well, they could not keep up with the rest of the elite. Still, the Julii were blessed with the legend that the founder of the family was the grandson of the goddess Venus. At Caesar's birth, Gaius Sr was quaestor and thus had just started his career as a government official. Gaius Sr had a brother, Sextus, Caesar's uncle, who had made it to the consulship. Gaius Sr died after he had attained the praetorship and stood a good chance to enter the consulship. This implies that the brothers were well on the way to restoring the old lustre of their patrician family.

The smart marital alliances established by the Julii boosted the career prospects of family members and helped turn the family's decline around. Julia, Caesar's aunt and sister of Gaius Sr and Sextus, married Gaius Marius, a political upstart. Marius, a victorious general, held several consulships and saved Italy from an invasion by Germanic tribes before becoming a leader in the civil war. The marriage was a win–win: Marius gained respectability by marrying into a patrician family, and the Julii secured access to wealth and prestige.

Gaius Sr married Aurelia Cotta, who would become Caesar's mother. Aurelia came from a plebeian family of excellent standing, the Aurelii Cotta. Her father became a consul when Aurelia was only an infant, and three of her brothers made it to the consulship. Aurelia's family had been part of the nobility for 150 years. She would have been around fourteen at her wedding, and her husband in his early thirties. Gaius Sr had only begun his career as a Roman magistrate, and Aurelia was quite a desirable partner, for she came with a valuable political network and a hefty dowry. Although her husband was far from rich, he did bring a solid pedigree. To agree to their daughter's marriage, the Aurelii Cotta must have seen potential in Gaius Sr, who, together with his brother Sextus, was starting to turn the Julii family's fortunes for the better.

The daughters of Aurelia and Gaius Sr, Caesar's two sisters, pursued the same strategy: Their aristocratic name was married to members of wealthy families not yet of senatorial rank. One of the Julias would become the grandmother of Octavianus, Caesar's nephew and successor and Rome's first emperor. Finally, Caesar himself married Cornelia, daughter of Cinna, Marius' political associate from a family of substantial wealth. The marriage formed another linchpin that tied the Julii to Sulla's enemies.

2 The Making of a Leader: Caesar's Early Life and Education

It is high time to turn our attention to Caesar's mother. Having grown up in a wealthy family, Aurelia now had to move into Gaius Sr's home, which was comfortable but located in a low-end neighbourhood. This did not seem to have bothered her, being discreet and not particularly interested in a luxurious lifestyle. In this patriarchal society, Aurelia had domestic responsibilities. She ran the household, its staff and the family finances while her husband was forging his career outside the home. Aurelia was a healthy woman who lived to the age of 64. In this pre-industrial society, women like her often gave birth to children who died at an early age. We know only of three children who made it to adulthood: two daughters, Julia Maior and Minor, and her youngest child, Gaius Jr., our protagonist. Aurelia took her role as matron seriously, working with her husband to make the Julii great again. She found promising wedding partners for her children.

Aurelia (Fig. 2.4) was 20 when she gave birth to Caesar. Although Gaius Sr was sometimes away for professional reasons, the family was mostly complete. As a child and a teenager, Caesar will have benefited from the attention of both parents. Aurelia and her husband had grand plans for their son. As a woman, she was without formal authority, but she was comfortable wielding her influence in the background using her wealth and network. She took responsibility for Caesar's schooling, and ensured that his teachers, usually slaves or freedmen from the Greek world, were excellent. The Roman historian Tacitus later deemed her an example of a mother who offered her offspring the best possible educational opportunities. Gaius Sr died in 85 BC. Aurelia, who was 35 then, had to bring up their son on her own. She never remarried and dedicated her life to supporting her son. When his father passed away, Caesar was about 15, formally an adult and now head of the family. This happened in the middle of the civil war. The following year, he married Cornelia—a union that must have been arranged and approved of by Aurelia.

Fig. 2.4 An impression of Aurelia from the Renaissance. Published by Guillaume Rouille (1518?-1589)—'Promptuarii Iconum Insigniorum', Public Domain, https://commons.wikimedia.org/w/index.php?curid=8799553

With Caesar's sisters having left, Aurelia, Cornelia and Gaius Jr. shared the family home in the same popular neighbourhood. Her son did cause Aurelia some worry. The civil war rendered the city prone to danger; even so, young Caesar enjoyed parties with his upper-class peers. Then, the civil war ended with the victory of Sulla, followed by purges, executions and expropriations in Rome. Caesar and his family had supported the losing side. As we have discussed before, Caesar refused Sulla's demand to divorce his wife and had to flee from the city. Aurelia was apprehensive about her son, but at the same time, she would have recognised her principled character in him. In any case, she did not fret but started working her network while Caesar hid in the Italian countryside. With the help of her family, Aurelia managed to get Caesar expatriated to the Eastern Mediterranean to serve on the staff of a provincial governor and friend of the family. For two years, Aurelia and Caesar's young wife resided alone in Rome, living off of Aurelia's dowry, which she had been able to protect. While away, Caesar made his mother both worried and proud. He obtained his first military experience, and his penchant for risk-taking earned him a decoration for bravery.

Relentlessly working in the background, Aurelia obtained a pardon for her son once Sulla died. As previously stated, Caesar returned to Rome to practice law. Now 22, he had grown up with a sense of purpose, entitlement and a burden to propel his family's status upwards—duties and principles that he shared with his parents. He played with high stakes, knowing his mother would always have his back. Through her family, Aurelia manoeuvred to get her son co-opted into the prestigious order of the priesthood of the *pontifices*. Aurelia continued to share the family home with her son, his wife and their daughter Julia, born in 76 BC. Following Cornelia's death in 69 BC, Aurelia cared for Julia until she left home to get married. The bond between mother and son was also evident in moments such as the morning of Caesar's election to the leadership of the priesthood (*pontifex maximus*). Caesar invested much money in his candidature, which Aurelia strongly supported and possibly initiated. He had run up enormous debts to acquire sufficient funding. On election day, Aurelia—in tears—walked him to the door to send him off. Caesar kissed his mother on the porch of the family home. According to both Plutarch and Suetonius—two biographers –, he declared the following: 'Mum, today I either come back as the pontifex maximus or go into exile'. Sigmund Freud perhaps had Caesar, rather than Oedipus, in mind when he said that *a man who has been the indisputable favourite of his mother keeps for life the feeling of a conqueror, that confidence of success that often induces real success*. Caesar triumphed in the election. Box 2.2 describes another example of Aurelia's involvement in her son's career.

> **Box 2.2 Aurelia Takes Charge**
>
> A year later in 62 BC, Aurelia again actively intervened to support her son. For good reason, as we will see next, Aurelia kept a close watch over Pompeia, Caesar's second wife. Pompeia hosted a women-only religious festival, with her sisters-in-law and mother-in-law in attendance. What happened next was something out of *Mission Impossible*. Publius Clodius, a 30-year-old noble playboy and future political ally of Caesar, dressed up as one of the girls playing music for the ceremony. It was a ruse to slip into the house after dark, unseen. He was on his way to Pompeia, who must have been about 20 years old then. Rumour had it that they had an affair. It was her maid who let him in. Yet, in the obscurity of the night, Clodius got lost in the large mansion that was now Caesar's residence as head priest. One of Aurelia's servants, whom she had positioned strategically in the house during the festival, spotted Clodius wandering up and down. The servant asked who 'she' was. Clodius gave her a woman's name and told the servant he was looking for Abra, one of Pompeia's maids. But his voice gave him away as a man, at which point the servant shrieked in shock. She immediately called all the women together while Clodius ran off. Aurelia then took matters into her own hands. She ordered all gates and doors shut and locked. She organised the women into search parties and sent them armed with torches to hunt the intruder. Unable to find a way out, Clodius hid in one of the maids' chambers. There, he was discovered and subsequently chased from the house in shame. For this sacrilege, Clodius was prosecuted. Aurelia and one of her daughters spoke at his trial. Caesar divorced Pompeia at once, claiming that the family of a high priest should be beyond suspicion. Aurelia, instrumental in getting her son into the priesthood and to the position of pontifex maximus, did what it took to protect his reputation. It must have been her idea to throw Pompeia under the bus. 'Good riddance', Aurelia will have thought.

To finish the story of his mother, three years after the divorce, Caesar married his third wife Calpurnia. She was 17 years old and Caesar 41. We can assume that Aurelia, as an active mother, had a hand in choosing Calpurnia and was surely adamant about avoiding the trouble that Pompeia had caused. Calpurnia came from a family that was as prominent as Aurelia's. People described her as shy. When Aurelia died in 54 BC, Calpurnia was 22, old enough for her mother-in-law to be comfortable that she would leave her son in safe hands and that the marriage would produce an heir. Calpurnia would remain with Caesar until his death. Like Aurelia, she was a mainstay of his career, but the marriage would remain childless. She seemed stoically accepting of Caesar's infidelities. Similar to Aurelia, she would never remarry after being widowed. The two women were very much alike.

The relationship between Caesar and his mother raises the question of what family expectations he carried on his shoulders? If anything, these expectations were considerable. Family continuity in name, prestige and wealth was essential for members of the elite. In Caesar's case, the family anticipated that he would assume his father's and uncles' mantle to lift the Julii Caesares out of the obscurity into which they had fallen. Aurelia had joined her husband in this quest. After Gaius Sr died before being able to complete the mission, she took it upon herself to support and motivate her only son during his career. Aurelia wanted Caesar to be no less successful than her brothers, her father and the man she married. She invested her energy, her wealth and her network in this purpose. By the time he became a teenager, Caesar had lost the male reference points that had accompanied him while growing up: his uncle Marius, his father-in-law Cinna and his father Gaius Sr. Financially and politically, he depended on his mother and her family, particularly after losing his father's inheritance and his wife's dowry. On his mother's side, he had relatives who had wealth and successful careers. She and her family worked actively behind the scenes, first, to protect him from Sulla's wrath and, next, to give him the best possible launching pad for his career.

As head of the family, Caesar was responsible for ensuring the future and continuity of the ancient Julii family. His sisters had done their part by marrying into wealth. Caesar proved successful in amassing wealth and prestige, but the survival of the family's name and tradition necessitated a male heir. This goal Caesar never realised until he met Cleopatra later in life. However, recognising a son born out of wedlock as heir was out of the question. Ultimately, Caesar would resort to adoption, a common practice among Romans.

2.4 Leadership Behaviours

Let us now turn to analysing Caesar's behaviour and career from a modern perspective. What competencies did Caesar leverage to overcome leadership challenges? How did he apply them? Each chapter in this book that describes a stage in Caesar's career serves as basis for exploring his leadership competencies, as reflected by his behaviour. The Global Executive Leadership Mirror (GELM®) will be used as a framework for the analysis. In the first stage of Caesar's career, between the ages of 16 and 30, Caesar had little opportunity to manage others. As head of the family, he managed household staff in Rome. At least on two occasions, he mobilised troops for military action in the eastern Mediterranean. Still, we have no details regarding his behaviour. Typically, the analysis of this initial career stage would be restricted to the first main competency identified in the GELM: *Leading Self*. However, because Caesar achieved exceptional feats, we will also evaluate his behaviour with respect to

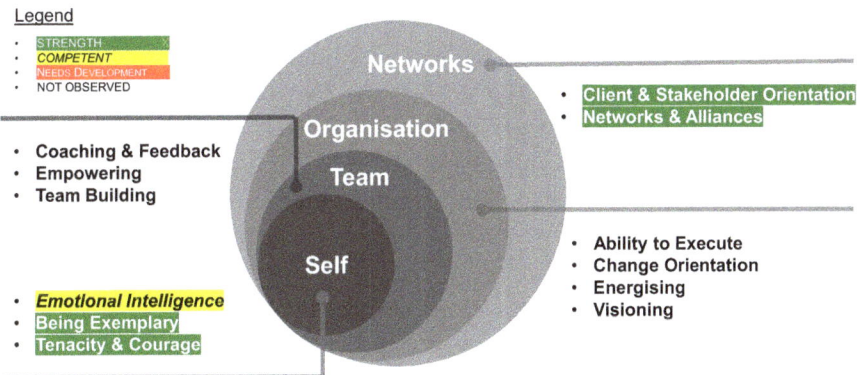

Fig. 2.5 Evaluation of Caesar's leadership behaviours during the early stage of his career according to the GELM. Author's adaptation based on GELM by KDVI

Leading Stakeholders and Networks. We will cover the most salient examples in this section. Figure 2.5 summarises the evaluation of Caesar's leadership behaviours during this period.

2.4.1 Leading Self

Regarding Emotional Intelligence, two instances shed light on Caesar's handling of his and others' emotions. The first is when Caesar refuses to divorce Cornelia at the behest of Sulla. The two men met in person to discuss the matter, but we have no record of their exchange. Given the haste with which Caesar had to escape from the city, Caesar underestimated Sulla's anger at his refusal. The second concerns the time he spent as captive of pirates. Caesar's challenging attitude, whether in sports and games or towards the pirates' negotiating strategy, seemed to have put the pirates in good spirits. Caesar spent his time in relative comfort until the ransom was paid.

We also get a glimpse of Caesar's Tenacity, that is, his ability to overcome setbacks and work towards a goal. Once more, let us return to Caesar's kidnapping. After being released unharmed, he could have simply continued onwards to Rhodes. The ransom had not cost him a penny. So why did he take the trouble to go after his captors? Was this driven by the belief that no one should get away with a crime? It would have sufficed for him to encourage the cities that had put up the funds for the ransom to recover their money and take measures to secure the seaways that were so important to their economy. Or was it a 'no-one messes with Caesar' type of reaction? This side was certainly evident in Caesar's character—initially reflected in his defiance of Sulla.

Another possible motivation appears from the wider context of events. Caesar left for Rhodes feeling only marginally successful. He seized the first occasion to do something remarkable in order to wipe his mediocre performance as a lawyer from public memory, preventing it from tarnishing his brand of success. It was a first occurrence that would transform into a pattern.

At this early stage, Caesar demonstrated loyalty to his values. Not only was he willing to act accordingly, but he was also prepared to suffer the consequences. The most telling example of his Being Exemplary, once again, is his refusal to divorce Cornelia. This choice was not only a matter of devotion to his wife and her family. It was also consistent with his political choice early in life. Although an aristocrat, Caesar was anti-Sullan. He supported the *populares*' cause of his father, his uncle Marius and father-in-law Cinna. So did his mother and her three brothers. All shared a desire to establish a more inclusive political system, more balanced towards granting non-senatorial groups a more significant say in the Republic's government. As a lawyer, Caesar sued two of Sulla's partisans. Once back in Rome as pontifex, he started campaigning to have Sulla's reforms revoked. His unwillingness to bow to Sulla's demand may also have been a show of independence. Caesar, nineteen at the time, had been the head of the Julii for a few years now, with a strong mother looking over his shoulder. Caesar may have been prompted to reset the power relationships within the family. Be that as it may, standing up against the dictator at nineteen was an act of great courage and so was his action on the battlefield at Mytilene a year later. Both almost cost Caesar his life. Not long after this, Caesar did something similarly courageous, albeit less risky. When Governor Juncus was dragging his feet to punish Caesar's kidnappers, the latter took justice in his own hands and had them executed himself. These examples of resoluteness when values are threatened says much about Caesar's character. The Rubicon loomed in the distance.

Another instance of consistency with values can be observed from Caesar's run-in with pirates. Crucifixion, a cruel method of execution, was the typical penalty for piracy and served as a deterrent. Caesar applied this sentence to his kidnappers, yet he spared them the most painful experience: Caesar had them strangled before they were attached to the cross. It was payback for his fair treatment while in captivity. Mercy was an essential value for Caesar.

2.4.2 Leading Stakeholders and Networks

Once back in Rome as pontifex, acting the part of a successful leader also served to develop a positive relationship with Stakeholders. Such stakeholders would include the inhabitants of the modest neighbourhood that Caesar called home. Sulla's reforms had reduced their influence and protection. These citizens would come together in the popular assembly that would elect the junior magistracy, for which he would soon be a candidate. It would also encompass the *equites*, the group socially below the senators and often wealthy business owners yet interested in reclaiming the influence that they had lost due to the dictator's reforms—causes for which Caesar actively lobbied. It laid the foundation for connections with Crassus and Pompey that we will explore in the next chapter. Caesar will have also supported his uncles on his mother's side, who, in the seventies, as consuls, managed to pass legislation to revoke some of Sulla's laws. During this period, Caesar benefited from his family Network. It protected him from the fallout of the civil war and restored him to the establishment. It is unclear how active he was in leveraging this network, but his mother certainly held the reigns. Caesar's lavish receptions were an opportunity to connect with the powers that be and those that will be.

2.5 Career Development: The Identification of a High Potential

Several individuals loomed large over the first 20 years of Caesar's life as role models and exemplars. When it comes to examples of formal leadership, there were first and foremost the three leaders of the civil war. Their successes and failures significantly affected Caesar's development. Intriguingly, of the three leaders, Sulla, the dictator, was the one with whom Caesar could identify most. Like Caesar, Sulla started his career with a good pedigree, little money and lost family status. Sulla even had to live for a while in a rented apartment. Thanks to his military achievements as an officer under Marius and to his marriage, Sulla could finance a political career and reach the consulship. To Caesar, Sulla was both a model and an anti-model. Sulla was a brave and successful military leader, adored by his men. He was merciless against his adversaries. He tried to restore order by turning the clock back, vesting the Senate with political power. He was not afraid to innovate, for example, by increasing the number of senators and magistrates to reinforce the government of the Republic. However, he could not be bothered about being appreciated by the general public. Sulla seized power through a military coup and did little to create a sustainable future for his country.

The second leader was Marius, Caesar's uncle. During Caesar's childhood, Marius was a military hero who had saved Rome from a barbarian invasion. Thanks to his military achievements, he attained the consulship several times despite being a social upstart. Marrying Caesar's aunt was his ticket into the highest circles. Marius felt competition from the younger Sulla, his most talented officer. He tried to resist Sulla's march on Rome, but the would-be dictator's army was too strong, forcing Marius to flee the city. When Sulla left Rome for Asia, Marius returned and took power in Rome with Cinna, Caesar's father-in-law, and the third civil war leader. Together, they started a bloody purge of current and former adversaries. Marius died soon afterwards. Cinna tried to calm the situation by making amends with the Senate and Sulla. He also attempted to stimulate the economy—two initiatives that Caesar would keep in mind. When Sulla refused to make peace, Cinna mustered an army. He was killed by mutinous troops, leaving a vacuum for Sulla to fill.

From his father, Caesar inherited a sense of duty to serve the Republic through the formal leadership structure of the *cursus honorum*. Gaius Sr also imbued his son with a sense of duty towards the family and to perpetuate its long-term success and continuity. Caesar learned about informal leadership from the women in his family, his sisters and particularly his mother. Their female power protected and propelled him towards his early career. Such power was, in the patriarchy of the Republic, by definition informal. It was wielded through family relationships, networking and the exchange of information and money. Caesar took good note of this.

In his twenties, Caesar had the opportunity to try out several endeavours—some by choice, some by chance. He sought opportunities to learn by doing and studying. His exile to the East, from age 20 to 22, when the ground in Rome was too warm under his feet after having stood up to Sulla, afforded him his first professional experience. He served on the staff of the governor of the province of Asia. It was akin to a traineeship in both civil and military service and a standard step in the career development of a junior member of the elite. Caesar could have avoided engaging in military action, but he didn't. During his service period, Caesar took part in two military campaigns: one on the island of Lesbos and one against pirates (not the ones that kidnapped him later) in what is now southern Turkey. On Lesbos, like a Greek hero under the walls of Troy, he saved a fellow soldier while storming the city of Mytilene. He was awarded the Roman equivalent of the Medal of Honour or the Victoria Cross (the *corona civica*), a crown of oak leaves to be worn in public. This head dress has been associated with Caesar until this day. It was his first leadership experience beyond managing household staff. By doing so, he made the experience he could win on the battlefield.

After returning from exile, he gave practising law a go with mixed success. After failing to secure victory in two lawsuits, he thought he needed further study. He departed to Rhodes to improve his skills in rhetoric. On his way to Rhodes and during his studies there, he twice took the initiative to unleash military action against his kidnappers and in nearby Cilicia. Caesar left

Rhodes to become pontifex in Rome, which offered the opportunity to engage in political discussions and networking. These he did with gusto, becoming a real socialite and spending a substantial amount of borrowed money in the process.

Yet from his experience as a lawyer, he did not learn what his real development need was. Possibly, he did not receive the feedback that learning to influence stakeholders would be more helpful than enhancing his public speaking skills in Rhodes. Upon his return to Rome as pontifex, he had four military successes on his record. At this point, he acknowledged that a legal career was not for him and that he would be better suited to follow the *cursus honorum*, oscillating between military and civil responsibilities. He could look towards several such examples in his family environment, both on his father's and mother's sides. Romans believed that a good leader in government could also be a competent military leader, and vice versa. The civil war leaders, however, had just demonstrated that this was not necessarily the case. Finally, we have no information on whether Caesar, in any of his activities and assignments, had the opportunity to learn how to work in a team configuration.

Living the high life in Rome, as Caesar did in his late twenties, is akin to 'acting the part', in the words of management author Jo Owen. It pays to learn from and imitate some of the rituals, values, behaviours and dress codes of more senior individuals in a hierarchy. In Rome, this meant mimicking a successful leader. Wearing a medal of valour and having some military success to show, he started to resemble one aspect of the ideal Roman leader—the victorious general. Establishing himself as a 'wealthy senator, who generously engaged in conspicuous consumption', Caesar acted the other part—the successful political leader.

Nearing the age of 30, Caesar was formally ready to start the *cursus honorum*, the leadership pipeline of the Roman Republic. How prepared was he for the first passage across the career ladder, that is, from 'leading self' to 'leading others'? According to the *Leadership Pipeline*, the most critical shift in this passage is a value shift: to value the work done by others for you and, by extension, to appreciate constructive horizontal and vertical relations with peers, stakeholders and bosses. In his early twenties, Caesar had some experience commanding troops and ships in military engagements. The little we know about his behaviour projects a top–down management style. In Rome, Caesar spent quite some time and effort on relationship-building with stakeholders. His track record thus far of invincibility in battle and excellence but vulnerability in the public domain (e.g. his foray into law) would repeat itself throughout his career.

After winning an election to military tribune, Caesar must have felt ready for the next step. His ambition was to follow the traditional path of Roman

Fig. 2.6 Marble head of Julius Caesar, eighteenth century. © The Trustees of the British Museum. Reprinted under license

leadership. Thus far, he had successfully overcome considerable hardship. He put himself in harm's way more than once, on the battlefield and by refusing to compromise his values. Remaining authentic and true to his values no matter what became part of his career vision. Caesar (Fig. 2.6) emerged victorious every time, owing to his actions as well as his mother and her network. He invested more than he could afford in building a support network and a reputation. He took out loans that he would never have been able to reimburse without a lucrative provincial or military assignment. Thus far, he had only learned that risks were well worth taking.

2.6 What Aspiring Leaders Can Learn from the Dawn of Caesar's Career

Caesar's behaviours and achievements in his early career demonstrated considerable leadership potential. Some of his accomplishments and actions were rather exceptional and put him in the public spotlight early on. He acquired a reputation as someone worth having on your team because of what he was able to deliver. Quite remarkable for this stage was Caesar's recognition of the importance of visibility and relationship-building with senior leaders in an organisation well before going through the first leadership passage. It gave him access to strategic information and helped him decide on the best course of action. Through networking and 'acting the part', he acquired the sponsorship that enabled him to launch his career.

Caesar was ambitious and driven by his family's expectations. He wanted to reach high without yet having a particular career goal. Grasping opportunities for early operational (military) experiences was paramount to launching his career and gave it direction. He tried out different types of jobs, and by the time he reached his late twenties, he was set on following the traditional career path of the *cursus honorum*. He was of his own mind in his choices but was also willing to follow advice, such as his mother's who arranged for him to become pontifex. He took risks—often tricky—and stood for his values, but it paid off in his development as a leader and his career progression.

The destruction, bloodshed and chaos that Caesar witnessed during his youth, which determined the zeitgeist, also impacted the development of Caesar's personality. Simultaneously, both the war with the Italian allies and the civil war had a zero-sum outcome. Caesar became convinced that cruelty and revenge were not the pathway to lasting peace. We are unaware of any close friendships dating from this period, except for Servilia, his teenage sweetheart. They would remain lovers for as long as Caesar lived. The treachery that Caesar saw during the civil war may have inspired a wariness of closeness with male friends. As a young adult, when he got into trouble by standing up against Sulla, he benefited from the protection of his mother. He soon learned through military action that he could use violence effectively.

Caesar met several senior leaders whose qualities and mistakes he took good note of. Later, once we have reviewed Caesar's development over his lifetime, we will see in the final chapter how these early experiences and encounters have forged Caesar's leadership personality. From the example of Caesar, leaders can learn that it is helpful to do some introspection to understand their values and where they originate from to gain better self-awareness. It is equally beneficial to go back into one's personal history to discover whether the ambition that drives a leader is really one's own. Caesar followed—at least to a significant extent—someone else's ambition, namely his family's. If that is the case, the leader needs to reflect on whether they are ok with that or whether they prefer to discover their personal ambitions and to follow these. In this book, we will see that Caesar's relentless motivation for excellence and his ambition to be always the best drove him to great heights, but not always to the best course of action.

At the dawn of his leadership career, Caesar made his mother proud, while at the same time causing her considerable anxiety for his fearless undertakings. By the examples he witnessed in his family and direct influence from his relatives, Caesar was filled with pride about where he came from, perhaps also with a sense of entitlement that greatness was his due. He was now ready to rise above the fray, for which he felt destined.

Bibliography

Greek and Roman Sources

Appian, *Roman History. The Civil Wars*, Book I–II.
Plutarch, Lives of *Caesar, Crassus, Pompey*.
Suetonius Tranquillus, G., *Life of Julius Caesar*.

Modern Works

Bleicken, J. (2004). *Geschichte der römischen Republik*. R. Oldenbourg Verlag.
Casson, L. (1991). *The ancient mariners. Seafarers and sea fighters of the Mediterranean in ancient times* (2nd ed.). Princeton University Press.
Charan, R., Drotter, S., & Noel, J. (2001). *The leadership pipeline. How to build the leadership powered company*. Jossey-Bass.
Crook, J. A., Lintott, A., & Rawson, E. (Eds.). (1994). *The Cambridge ancient history* (The last age of the Roman Republic, 146–43 B.C.) (Vol. IX, 2nd ed.). Cambridge University Press.
Freud, S. (1940–1952). *Gesammelte Werke. Chronologisch geordnet*. Imago.
Gelzer, M. (2008). *Caesar. Der Politiker und Staatsmann*. Franz Steiner Verlag.
Griffin, M. (Ed.). (2009). *A companion to Julius Caesar*. Wiley-Blackwell.
Gruen, E. S. (1995). *The last generation of the Roman Republic*. University of California Press.
KDVI. https://kdvi.com/tools/
Meier, C. (1997). *Caesar*. DTV.
Morstein-Marx, R. (2021). *Julius Caesar and the Roman people*. Cambridge University Press.
Owen, J. (2009). *How to Lead. What you actually need to do to manage, lead and succeed* (2nd ed.). Pearson Education.
Vanderbroeck, P. J. J. (1987). *Popular leadership and collective behavior ca. 80–50 BC*. J.C. Gieben.
Vanderbroeck, P. (2012). Crises: Ancient and modern. Understanding an ancient Roman crisis can help us move beyond our own. *Management & Organizational History, 7*(2), 113–131.

3

Rising Above the Fray: From High Potential to Leader

> *….Sweating beneath the weight of their white woollen candidate's togas, the trio of contenders stood upon the elevated platform. A canopy provided some shade from the searing sun on this summer's day. They watched a vast sea of toga-draped citizens slowly moving row by row across the field as they ascended the bridges to deposit their votes into the urns, Suddenly, the senator overseeing the voting process called a halt. He announced the first candidate who had passed the post and was elected consul of the Roman Republic. Raising his arm and stepping forward to receive the thunderous ovation from the assembly, the new consul's eyes sought out his mother. He caught her eye as she was standing at the far end of the field, his daughter in her arms, watching the proceedings that brought her son to power…*
> (This quote is fictional and created by the author for illustrative purposes.)

When Caesar was 30 years old and at the minimum age to begin the *cursus honorum,* the career structure of Roman government, he was already at an advantage. He had received the best possible education. He had shown courage in battle and pronounced political principles. He had secured his first election victory and obtained a prestigious priesthood. From his father, he had inherited an aristocratic pedigree; moreover, his mother and her powerful family provided a support network that Caesar expanded through his socialising. He had become known for the fact that he lived among the people and for 'looking the part' of a Roman leader. What he was lacking, though, was sufficient funding for his election campaigns. Living above his means, he was at risk of running out of money before he could even get his career on track.

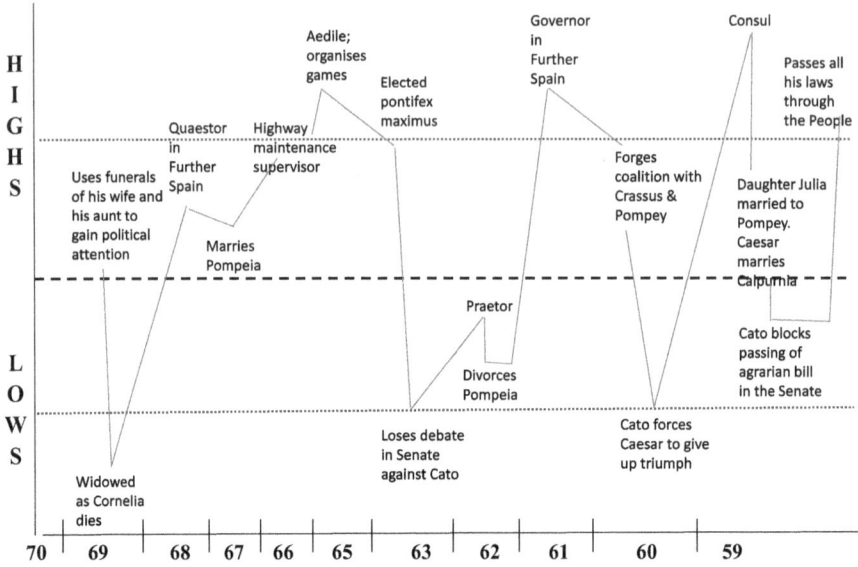

Fig. 3.1 Caesar's leadership timeline: Highs and Lows 70–59 BC. Author's own illustration

In this chapter, we will examine the next ten years of Caesar's career as a leader in the service of the Republic (Fig. 3.1). This period, where Caesar ascended through all the ranks of the Roman professional hierarchy, is particularly relevant in terms of career progression. We will find answers to the following questions: How did Caesar leverage his strengths and minimise weaknesses to realise a career and performance that lived up to his potential? What were the key elements that built his career? How did he adapt to his surrounding context? What competition did he encounter from peers, and how did he handle that? How did he establish his brand as a leader? How did he exercise leadership?

3.1 Caesar's Life and Mid-Career

The civil war and the rule of Sulla and his partisans strongly influenced Caesar's first 30 years of life and early career. In the year 70 BC, Pompey and Crassus, as consuls, did much to re-establish the balance of power between the People and the Senate, notably by restoring the powers of the tribunes of the plebs. However, the competition between the two major factions—those in favour of Sulla's conservative reforms (*optimates*) and those in opposition (*populares*)—for the next ten years would dominate Roman politics. Caesar now openly sided with the anti-Sulla faction. In 69, Caesar, being the head of the Julii family, gave a eulogy at the funeral of Caesar's aunt and Marius's widow, Julia. Innovatively, he displayed portraits of his uncle, Marius, at the funeral cortege, thus resuscitating Marius's memory in a post-Sullan world that had banned his image. This defiance against the Sullan establishment garnered Caesar great popularity with the People, who had considered Marius to be their patron and a saviour of Rome.

Soon after, Caesar lost his wife, Cornelia, and Aurelia took their daughter, Julia, under her wing. Again, he gave a funeral speech at the well-attended Forum. Caesar apparently used his rhetorical skills to fill his speech with emotion and passion, leaving the attendees in awe. Incidentally, a funeral speech for a younger woman (Cornelia was 28 when Caesar was widowed) was unprecedented and another of Caesar's innovations.

During that same year, Caesar was elected by the People to the office of quaestor for the year 69. He was 31 when he held the office. There were twenty quaestors in total, and they represented the first rung on Rome's public service career ladder. Though it was an introductory management position in government, it presented unique challenges: For most quaestors, it was their first time supervising staff who were neither slaves nor on their personal payroll nor part of the disciplined, hierarchical organisation of the army. The tenure was one year. Caesar was among the quaestors sent abroad. He was assigned to Further Spain (modern-day Andalusia). Here, he served in the provincial administration by presiding over the courts and dealing with financial matters.

The quaestorship also was the entry point to the Senate. Once a senator, Caesar could add a broad purple band to his *tunica*, worn under the toga but still visible so that all could recognise who was a senator. Purple was the colour of kings. On the dress of a senator, the colour purple symbolised the authority that the Senate had seized from the kings after the revolution that had established the Republic almost five centuries before. Caesar continued to wear his clothing in his distinctive style: loosely fitting, giving him a distinct air of youthful nonchalance. He also became known for his skilful speeches, which he now could display before the Senate. He had an elegant yet uncomplicated rhetorical style. As a junior senator, Caesar made himself heard by partaking in the discussions in this illustrious body.

Caesar remarried in the year 67. Surprisingly, he took Pompeia, a granddaughter of Sulla's, for his bride. Supporters of Caesar's uncle, Marius, had killed Pompeia's father during the civil war. Such an arrangement could have been an attempt at reconciliation with the supporters of Sulla. Still, two years later, Caesar prosecuted two men accused of crimes committed on Sulla's behalf.

During that time, pirates threatened trade in the Mediterranean and, thus, Rome's corn supply. Some senators proposed to grant Pompey extraordinary powers and resources to solve this problem. Pompey (Gnaeus Pompeius) was Rome's most successful general at that time, and therefore nicknamed the Great (Magnus). The proposal was controversial because it would confer Pompey far more power than a usual general or provincial governor. With the civil war still fresh on their minds, the senatorial majority considered it too risky to put so many resources in the hands of one individual. However, Rome's inhabitants and merchants—who depended on a reliable corn supply and safe trade routes—needed an immediate solution to this problem. Caesar, consistent in his position, stood with the minority in the Senate. Besides, he knew from personal experience how dangerous the shipping lanes had become. Although a junior senator, he vociferously championed the People's opinion. Pompey was granted the assignment by popular vote and, within a few months, he swept the Mediterranean free of pirates. In the year 66, Pompey received another extraordinary assignment: to remove the threat of King Mithridates once and for all in the Eastern Mediterranean and Black Sea, again with Caesar's support. Pompey, an erstwhile supporter of Sulla, had been leading the 'desullanisation' of the Roman state. Now, Caesar was firmly on the side of the People's faction, the *populares*. This shift was the start of the coalition between Caesar and Pompey.

In 66, Caesar won his subsequent election as curator of the Via Appia, one of Rome's oldest roads, which connected the city with the Port of Brindisi on the Adriatic. The curator's role was to maintain this vital highway and its infrastructure, including bridges and waystations. It offered Caesar an opportunity to make a name for himself. Roman civil service jobs typically allotted insufficient staff and budget. Caesar took out hefty loans both to fulfil his duties and to make sure his accomplishments were not forgotten. He put his name on the infrastructure he built or repaired, as was customary for curators to do. In Rome, he continued to finance a luxurious lifestyle on credit, building himself a mansion in the surrounding hills.

He was elected to become aedile the following year, in 65. It was the next stage on the career ladder. Aediles were responsible for public order, urban infrastructure, markets, water and food supply in the city. In addition, and most importantly when it came to image-building, they oversaw the games. Caesar took the opportunity to stage lavish games, and he ensured the public was aware that he had personally financed them as proof of his generosity.

Furthermore, as part of his management of urban infrastructure, Caesar restored the monuments dedicated to his uncle Marius's victories against foreign enemies, which had been taken down as part of Sulla's purges. Caesar also had copies made of the monuments that had been destroyed. However, he had this work done in secret. During one night, he had monuments restored to their original place at the Forum and the Capitol. When the sun rose, the surprise had its desired effect on the public, who was duly awed. They flocked to the city centre to admire and applaud the sight. This stunt elicited the ire of many senators, who wished to keep the memory of Marius swept under the rug.

These roles undoubtedly contributed to his successful election to *pontifex maximus* in 63, where he became head of the priesthood of which he was already a member. Though pontifex maximus was a position for life and outside the government career track, it awarded considerable prestige to its incumbent. The priests were co-opted, but their president was elected by the popular assembly. When the pontifex maximus died, Caesar seized the opportunity to stand for election. Caesar's popularity secured him the victory, even if the position was traditionally reserved for the oldest pontifices. With the prestige of the office came a residence near the Forum, on the Via Sacra, right in the middle of Roman political activity. At 37, Caesar and his family left their dwelling in the popular neighbourhood and moved into their new prestigious home.

That same year marked another political crisis in Rome, in which the Republic came close to civil war. Heavily indebted after losing another election for consul, the senator Catiline staged a desperate revolt. Promising debt relief, many from the middle and upper classes in Rome and the countryside were enchanted by this tune. He also sought support from the urban poor. However, Cicero (Fig. 3.2), the elected consul, thwarted the attempt, and the Senate declared a state of emergency. Cicero proposed to deal with the apprehended conspirators swiftly and decisively through execution, a stance with which Cato the Younger, another opinion leader in the Senate, agreed. Caesar, however, pleaded for an alternative punishment in the ensuing debate. Although Caesar initially managed to get the Senate to agree to his proposal for imprisonment, Cicero's death penalty proposal was ultimately favoured. Henceforth, Cato and Caesar were political rivals.

Caesar was elected praetor to serve in 62. During this time, he supported legislation that served Pompey's interests, but was unsuccessful. At the end of that same year, Caesar divorced Pompeia after the scandal at his home, which was discussed in the previous chapter. Soon after, he was set to leave Rome for

Fig. 3.2 Nineteenth century impression of Cicero's speech against Catilina in the Senate. Fresco by Cesare Maccari (fragment), Palazzo Madama, Rome. Public domain; Wikimedia Commons. https://commons.wikimedia.org/w/index.php?curid =132651272

his next assignment as governor of Further Spain in 61. After their tenure in Rome, praetors were usually expatriated to govern a province, a role that did not require an election. This system was probably for the better in Caesar's case, given how he handled the praetorship. Financing another election would have only added to his already vast debts and made it difficult to raise funds. Caesar was nominated to govern the province of Further Spain on the western fringe of the empire, the same province where, eight years prior, he had served as quaestor on the governor's staff. However, there was a roadblock. Caesar's creditors prevented him from leaving before he repaid his debts, lest he die overseas. Moreover, since Caesar's praetorship had not proven particularly successful, he seemed less worth the investment than initially thought.

Caesar went to Marcus Licinius Crassus, who was at the time the wealthiest man in Rome. Crassus was a real estate tycoon who had started his business by buying and selling the properties Sulla had confiscated during the post-civil war purges. Crassus was the informal leader of Rome's business community. (One could compare him to Silvio Berlusconi, the former Italian nouveau riche tycoon turned politician.) Crassus saw the potential in Caesar and thought he could do with Caesar's support to keep up with Pompey in power and influence. Thus, Crassus put up a pledge for Caesar's debts that allowed him to leave. Caesar became an effective governor and general during his time in Spain. He reformed taxation and improved governance in the interest of a sustainable administration of the province. As a general, he waged war against the Iberian tribes that Rome had not yet conquered in modern-day Portugal to secure the borders of the province. He was victorious, and the resulting plunder was enough to repay his debts in Rome. After winning the war, Caesar returned to Rome entitled to a triumph—a Roman victory parade.

Back in Rome, Caesar established an effective political coalition with Pompey and Crassus, the so-called First Triumvirate, in the year 60. The following year, Caesar, as consul, managed to pass a series of laws that were in his and his partners' interests as well as solved pressing problems. After leveraging their support to get himself elected, Caesar, as consul, could pass laws that would benefit his allies after they had failed to obtain a majority in the previous years. Caesar's consulship was full of legislation and often vehement debate. He cemented the coalition by marrying off his only daughter, Julia, to Pompey. This marriage was a copy-paste of the bond between Marius and Caesar's aunt: a successful general and social climber weds the daughter of an aristocratic family. Julia married into money; Pompey into social standing.

At 41, Caesar had already reached the highest rung of the government career ladder, consul. He had now finally surpassed his father Gaius Sr. Aurelia must have been as proud as her son. While in this office, Caesar secured the promising assignment of governing the Gallic provinces after the consulate. He spearheaded social and economic reforms and influenced the governance of the empire. He positioned himself firmly and consistently on the *populares* side of the political spectrum. He maintained a strong alliance with Pompey and Crassus, Rome's most powerful politicians. He needed only to add significant military victories and substantial wealth to his record to become an equal partner in the triumvirate.

This chapter mentions many elections and legislative activities. Therefore, it may be helpful to be reminded how the different institutions of the Roma Republic worked by repeating Fig. 3.3.

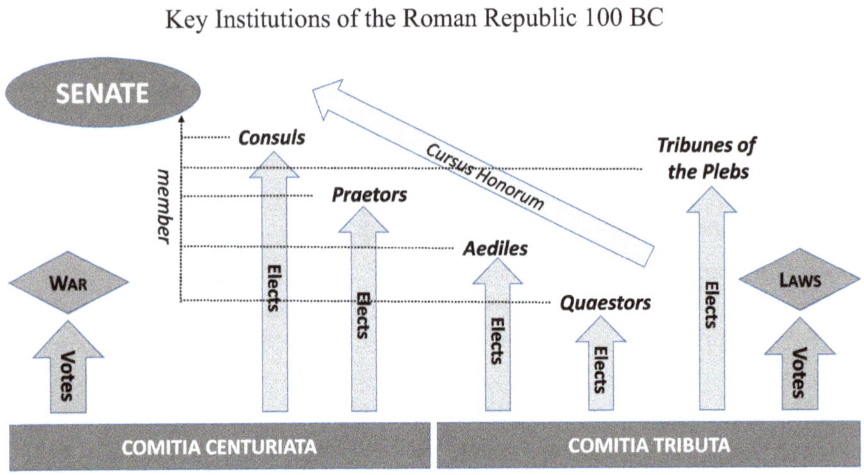

Key Institutions of the Roman Republic 100 BC

Fig. 3.3 Key institutions of the Roman Republic 100 BC. Author's own illustration

3.2 Caesar's Mid-Career Achievements

After the overview of Caesar's career in the 60 s BC, let us now look in more detail what Caesar achieved and did not achieve as he moved up the career ladder and how he did that.

3.2.1 Performance in Different Roles

From the start, Caesar took his role as a senator seriously. He actively participated in the debates over granting Pompey the power to extinguish the pirates and Mithridates' forces as well as the handling of Catiline and his conspirators. When Caesar was responsible for public services in Rome and Italy—as curator of the Via Appia and then as aedile—he performed exceptionally well in improving the city's infrastructure and facilitating leisure activities. He then upped the ante: As aedile, he found it opportune to stage gladiatorial fights in honour of his father, Gaius, who had died 20 years before. And his work did not end at just the fights. Caesar surpassed previous shows through sheer scale (he had 320 pairs of gladiators engaging in bloody combat) and spectacle (each of the gladiators appeared in silver armour). Buying gladiators was expensive, and so he ran up considerable costs funding these games.

He also performed well during his two overseas assignments in Spain as quaestor and governor, particularly during the latter, where his achievements truly stood out. Because of his military success, he was even awarded a triumph—a recognition of exceptional achievement. Ultimately, the spoils of his efforts abroad were enough to clear his debts. Caesar's tenure in Spain gave a foretaste of what he would later carry out in Gaul at a much larger scale. In Spain, Caesar showed an early interest in empire-building: He released local cities from an exploitative tax burden while at the same time issuing guarantees for Rome's private tax-collecting companies. Also, he improved the governance of the cities. He reformed laws, which, it is worth mentioning, put an end to the practice of human sacrifice where that was still carried out.

Caesar's performance as praetor (in the year before he went to Spain for the second time), however, was less brilliant. Caesar shared the office with seven colleagues. Regarding his primary responsibility, overseeing the judicial system, he appeared to simply fulfil his objectives, performing his primary duties of presiding over the jury courts without meriting either criticism or praise. When it came to his legislative tasks, however, he failed to reach his goals. As we will discuss later in this chapter, the resistance he received from Cato and others was overpowering. Fortunately, when he became governor of Spain immediately following the praetorship, he was able to turn things around.

During the election campaign for consul, Caesar brought Pompey and Crassus together to build the coalition that went down in history as the First Triumvirate. The solution they negotiated was that they would mutually support each other to realise the following objectives during Caesar's tenure: Caesar would receive a sizeable provincial command after his year as consul was up, Pompey would get his settlement of the East and land for his veterans, and Crassus would get a much better deal for the tax-collecting companies that formed an influential part of his constituency.

Upon starting their office, newly elected consuls called a Senate meeting to express their view of the state of the Republic and to outline their plans for the year. After introducing their vision, they called upon individual senators to comment. On this occasion, Caesar would have donned his official toga, which distinguished itself by its very visible broad purple stripe on the border. Accompanied by twelve formally dressed lictors—civil servants who acted as bodyguards and attendants—he walked in formal procession the short distance from his new residence on the Via Sacra to the Senate building. The city centre was usually crowded. Throngs of citizens and visitors bore witness to this spectacle of power and standing. After speaking to the Senate, the consuls held a speech before the people. Consul Caesar's first decision was an innovation within Rome's political sphere. It entailed that, henceforth, scribes would record and publish a transcript of every meeting of the Senate and popular assembly. It was called *acta diurna* or daily news. After being posted up in public, they were archived in an *album*. There were private companies who made a business out of distributing copies in Italy and the provinces. This act of transparency and documentation was Caesar's measure against political obstruction and false testimony, as the senatorial debates themselves were not public. It also presented an early example of how Caesar wanted to involve the Roman citizens in his government.

Caesar had prepared his consulate. Within a few days, he proposed his agrarian bill to the Senate. The proposal offered land to Pompey's veterans and members of the urban poor to alleviate some of Rome's socio-economic tensions. Such laws had been proposed before but had not always been successful. With the professionalisation and demobilisation of the army, such proposals became commonplace. Caesar's bill foresaw the distribution of available public land and, in addition, the purchase of private land financed from the windfall of Pompey's campaigns in the East. It was a balanced proposal because it did not involve displacing landowners or any additional taxation. However, as we will see later in this chapter, the opposition of Cato and others prevented the bill from being approved in the Senate. Caesar subsequently initiated his backup plan: proposing the bill to the People without the Senate's endorsement.

Next, the popular assembly ratified Pompey's enactments in the East and the rebate for the tax farmers, which was Crassus's wish. At his own initiative, Caesar admonished the tax farmers to stop overbidding for contracts. Finally, Caesar was voted governor of Cisalpine Gaul, a post he would begin after the consulate. Within just a few months, Caesar had already realised the objectives of each of the triumvirs. However, Caesar did not stop there. In May, he passed another agrarian bill. This time, rich public land was to be distributed to large families in the city. Caesar was also assigned to govern two additional provinces—Transalpine Gaul and Illyricum. Planning ahead now, he tried to position himself again at the fringe of the empire, which in previous years had granted him the opportunity to seize military glory and financial gain in Spain. In Gaul, incursions from across the Rhine posed a potential threat to the territories under Roman rule. This was just the opportunity Caesar needed.

In August, he passed a law on the provincial government—a far-sighted and far-reaching law that would be enforced until the end of the Roman Empire. It resembled our modern-day Sarbanes–Oxley Act in its intent and construction. This act was a reaction to a number of major corporate and accounting scandals. It provides compliance regulations for bookkeeping and reporting for corporations listed on the US Stock Exchange. Caesar had been part of a provincial administration three times, once in Asia Minor and twice in Spain, where he had witnessed first-hand the right way to govern and the wrong way. Prosecution for purpose of extortion regularly occupied Roman courts. Governors and tax farmers alike frequently exploited the provinces for personal gain. The case of Verres, who was sued by Cicero ten years earlier on behalf of the exasperated Sicilian public, has gone down in history as an extreme example. As governor of Sicily, Gaius Verres was responsible for the collection of taxes and for buying corn to supply the city of Rome. He manipulated financial data and siphoned off taxes and government funds meant for the purchase of corn to his own account. This money he then loaned at high interest to whoever needed cash. He met his targets in taxes and corn by forcing the Sicilians to pay higher taxes and sell corn at a lower price. In Spain, Caesar recognised that such common practice was not a sustainable way of generating income for the state. As consul, he warned the tax farmers to stop overbidding for contracts, because it led to exploitation.

What's more, instances in Spain had demonstrated that unhappy provinces could give rise to revolts and provide a support base for civil war rebels. Therefore, Caesar's law outlined how Roman officials abroad were to govern the provinces and set rigorous limits on the reimbursements that provincial governors could claim from the treasury and provincials. It also required strict accounting, including duplicates of records, to create an audit trail. The law concluded a year of high-intensity legislation and served as a prelude to when Caesar was in full command of the city and the empire after ending the civil war.

Except while praetor, Caesar proved to be a high performer in each of his positions between 70 and 59. His achievements within these roles were recognised as well above average. Each time, his accomplishments helped propel him to the next level—and through the elections he needed to win to get there. He excelled when he was in a position of autonomy with clear boundaries. Once Caesar was in the senior leadership positions of governor and consul, his performance reached strategic proportions: He introduced well-thought-out reforms and legislation that had long-term positive effects on the city of Rome and the empire.

However, when he had to deal with soft boundaries and depend on his influencing skills alone, Caesar struggled to perform at the same level. These hurdles had already troubled him before, both as a lawyer and during the debate on the Catilinarian conspirators. Caesar found it difficult to broker a deal with stakeholders behind the scenes. Once consul, his leadership organisation, which will be discussed next, compensated for the lack of influencing skills. Caesar would use this key advantage to continue to perform above and beyond in his role. Still, as we will see in the subsequent chapters, his development need in influencing would come back to haunt him several times during his career.

3.2.2 Building a Leadership Organisation to Mobilise Followers

Leaders during Caesar's lifetime could follow either of two approaches to secure agreements and, thus, initiate change. The traditional and most harmonious way was to achieve a majority vote in the Senate, an approach that would also guarantee buy-in from the higher levels of society. This was the way the oligarchy was expected to function, and those who pursued that method were referred to as *optimates*. The alternative, which the Gracchi brothers had introduced some 30 years before Caesar was born, was to bypass the Senate or ignore its advice and propose a bill directly to the popular assembly. Those who primarily counted on the People to get things done were called *populares*.

Winning the vote (Fig. 3.4) in the popular assembly was a matter of influencing public opinion and mobilising voters. The most successful leaders employed a 'leadership organisation', which was an informal organisation with a three-level leadership structure: top, middle and first level. Since Roman statesmen were not allowed to propose a bill for their own self-benefit, a top leader, say Pompey, would informally engage mid-level leaders to enact their plans. At the mid-level position in the leadership structure were junior magistrates, particularly tribunes of the plebs, whose legitimate formal authority permitted them to convene public debates and popular assemblies, preside over these meetings, introduce bills and conduct a vote. Additionally, the tribune's ability to veto the decisions of all other magistrates and in the assembly was effective in blocking decisions that endangered their patron's agenda.

Fig. 3.4 Coin from 63 BC showing Roman citizen casting a vote at the urn. © Museum of Cultural History, Oslo, M214023. Reprinted under license

Moreover, the lower orders recognised that the original purpose of tribunes was to promote the interests of the people, which gave tribunes an edge in mobilising a following on behalf of their patron. These mid-level leaders were in turn supported by first-level leaders who directly interacted with the electorate. First-level leaders were recruited from members of the plebs. Though they did not hold any formal authority, they were able to rally followers thanks to their elevated social status (typically they were the heads of a professional, neighbourhood, or religious association) and network.

Being part of a top leader's organisation had its benefits; those outside of the Roman elite stood a better chance of climbing the social ladder and becoming military officers or higher-level magistrates if they aligned themselves with a leader from the *populares*. Operating as a first-level leader could be the first career step towards entry into a higher social order or a magistracy for themselves or their offspring. However, there were challenges to making this plan work. Pompey himself obtained mixed results. In 67, the tribune Gabinius managed to pass a law through the assembly granting Pompey special command over forces that would crush the pirates. Despite this success, in 62, the tribune Metellus Nepos and Caesar as praetor failed to secure a bill that would give Pompey a similar command against Catiline. Learning from this experience—and having discovered in Spain what he was capable of when granted full executive autonomy—Caesar devoted much effort into improving his leadership organisation before starting his consulship in 59.

Publius Vatinius is a case in point of how Caesar developed and used his leadership organisation. Vatinius won the election for quaestor in 63 and became a senator. In 62, Vatinius was assigned as quaestor to the province of Further Spain to serve on the staff of the governor, the same position Caesar had held in 69. However, on his way to Spain, he took a detour via Africa to do some investigative work on behalf of Caesar, who as praetor was involved in a court case regarding the African kingdom of Juba. Because Caesar became governor of Further Spain in 61, the two interacted during the handover between Caesar and Vatinius' boss, Governor Gaius Cosconius. Caesar and Cosconius had a good relationship. Later, as consul, Caesar would put him on his commission for land distribution to veterans, and perhaps Vatinius even recommended his former boss for the commissioner job. Vatinius, backed by Caesar and the other two triumvirs, was elected to become tribune of the plebs in 59. During that year of Caesar's consulship, Vatinius served as Caesar's foremost mid-level leader.

Vatinius came from a family outside of Rome. As the first of his family to enter the Senate, he was a *homo novus* ('new man'), hence a social climber. In a society where social status counted much, it was somewhat unusual for someone like Caesar to recruit a person of a modest background for an important position. Vatinius was quite ambitious, and he let it be known that his long-term career goal was the consulate. He would later follow Caesar to Gaul as a military officer, where he would make a fortune. Living up to his promise to develop Vatinius' career, Caesar decommissioned him to return to Rome to stand for election, and Vatinius became praetor in 55. Subsequently, Vatinius returned to Caesar's army in Gaul and acquired several military victories. He stayed loyal to Caesar throughout the civil war. In 47, his dream to become consul came true, followed by his governorship of Illyria.

While a quaestor in Spain, Caesar met one of his most important and loyal staff members: Lucius Cornelius Balbus. Eight years later, in 61, Caesar, now governor, recruited Balbus as his *praefectus fabrum*, or chief engineer and head of army logistics. Balbus served Caesar well during his military campaign in Spain. Caesar would employ him in the same job during his campaign in Gaul. From Spain, Balbus followed Caesar to Rome to serve on Caesar's staff alongside Vatinius while Caesar was consul. Rather than serve in a formal function, Balbus was more like a middle-man. For example, Caesar sent Balbus to Cicero to invite him—albeit unsuccessfully—to join the coalition with Crassus and Pompey. When Vatinius in 62 arrived from Africa to serve in the province of Further Spain, where Balbus was an important figure, both were already part of Caesar's network. The two would go on to lay the groundwork for Caesar's governorship a year later.

Living in the Suburra, and later in the city centre (Fig. 3.5) in his official residence, turned out to be an advantage. The citizens who made up the bulk of the popular assembly were right at Caesar's doorstep. It was there that he could observe and interact with artisans, shopkeepers and pub owners. He could, for example, become familiar with the person who conducted the religious ceremonies in the small temple down the street. He could build relationships with the presidents of butcher or vendor associations, who might be candidates to serve as first-level leaders to mobilise voters for the popular assembly. Others would have been in his employment when he was funding public works and organising games, such as foremen, small entrepreneurs and gladiator trainers. We know from his time in the military that Caesar easily connected with people from a less privileged background. This facilitated recruiting talent to complete his organisation. Box 3.1 gives an example of how Caesar mobilised followers.

3 Rising Above the Fray: From High Potential to Leader 61

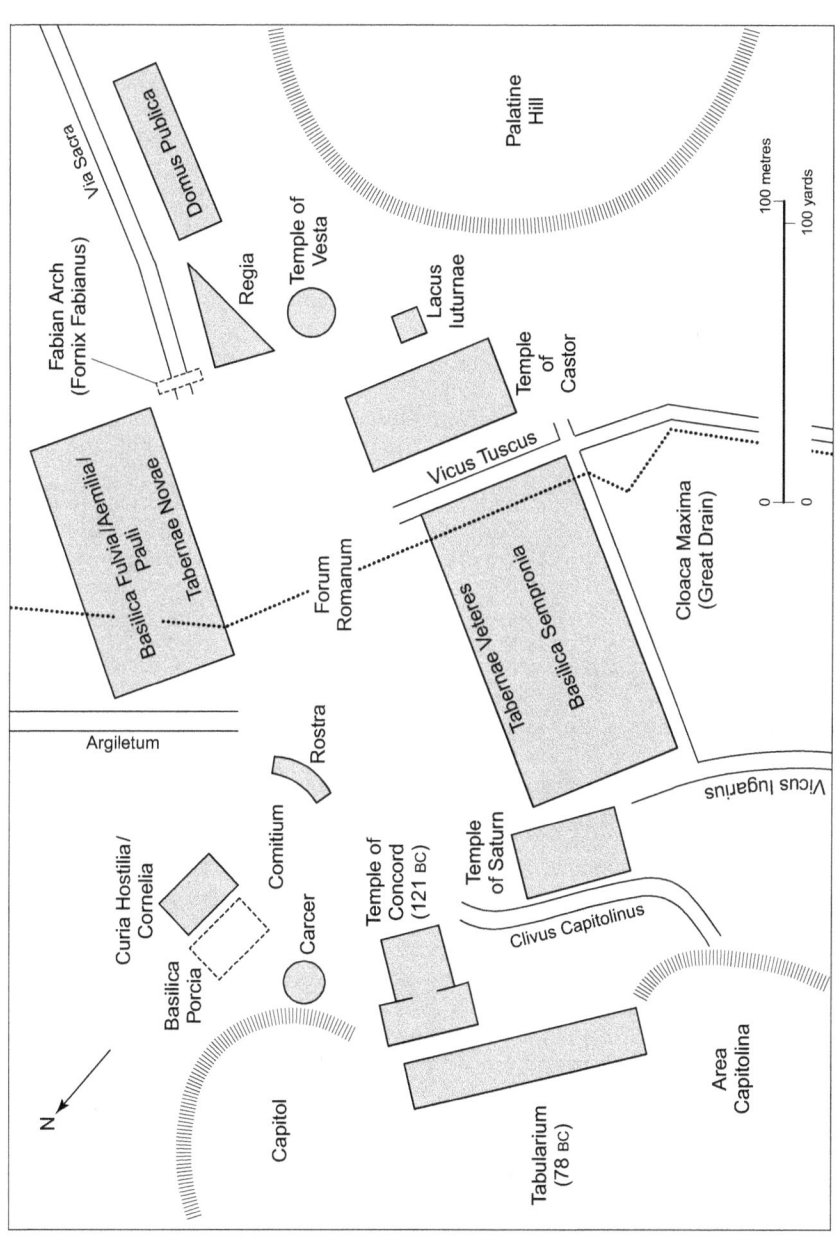

Fig. 3.5 The Roman Forum during the time of Julius Caesar. From: *A Companion to the Roman Republic* © John Wiley & Sons 2007. Reprinted under license

> **Box 3.1 Mobilising Followers**
>
> So how did this pan out in practice? Caesar started his consulate in early 59 by proposing a land distribution bill for Pompey's veterans in the Senate. Cato sabotaged that endeavour. Caesar then employed his leadership organisation to enact Plan B: putting the plan before the People. It was customary to hold a public debate before the vote, a kind of town hall meeting. Caesar called such a *contio* and Vatinius helped him mobilise participants. He asked his fellow consul and Cato's ally, Marcus Calpurnius Bibulus, to express his opinion on the law. Bibulus, as a true conservative, merely stated that he would not tolerate any other innovations this year. Caesar announced that the law would pass only if Bibulus agreed to it. He encouraged the crowd to join him in imploring his colleague to relent. Bibulus, visibly irritated, briskly shouted that there would be no law even if the People wanted it before he abruptly left the assembly. By provoking Bibulus to publicly express his intention to ignore the will of the People, Caesar had set a clever trap for his colleague that Bibulus had walked right into. Moreover, thanks to Caesar's innovation, interested people could now read the records of the Senate meetings and form their own opinion on how the Senate had handled Caesar's proposal. Some arrived at the *contio* already having formed an opinion about who was the 'good guy' and who was the 'bad guy'.
>
> Next, Caesar called the senior leaders, Crassus and Pompey, to the podium to express their opinions. Pompey voiced his support and detailed the provisions of the law. He also made it clear that there would be no problem funding the law, thanks to the wealth that his conquests had brought to the treasury. It was only fair that veterans and other citizens benefit from these achievements. The audience reacted approvingly. Caesar then beseeched the crowd to join him in asking Pompey if he was willing to help overcome opposition to the law. Pompey, noticeably pleased with this attention, said he would do whatever was necessary. Crassus joined him in this statement.
>
> In the next few days, Bibulus unsuccessfully employed procedural delays to prevent the vote. Caesar set the day for the bill to be put before the People. Many voters, including veterans, assembled on the Forum the night before. The following day, after the assembly had started and Caesar had begun reading the bill, Bibulus pushed himself through the crowd. He climbed the podium and interrupted Caesar's speech to voice his opposition. Under the leadership of Vatinius and Fibulus, one of his first-level leaders, citizens, incensed by this act of obstruction, intervened and pushed Bibulus and his retinue away. They also broke his fasces, which symbolised his consular authority. This was not an act of rebellion; it was the People's admonition of a consul who had forfeited his legitimacy through his negation of popular sovereignty. To add insult to injury, someone emptied a bucket of manure over his head. The law was voted through. Caesar's organisation kept a stronghold on the assembly for the remainder of the year and enabled him to realise his political programme.

To execute his programme as consul, Caesar built a leadership organisation that allowed him to influence public opinion and obtain majority votes for the bills he proposed in the popular assembly. The organisation was highly successful in its aims, permitting Caesar to keep the support of the People

3 Rising Above the Fray: From High Potential to Leader

throughout the entire legislative period, which was exceptional. Most leaders could not manage to maintain that support beyond one bill or assembly.

3.3 Caesar's Mid-Career Leadership Behaviours

Returning to the Global Executive Leadership Mirror (GELM®)'s framework, we will analyse Caesar's leadership competencies based on his behaviour, covering the most salient examples. Figure 3.6 summarises the evaluation of Caesar's leadership behaviours during this period.

3.3.1 Leading Self

Regarding Caesar's willingness and ability to learn from his mistakes, his building of a leadership organisation is a telling example. Caesar's limited success as praetor taught him the value of adapting his strategy to sway the vote in his favour, chiefly through the popular assembly. His Emotional Intelligence, meanwhile, was mixed, notably regarding persuading large groups of people. He was successful when he could leverage hierarchical power, such as when he was a governor or general. When he had to do so without authority—i.e. through influencing—he was less successful. However, leading without authority was a skill a politician needed to get elected, pass bills in the assembly and get the Senate to decide in one's favour. Though resistance from competing leaders obstructed Caesar from passing bills in the popular assembly as

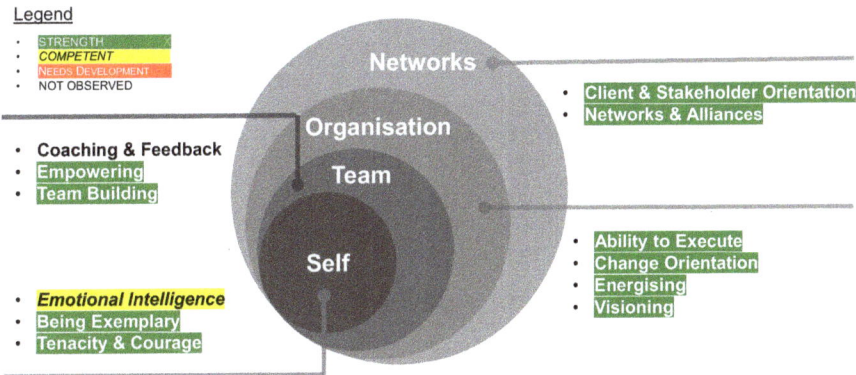

Fig. 3.6 Evaluation of Caesar's leadership behaviours at mid-career according to the GELM. Author's adaptation based on GELM by KDVI

praetor, he found a way around it by employing an organisation to influence and mobilise followers directly when he became consul. Yet he failed in every attempt to sway a majority of senators to his side. The agrarian law in 59 is a case in point: The Senate refused to approve the bill despite finding nothing technically wrong with it.

What could explain the difference between Caesar's skill in leading with and without authority? To begin with, as a leader who defended the People's interests and an opposer to the Sullan establishment, Caesar appeared less credible in the eyes of the conservative majority. Box 3.2 gives a first example of Caesar's struggle to get the Senate on his side.

> **Box 3.2 Power Struggle with Cato Act 1**
>
> But the matter runs even deeper. For this we need to look at the confrontation between Cato the Younger and Caesar in 63 on what to do with the captured Catilinarian conspirators (mentioned in the first section on Caesar's life and career) in more detail. Cicero, then consul, invited the Senate to meet in the temple of Concord in the Forum, hoping that the goddess would bless the senators with harmony. The senators entered through the colonnade into the walled interior that allowed them privacy. Many senators showed up. About 500 toga-clad men were crammed into a room not bigger than two tennis courts, each angry and anxious about the situation before them. For both the fate of the Republic and their own position hung in the balance. Cicero suggested that the perpetrators be executed. Caesar and Cato, two ambitious junior senators, crossed swords in the ensuing debate in the senatorial arena. On one side stood Caesar, fashionable in his toga, enhancing eloquence with elegance. He faced Cato, unkempt in an old toga, spurting out words in his unsophisticated style.
>
> Caesar spoke first, arguing in favour of indefinite imprisonment rather than summary execution. He bolstered his position through three main points: the risk of angering the people, the risk of creating a precedent for unlawful violence and the risk of infringing upon the law forbidding the execution of a Roman citizen without trial. Noticing that the Senate was beginning to be swayed by Caesar's argument, Cato stood up and made his case. The Senate had the obligation to restore order, he sternly reminded his colleagues. He warned against leniency in the face of the clear and present danger of an ongoing uprising, especially with Catiline and his supporters still at large in the countryside. But most importantly, Cato's proposal promised to protect the possessions of the senators—a key difference between his argument and Caesar's. Cato gave it to them straight:
>
>> But, in the name of the immortal gods, I call upon you, who have always valued your mansions and villas, your statues and pictures, at a higher price than the welfare of your country, if you wish to preserve those possessions of whatever kind they are, to which you are attached; if you wish to secure quiet for the enjoyment of your pleasures, then arouse yourselves, and act in defence of your country. (Sallust, *Conspiracy of Catiline*, 52 (transl. Watson 1899))

> The Senate ultimately chose personal profit over principles. Cato gained the senators' backing because he was able to identify and speak to their worst fear. Successful persuasion requires empathy to understand the other party's interests, desires and feelings. Caesar seemed to lack sufficient Emotional Intelligence for the senators as a collective.

The debates around the agrarian law, when Caesar was already consul, provide insight into Caesar's Emotional Intelligence towards individuals. In the Senate, Caesar had difficulty understanding and controlling his emotions. For instance, he failed to act constructively after becoming impatient with Cato's obstruction, which will be discussed in detail later as an example of career competition. Cato managed to trigger an adverse reaction from Caesar, and Caesar had him hauled from the Senate. Caesar, however, had not anticipated that the other senators would react unfavourably to his impatience, which forced him to backtrack. It was only later that he was able to understand the emotions of others and act upon this knowledge. He used these skills to trigger a reaction from Bibulus, who was as conservative and inflexible as Cato, and influence the opinion of those attending the popular assembly. On the same occasion, Caesar played on Pompey's need for recognition, which earned him the full and public support of the senior leader.

Caesar's most explicit example of Leading Self was the steadfast consistency with which he spoke and acted according to his values—something that would become a pillar of his leadership brand. He expressed a desire to do things on behalf of the People and through the People (essentially his *popularis* stance), which manifested as generous involvement in public works, support for Pompey and Crassus and their plans, taking the people's interests into account in the wake of the Catilinarian conspiracy, initiating public records of the meetings of the Senate, and passing the agrarian laws. Additionally, Caesar's support of due process for the Catilinarians and of a law to instil more transparency and control in the governance of the empire made it apparent how much weight he gave to integrity. He also demonstrated clemency towards perpetrators by advocating for life imprisonment instead of the death penalty for the conspirators. (In the previous chapter, we saw that Caesar had already conveyed this value by sparing the pirates a painful punishment.) Undoubtedly, these behaviours served Caesar's interests, as well. Yet, at the same time, these choices were met with considerable resistance and put his career at risk. The value he attached to transparency (no doubt spiked with over-confidence in his persuasive abilities) stopped him from brokering a deal behind the scenes in the Senate and the courts. Even so, he tenaciously persisted. Finally, after his mediocre performance as praetor, Caesar in 61 turned his frustration into a motivation to outperform as governor in Spain, his next job. It reminds us of the Tenacity with which he went after his kidnappers six years earlier to compensate for his lack of success as a lawyer.

3.3.2 Leading Teams

From 69 to 59, Caesar held several positions with a strong operational component that involved leading direct teams, suppliers, and, later, organisations. This competency became most evident when Caesar was consul. He proved effective in bringing together the right people with the right skills to fulfil different roles in an organisation. Empowering team members like Vatinius and Fibulus to operate autonomously was a crucial element to this; otherwise, they would be ineffective in mobilising followers on behalf of their leader. Caesar demonstrated a particular eye and appreciation for diversity. Recruiting Vatinius, a provincial upstart with few connections to the elite, proved a long-term success. The same goes for Balbus, the Spanish foreigner turned immigrant. During his youth, Caesar had witnessed how citizenship was extended to all peoples in Italy. It took a few years to inscribe all new citizens, but once completed the number of Roman citizens had doubled. It was a major political shift. The new citizens provided an opportunity for Roman leaders to increase their followership. For Pompey, for example, the Italians were a source of volunteers for his armies and offered voting support in elections and legislative assemblies. Only Caesar truly recognised the enormous talent pool that had become available. Harvesting that talent for his organisation and the Republic became a distinguishing feature of his leadership.

3.3.3 Leading Organisations

An early glimpse into Caesar's Visioning appeared in the debate on what to do with the conspirators. He knew summary execution would have implications, such as setting legal precedents and an adverse reaction of the general public, that would extend beyond simply re-establishing law and order. Once Caesar attained a general management position, his strategic insight became even more apparent. His measures to ensure sustainable management of the province of Further Spain and then of all provinces through his extortion law were examples of improving governance with a long-term perspective. The laws he introduced as consul regarding land distribution, taxation and reorganisation in the East addressed issues of strategic importance for the Republic. Moreover, the land distributions came with a solid financial plan and a dedicated organisation of land commissioners to ensure efficient Execution. Regarding Caesar's career strategy, he made the right decisions even when the payoff was not set in stone. Notably, he was willing to forego the triumph he had earned for his military accomplishments for the uncertain opportunity of winning the election for consul (details in the next section).

When it comes to Energising followers, Caesar won every election he stood for. As he moved up the ranks, he had to win over different constituencies: first, the citizenry at large, and then, in his bids for praetor and consul, the wealthier members of the electorate. Driving a successful campaign and effectively reaching supporters, some of whom may have needed to travel to Rome, was essential. Campaigning also meant securing public endorsement from senior members of the elite. In addition, voters wanted to see past, present and promised benefits to themselves and the state and sided with whoever provided those benefits. In Caesar's case, his performance in past roles had benefitted the people as well as specific interest groups (benefits such as public works, games, military achievements and anti-pirate measures). As a candidate, Caesar's promises were attractive (e.g. agrarian law and reforming taxation). During electoral campaigns, he invested heavily in providing present benefits by offering largess—mostly gifts and financial support—to the point of heavily indebting himself. It was a common practice; in fact, giving back to the community was expected from the privileged. Caesar successfully created a followership among the electorate by offering tangible benefits that responded to concrete needs.

Caesar was innovative in his communication. He used images and speeches at his aunt's and his wife's funerals to express a political message to build his leadership brand. He restored Marius's monuments to the same effect. The games he organised were spectacular in themselves, but he also built anticipation—and ensured that he got all the credit—by displaying illustrations of the shows in the city centre in advance. Introducing public records of the discussions in the Senate was innovative and an act of political transparency. Finally, it is worth mentioning that Caesar was the first to send letters to friends and acquaintances within the city of Rome. While correspondence with people outside or abroad was common practice, Caesar was the first to adapt to the growth of the metropolis and the resulting challenge of meeting people face-to-face. He started doing this to be quicker and more efficient in his interactions. Yet, as we will see later in the lead-up to the eventful crossing of the Rubicon—which started the civil war –, he underestimated how reducing face-to-face communication negatively impacts influencing.

3.3.4 Leading Stakeholders and Networks

Over the course of the ten years covered in this chapter, Caesar became increasingly effective at Leading Stakeholders. It was one of the skills that made his consulate so effective. During this time, his policies chiefly concerned landowners, the business community, veterans and the poorer city-dwellers. Thus, he developed a political network, the triumvirate, with two foremen of important stakeholder groups. He promised to consider stakeholders' interests, and he followed through on that promise. Both the agrarian law and the law on provincial government were so well-constructed and balanced that no stakeholder, including the Senate, could find fault with either.

3.4 Caesar's Career Development

The leadership development system of the Roman Republic was designed to grow generalists able to lead both in peace and in war. After climbing the ranks and fulfilling three specialised roles of increasing responsibility, a leader could reach the top as a consul. Getting there required a combination of achievement, renown, sponsorship, networking and successful election campaigns. These career steps were supplemented with assignments in the provinces and other civil service positions, where a leader could gain further experience in government and military matters. Fierce competition and low life expectancy meant that few reached the apex of the Roman career ladder. In spite of this, Caesar demonstrated a steep rise to power during this period, climbing from junior magistrate to the Roman Republic's highest position within only a decade. Caesar entered into each career stage at the minimum age required and never lost an election. Between 69 and 59, Caesar made more career moves than in any other decade of his life, which makes this particularly rich from the perspective of analysing how his career developed.

3.4.1 Career Competition

The first jobs happened by election in the assembly in which the votes of all citizens counted equally. Promotion to praetor and consul required overcoming a different electoral challenge since the two senior offices on the career track were elected by a separate popular assembly. In these elections the votes of the wealthy counted much more, including those of wealthy citizens outside the Senate. Hence, Caesar had to gain the support of the upper classes to succeed. Moreover, following Sulla's expansion of the Senate, competition for the senior offices had become much steeper as there were now more potential candidates. When it came to support from elites, Caesar could count on his mother's family and the wealthy families into which his two sisters had married. Plus, he was still married to Sulla's granddaughter, which won support of those who had previously been his political adversaries. Additionally, a few years earlier, Caesar had gained approval among the business community by strongly supporting Pompey's efforts against the pirates. Significantly, he had obtained the support of the two most powerful men in Rome, Pompey and Crassus. These factors, in addition to the impact of his networking and generosity, allowed Caesar to secure sufficient support to win the election to praetor and consul.

3.4.1.1 Competing with Cato: Catiline and Caesar's Praetorship

Caesar now faced stronger peer competition both for jobs and for followers. As he climbed the career ladder, Caesar notably encountered Cato the Younger and his sidekick, Bibulus. The latter's career was synchronous with Caesar's. Only two years his senior, Bibulus came from a noble family. Both were aediles in the same year, and both devoted considerable funds towards their office. Caesar, however, used the spectacle of the games he produced to get all the credit for the spending. The two would be dissenting colleagues again as praetors and consuls. As for Cato and Caesar, their competition would endure even beyond their deaths in the ongoing debate among Cicero and others about who had been the better leader. Cato was a few years younger than Caesar but of the same generation. He started his career like Caesar: military service followed by election to quaestor. He eloquently argued in support of decisions that reinforced the traditional oligarchy and, as a senator, consistently opposed any exceptions to these rules. As a quaestor, Cato took decisive measures against tax evaders and corruption, which boosted his popularity and cemented his reputation as someone who unselfishly had the Republic's best interests in mind. Cato was at odds with Caesar, whose pragmatic approach favoured innovation and pushing boundaries. Even their appearances were different. Cato preferred simplicity to the point of going barefoot and looking unkempt. Caesar, on the other hand, took great care to look stylish and fashionable.

The debate in 63 regarding the sentence for the conspirators was the first confrontation between Caesar and Cato and ended in a political defeat for the former. However, as is often the case with career competition, the conflict between Cato and Caesar was about more than just their rational disagreements. The latter was intimately involved with Servilia, Cato's half-sister. Servilia, though married, was Caesar's lover for most of his life. It was a point of contention between the two opponents. Servilia's behaviour did not align with the virtuous image of Cato's family. For example, during the same debate, a handwritten note was given to Caesar. Suspicious that it might have to do with the plot, Cato bade Caesar to read the note aloud. Instead, Caesar handed the note to Cato; it turned out to be a sexually suggestive message from Servilia. Angry and frustrated, Cato threw the note back at Caesar. One year later, Caesar, to protect his reputation as a newly elected high priest, divorced his wife Pompeia after she was accused of having an extramarital affair. Cato must have balked at Caesar's hypocrisy. In any case, the first match went to Cato. Next, he made an intelligent move that taught Caesar a lesson in stakeholder management. Cato observed that Catiline's uprising, rather than appearing out of the blue, was the result of real economic distress among some groups. Harsh policing was not enough to ensure lasting order. Recognising that Caesar had a point in fearing the people's reaction, Cato convinced the Senate to offer a generous new grain subsidy for the poorer citizens of Rome. Cato continued to stand in Caesar's way (Box 3.3).

> **Box 3.3 Power Struggle with Cato Act 2**
>
> The following year, 62, Caesar was installed as praetor alongside Bibulus, while Cato became tribune of the plebs. Caesar, out of equal parts loyalty and conviction, from the outset supported Pompey's interests. He teamed up with the tribune Metellus Nepos, formerly a military officer with Pompey and now Cato's colleague. Nepos proposed a bill that would recall Pompey and this army from the East to mop up the Catilinarian insurrection still ongoing in the Italian countryside. Faced with Cato's fierce opposition Nepos failed to get the okay from the Senate.
>
> With Caesar's support, Nepos brought the bill before the popular assembly. When the meeting had begun, Cato, consistent in his wariness of vesting one individual with too much power, wanted to put a stop it. He shoved through the crowd towards the podium with a colleague in tow. Cato then sat between Nepos and Caesar, interrupting the herald as he read the bill. When Nepos took over from the herald, Cato grabbed the text himself. Nepos then proceeded to recite it from memory, prompting Cato's colleague to put his hand over Nepos's mouth. Frustrated, Nepos cancelled the meeting. Many of the people present were angry with Cato, and they pelted him with sticks and stones. When Nepos tried to reconvene the assembly, Cato and his supporters returned. Though they were eventually able to disperse him and his adherents, Cato, no doubt due to his reputation for being incorruptible and the credit he gained among the people for initiating the corn subsidy, was able to swing the mood in favour of aborting the vote.

> For the rest of Caesar's tenure as praetor, Cato, influential in the Senate, held sway over political decision-making in Rome. Caesar and Nepos also lobbied to allow Pompey to stand for the consulship in absentia and to keep his military rank within the city, so that he could hold a victory parade. Cato successfully frustrated these proposals by convincing the Senate not to go along with it and again obstructing the vote in the popular assembly. Pompey chose to hold a triumph and forego a second consulship. Caesar's fellow praetor, Bibulus, did what he could to hinder Caesar's actions, as well. For his role in the riot between Nepos and Cato, Caesar was suspended from office for a while until popular demand called for his restoration. Consequently, the praetorship became the office where Caesar achieved the least. After the debate regarding the captured conspirators, the second match, too, had gone to Cato.

While Caesar was away in Spain in 61, the two bigwigs, Pompey and Crassus, tried to arrange things in favour of their stakeholders. Cato, again abhorring the idea of individual magnates having disproportionate influence on a republic in his view based on the collective rule of the elite, successfully frustrated these plans through his continued influence in the Senate. Enter Caesar, reappearing from his foreign assignment laden with success. Caesar, entitled to a triumph and in the running for the consulship, asked for an exception to the procedures to do both, as Rome's fear of military coups typically prevented military commanders from entering the city. However, standing for election required physical presence. Additionally, one needed to maintain one's military rank until the day of the triumph. Thus, Caesar could not stand for election while a general and could not hold a triumph once he left the military. Neither did the timing allow him to do one after the other. Caesar's demand was not unprecedented. He had lobbied to grant Pompey the same exception two years earlier in 62. But then and now Cato was not one for exceptions. Filibustering (speaking without interruption until the end of the meeting) in the Senate, Cato prevented a decision on Caesar's request, forcing Caesar to choose between the options. Caesar, to the surprise of all, opted for the uncertain election over the guaranteed triumph. A triumph offered prestige, but the consulate would provide him with true power. For he had seen how Pompey had made the opposite choice and despite the prestige had been unable to get what he wanted.

By this point, Caesar had developed a considerable track record and name for himself. He had achieved substantial military success. The effect of his efforts from previous magistracies through games and infrastructure was visible and highly appreciated. He had supported initiatives favouring the interests of the people and the business community. He had managed to enlist the support of two of the most powerful men in Roman society, Pompey and

Crassus. Caesar now took the initiative to pool resources and interests into what became known in history as the First Triumvirate. Although successful in war, Pompey had not fulfilled his aspirations after returning from his campaigns. His restructuration and pacification proposals for the provinces in the East were still awaiting ratification by the Senate. Not to mention, that the land distribution for the retirement of Pompey's veterans was still pending. Crassus, on the other hand, was hoping for an improved deal for the tax collectors whose interests he represented. By foregoing the certainty of the triumph for the uncertainty of winning the election, Caesar was making a risky investment in his future. He had plans to use this position to achieve more extraordinary things during and after his tenure.

3.4.1.2 Competing with Cato: Caesar as Consul

After frustrating one of Caesar's options—the triumph—Cato proceeded to try to sabotage the other. In the time running up to the elections, he lobbied to ensure that Caesar, should he be elected, would achieve little during and after his consulate. Adamant about preventing the rise of a third magnate next to Pompey and Crassus, and having seen what Caesar was capable of once in command of a province, Cato was keen on destroying Caesar's chances at another victory. Hence, he convinced the Senate to allocate the 'forests and paths of Italy' to the consuls after their tenure. Compared to governing a substantial province, little glory was to be had from such a job. Cato rightly expected that Caesar, as consul, would pursue the programme that Crassus and Pompey had designed. Therefore, he put a spoke in Caesar's wheel by promoting the election of Bibulus, now also Cato's son-in-law, as second consul. Caesar, backed by the financial means of Crassus and others, resorted to buying votes. In retaliation, Cato and his allies went around matching whatever Caesar offered. Cato admitted that though this tactic was contrary to his principles, Caesar's power had to be curbed by any means necessary (Box 3.4).

> **Box 3.4 Power Struggle with Cato Act 3**
>
> The consular elections were held in July. It brought thousands to Rome from all across Italy, which was something that the candidates and their support networks had campaigned for. To support Caesar, Crassus mobilised wealthy business owners who would stand to benefit from the triumvirate's plans. This was crucial because, in consular elections, the votes were weighted according to one's social and economic standing. The election day was a festive and ceremonial occasion. Priests performed sacred rites to invoke the blessings of the gods.

All male citizens who had turned up to vote assembled on the Campus Martius, the military training ground just outside the city; orderlies helped the citizens line up according to their social class in groups called centuries, a term that recalled the organisation of the Roman army. Both the location and the formations reminded everyone that they once had been citizen-soldiers. The groups were cordoned off from each other. After entering their century and proving their identity, each person received two tablets—representing the two consuls to be elected. Next, the candidates walked onto the podium and were presented to the public by the assembly's chairman. The candidates wore a bright white toga, symbolising the honesty of their intentions. (From this *toga candida* originates the word 'candidate'.) The centuries, one after the other, approached the voting urns to cast their votes. The process took hours to complete. Caesar's votes passed the post first, Bibulus came second. Both had had now reached the highest elected office and rank in the Roman leadership hierarchy. For the third time, Bibulus and Caesar became colleagues in office and the power struggle between Cato and Caesar ended in a draw.

In previous years, Caesar had observed Cato's effectiveness in swaying the Senate's opinion, using its procedures to his advantage, and commanding the popular assembly as a tribune. Caesar was armed with a Plan B this time. Now that he was in charge, he could leverage the leadership organisation he had established to recruit and mobilise followers. He forged the loose alliance with Pompey and Crassus into a three-way coalition. But against a rival as formidable as Cato the Younger, putting his plans in motion would not exactly be a cakewalk (Box 3.5). With an ambitious agenda and only a one-year tenure, Caesar immediately took action once installed, the first being the publication of the proceedings of the Senate and the popular assembly.

Box 3.5 Power Struggle with Cato Act 4

The next item on Caesar's agenda was the agrarian bill, one of Pompey's long-standing goals. While Caesar devoted much effort into making the bill critique-proof, he chose to go the harmonious route first. He expressed his intentions to propose the bill to the Senate first so they could amend it before putting it to the people for approval. Still, Caesar's persuasive measures would not hold up against Cato's opposition. After reading the bill in the Senate, Caesar asked each senator to express their views and suggest amendments. Caesar's bill had taken into account all eventualities and interests. In the subsequent debate, senators for and against took the stage, neither side offering concrete objections or suggestions. After almost a full day of discussions, Cato took the floor. He argued that even if he found nothing at fault with the proposal, there was still no need for a new law. He started a filibuster to prevent the vote in the Senate. Caesar, chairing the meeting as consul and growing impatient, accused him of obstruction and commanded an orderly to arrest Cato. Cato offered no resistance. When a large group of senators stood up to follow Cato to the jail in protest, Caesar backed down and adjourned the session. Before leaving, a frustrated Caesar told the Senate that since they had refused to offer their opinion on the bill, he would let the people decide instead. Caesar managed to get the law passed in the assembly against considerable pushback thanks to the influence of his leadership organisation, as has been described in detail in Box 3.1 above.

Afterwards, Cato's ally, Bibulus, protested to the Senate to no avail. Cato and Caesar's other opponents proceeded to boycott the political process, hoping for a government shutdown. Cato spoke out in public several times against Caesar's proposals but could not influence the vote. Bibulus began isolating himself in his home, frequently announcing that he saw 'unfavourable omens' in an attempt to invalidate proceedings. Many senators, including Cato, refused to attend Senate meetings. None of this had any effect. Caesar was on a mission to get his ambitious programme approved by the People, including a more promising provincial assignment after his tenure. This time, the match went to Caesar.

Reaching the highest office did not need to signify the end of a career. A two-year assignment to govern one of the larger or several smaller provinces was typically the next step. While consul, Caesar secured his eventual government of Cisalpine Gaul and Illyricum for five instead of two years, replacing the low-level assignment in Italy that Cato had reserved for him. Plus, he was set to assume command over three legions. Together, these agreements represented an attractive package offering opportunities for further prestige and income. Before he left the office, Caesar managed to add Transalpine Gaul and another legion to this list. When he had first joined the triumvirate, Caesar was merely a junior partner. By late 59, when his consulship ended, Caesar had proven so effective that he emerged as an equal partner in the alliance. However, he had yet to match Pompey's military success or Crassus's wealth. He was about to embark on a journey that would allow him to do just that.

3.4.1.3 Two Visions of Government

Caesar would be away from Rome for the next decade. The competition between him and Cato would persist, but it would now involve representatives. The two would never meet face-to-face again. Their rivalry was as much about principles and power as it was about personal enmity. However, they could both agree on the importance of effective governance. As magistrates and governors, both took measures that would discourage the exploitation of the provinces while favouring responsible accounting, reporting and control.

3 Rising Above the Fray: From High Potential to Leader 75

Fig. 3.7 Bust of Cato the Younger. From the Musée de l'Histoire et des Civilisations in Rabat, Morocco. Photo by Ángel M. Felicísimo during the 'Around the Pillars of Hercules' temporary exhibition at the Museo Arqueológico Nacional de España 2022. CC BY 2.0. https://flickr.com/photos/8146925@N08/52340687524

Even so, each pursued contrasting organisational concepts to achieve effective governance. For Cato (Fig. 3.7), the Senate was the primary institution of the Republic, and its leaders merely served to execute the will of the Senate. Therefore, he did not diligently climb the Roman career ladder. Contrary to Caesar, who never lost an election, Cato failed twice. His career did not reach higher than praetor. For Cato, magistrates were a means to an end; he saw his primary responsibility in the Senate. However, he demonstrated considerable talent, performing exceptionally both as quaestor of the treasury and governor of the newly acquired Cyprus. For Caesar, the executive leadership was the Republic's primary institution. The role of the Senate and the popular assembly was to approve and control that leadership. Climbing the career ladder, in this view, was a goal in itself.

3.4.2 Leadership Brand and Reputation

Objective factors, i.e. performance and competencies, were as important in Rome as they are now for career development. However, the same applies to subjective factors. As an HR executive and executive coach, I have encountered numerous leadership and career development processes. From these experiences, I have learned that leaders tend to underestimate the importance of subjective factors when it comes to promotion decisions. Of course, nowadays, organisations try to make such decisions as objectively as possible with scientifically developed selection methods, clear criteria, fact-checking and transparent processes. Still, when push comes to shove and a decision between two or three remaining candidates must be made, subjectivity and bias play a role nowadays just as they did in Caesar's time. For any ambitious leader, understanding this game—and how to influence it—is essential. Given the absence of systematic selection processes, Caesar's career progression is an ideal case for observing how subjective decision-making works in practice.

Let us review two phenomena that influence and represent the subjective evaluations of followers and career decision-makers: brand and reputation. Both of these contribute to building a leader's renown, as well. A personal brand reflects the emotional attachment to an individual leader, which reassures followers that they have chosen the right person to follow or prompts decision-makers to promote this person over another candidate. This brand is influenced by the leader's values and vision as well as the experiences the organisation or followers have had with the leader over time. If done well, the brand creates a positive label that remains in force over an extended period, often over the duration of a career. Reputation, meanwhile, has a shorter lifetime and changes from one position to the next. Reputation is the evaluative consensus that followers and stakeholders form based on a leaders' recent actions. Brand and reputation mutually influence each other. The credit of a strong personal brand makes it easier to repair a dent in a reputation. On the other hand, a consistently positive reputation reinforces a brand. And, of course, both are shaped by a leader's achievements and behaviour.

Some of Rome's most powerful families developed a collective brand over time that aided them in their pursuit of position and power. The Scipio family, for instance, was famous for producing victorious generals since the war against Hannibal. Mettelus Scipio would fight Caesar's forces several times during the civil war. The final battle between the two occurred near the site in Africa where Scipio's ancestor had ignited the flame of the family's fame by defeating Hannibal. Here, reminiscent of Rome's most formidable foe, Scipio fielded elephants against Caesar. Pompey constructed an individual brand as

Rome's primary trouble-shooter, solving problems like revolts, rebellions, piracy and the logistics of the corn supply. It compensated for his lack of pedigree and allowed him to pursue a non-traditional and accelerated career path. The Catos, a powerful and prestigious family, were known to consistently uphold traditional values ever since Cato the Elder relentlessly called for the destruction of Carthage. Cato the Younger would perpetuate the virtuous conservatism of the family brand in his political positions.

The Roman historian Sallust asserts that, in terms of personal brand, Caesar became known for his generosity and clemency, and Cato for his austerity and severity. Caesar's ambition was to demonstrate his talents through leadership. Cato was driven by a desire to be virtuous and uncompromising. Whereas Caesar could see several sides to an issue, Cato was a *Prinzipienreiter,* as Germans would call it, a stickler for principles. Sallust also seems to imply that Caesar was more pleasant company. Yet, there was more to Caesar's brand. By the time he arrived at the middle-management level, on his way to stand for the praetorship, he had firmly established his brand as a *popularis*. Cicero said as much during the infamous Senate debate on what to do with the Catilinarian conspirators, in which he distinguished between irresponsible demagogues and a real *popularis* like Caesar, who was both loyal to the Republic and concerned about the well-being of the people. Cato and Caesar each constructed a successful personal brand to support their careers. Moreover, having opposing brands helped both in gaining support. Cato's unyielding conservatism made it easier for Caesar to position himself as the leader of progress and reform. Caesar's consistent promotion of the interests of the People made it easier for Cato to be perceived as the force of reason. In that respect, they depended on each other even if they didn't like each other.

Reputation stems from followers and stakeholders determining 'how good' or 'how suited' a leader is. The GELM, which we have been using to evaluate behaviours, also measures reputation through *Perceived Leadership Performance*. This approach involves a series of questions related to achieving results (meeting organisational expectations and objectives, decision-making, contributing to the success of the organisation and reaching career performance goals) and to developing others (bringing out the best in people and leading them to high performance, developing strengths and valuing contributions). In the workplace, gossip can strongly influence a leader's reputation. Gossip is essentially the informal evaluation of a leader when they are not present—in other words, talking about a colleague or boss around the water cooler. Gossip about leaders in the spotlight was rife throughout all layers of Roman society. For instance, Cicero's letters to his friends and family are full of it. Cicero once wrote to his friend Atticus that Cato was too principled. Rather than recognising the reality of Rome's politics he behaved like a fictional character straight from Plato's philosophy. In his correspondence, Cicero nastily accused fellow-senators with a more privileged upbringing of paying more attention to their expensive fish ponds than the state of the Republic. Caesar's alleged love-affair with a foreign king was a running gag among his troops.

3.4.3 Leadership Pipeline

3.4.3.1 From Leading Self to Leading Others and to Functional Leadership

Looking at this period through the lens of the *Leadership Pipeline* (Fig. 3.8), Caesar had to manage several leadership passages on his way to the top. First, he transitioned from individual contributor to managing others when he was elected quaestor. He held similar positions with increasing levels of responsibility as highway curator, aedile and praetor. In these roles, he managed a small group of specialised civil servants supplemented by staff paid from his pocket. The tasks of the lower magistrates had a strong emphasis on execution. According to the *Leadership Pipeline*, the most necessary shift in this passage is a value shift: towards valuing the work done by others for you and, by extension, to valuing constructive horizontal and vertical relations with

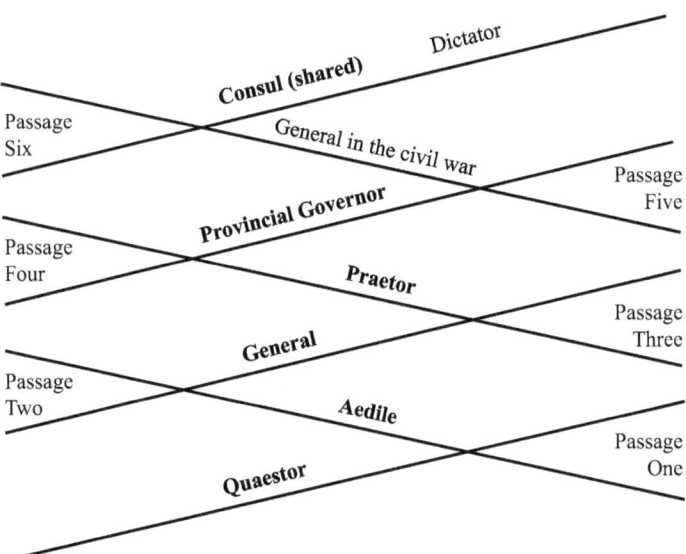

Fig. 3.8 Julius Caesar's mid-career passages in the Roman Career System. Author's adaptation: based on Charan et al. (2001)

peers, clients, suppliers and superiors. Valuing work by direct reports means a willingness to delegate, plan the work of a group and develop staff. Even from a modern perspective, these first career steps were crucial—especially given the fact that relatively inexperienced professionals were carrying fairly large responsibilities in a sizeable city and were required to make decisions that had ramifications throughout the empire.

Magistrates received a small staff of state employees to exercise their duties. Some of these staff members were rather specialised, such as the financial experts of the treasury who reported to the quaestors assigned to manage the state's finances. The inexperienced magistrates often found it challenging to manage a group of experienced civil servants. Cato the Younger, ever-diligent, delayed becoming quaestor of the treasury until he had learned all the ins and outs of the function as well as its rules and regulations. When he started at the post in 64, he used this knowledge to introduce changes that would improve the office's performance and eradicate corruption. He cleaned up the accounts by collecting overdue debts and repaying loans. Though successful, he had to overcome considerable resistance from his staff and lay off several incompetent and recalcitrant employees. Cato's responsible management of the position earned him much admiration from the Roman public.

As quaestor, Caesar was assigned to a provincial administration. Effective people management was less critical in this role. He achieved his actual passage to managing others when he became a highway curator. Apart from visibility, the job offered a development opportunity. Since curator was a purely optional part of the career track, this decision was simply an intelligent move by Caesar. It prepared Caesar well for the next responsibility of aedile, where he would oversee the organising of games. It was a position that demanded real operational and managerial prowess. Given Caesar's considerable output as curator and aedile, he valued the work done by others and, therefore, mastered these transitions well. In addition, Caesar's successful horizontal relations were evident in his obtainment of private funding for his shows and public works. Finally, Caesar appreciated constructive vertical relations, notably upward, by increasingly aligning himself with the interests of Pompey and Crassus.

For Caesar, the passage to praetor was the most challenging one. In his previous offices, he had worked hard to secure achievements that benefited both the state and his reputation. Now, for the first time, he participated in partisan politics not as a senator but as a high magistrate. Consequently, the headwind he received was more substantial—to the point that his actions almost backfired and resulted in his suspension. What made this passage so tricky for Caesar? The praetorship was a complex role, particularly if one engaged in general politics rather than limiting oneself to the core tasks of the position (i.e. dealing with jurisdiction). In politics, coalition-building and strong horizontal and upward relationships are key. As Caesar had experienced the year before during the Catilinarian conspiracy, the opposition from the conservative majority, led by Cato, was too strong to overcome. He was working for the absent Pompey, whose support network in Rome was too unorganised to stand up against a determined senatorial majority. The alternative route, through the People, was also foiled by Cato.

Caesar found managing boundaries challenging. In modern matrix or network organisations, this facet is of particular relevance. Previously, as quaestor and aedile, Caesar's boundaries were relatively straightforward. Responsibilities and resources were well-defined and execution-oriented. Whether they achieved a little or a lot, the incumbents could go about their business relatively independently. Interface with other institutions was limited. For the lower magistrates, the senator's role did not interfere much with their role as magistrates.

Praetors, just below consuls as the most senior government positions, were somewhat dependent on what happened outside their influence. As president of the jury courts, a praetor could take the initiative to bring cases before the court, but otherwise, they could not predict or influence what lawsuit was brought before them. This role corresponds with the functional leader role in the Leadership Pipeline and had clearly defined responsibilities. When engaging in legislation, however, praetors often encountered blurred boundaries between their role as a magistrate and being a senator. Consequently, to be successful, a praetor had to deal with other magistrates (consuls and tribunes) with overlapping legislative authority, with the popular assembly and with the Senate. Add to that the various interest groups connected to these individuals and institutions. Caesar struggled with managing those boundaries. As a lawyer and senator, he had to discover that his excellent rhetorical skills were not enough to sway larger groups' decisions in his favour. It was largely the effect of his achievements, charisma, transparency and networking that convinced people to choose him over others during elections. When it came to persuading senators to approve his proposals, however, he was less successful. Caesar's persuasive skills were clearly missing something. Caesar felt more comfortable a position with clear boundaries and direct authority than in a position with unclear boundaries and indirect authority.

3.4.3.2 From Leading Others to Leading Managers and to General Manager

Governor of Further Spain in 61, at age 39, was Caesar's first job as a general manager—or business leader, according to the *Leadership Pipeline* –, which in Caesar's case involved several simultaneous passages. First, Caesar had to transition from leading others to leading managers in government and the army. Each governor had a small administration to manage, and city councils and local chieftains reported to him, as well. A general, meanwhile, commanded several officers. Navigating this passage effectively requires a manager to become a full-time leader with little time for individual contributions. Furthermore, strategy is now part of the leader's responsibility. Caesar proved to be adept at these transitions. As a general, he did not just command battles; he led an entire campaign into Lusitania (modern-day Portugal), an impossible feat without an airtight strategy.

The second passage involved Caesar's official transition to business leader, namely governor of a province, which requires a forward-thinking, profit-oriented perspective. Caesar achieved this passage through taxation and government reforms in his province. The business leader position typically grants considerable autonomy, which was certainly true in Caesar's case as governor, especially given the province's geographical distance from Rome. The position put Caesar in his comfort zone of clear boundaries and direct authority. A successful transition to business leader also hinges on the manager's appreciation of specialised support staff. Caesar found one of his best staff members in Spain, Balbus, who would work for him by handling logistics during the military campaign. As a Romanised local, Balbus also advised Caesar on how to improve local government. He would serve Caesar from that point onwards.

3.4.3.3 From Leading Managers to Group and Enterprise Leader

The last passage in the Roman career system was from governor to consul. This passage is more difficult to fit in the *Leadership Pipeline* model, because of the specifics of the leadership structure of the Roman Republic. The position of consul bears elements of both group leader and enterprise leader. As highest magistrates in the republican hierarchy, the consuls ruled the state. The fact that there were two consuls did not diminish their individual authority. In times of war, when the whole nation was at stake, they would lead the army. All this would plead for liking the consul to enterprise leader or CEO in the *Leadership Pipeline*. Yet the empire, namely the governors of the provinces, reported to the Senate. Due to expansion, governing the empire became increasingly important in the Republic. As a result, by the time of Caesar, the authority of the consuls had relatively shrunk over time compared to the Senate and big governors. The Senate also decided on the state finances. Therefore, the consul does not fully meet the criteria of enterprise leader and can be compared to group leader. Group leader exist in large corporations to manage several business managers in order to reduce the span of control of the CEO. In Rome, all other magistrates reported to the two consuls, which was the only generalist position. However, since the consuls had the right to propose laws and because they presided over the Senate, they were more senior than group leaders in a modern corporation. The conclusion therefore is that the consul sits in between group leader and enterprise leader. To understand Caesar's career development, it makes sense to look at both passages.

Mastering the passage from business to group leader requires adopting a holistic perspective and acquiring four critical skills: strategy development, leadership development, managing a portfolio strategy and developing capabilities to win. Caesar ticked all the boxes. His legislation successfully adopted a holistic approach, dealing with socio-economic issues, taxation, governance, organisational structure and defence all during his one-year tenure. He demonstrated strategic skills by funding land distribution through income from Pompey's conquests in the East. Furthermore, he showed leadership development skills by preparing his leadership organisation to effectively execute its plans. Caesar's skill in managing a portfolio strategy to ensure a sustainable organisation was apparent in his laws regarding tax farming, provincial government and land distribution. Lastly, he demonstrated his capacity and drive to win by switching his focus from the Senate to the popular assembly and by putting an organisation together to mobilise the following that voted his bills into law. Transitioning to group leader from business leader often means letting go of a job that gave the incumbent much satisfaction, because of its immediate and tangible results. That was certainly the case for Caesar when he exchanged the governorship for the consulate. However, Caesar was able to quickly arrange things in such a way that he could influence events directly.

The passage to enterprise leader involves a shift in values and perspective. Enterprise leaders consider the business and the organisation an entity, and their decisions support a long-term strategy. Their success depends on a few high-impact decisions and their effective execution. It requires assembling a high-performing team that looks after the individual operations so that the enterprise leader can focus on the whole. Caesar's few laws went beyond Rome and Italy, impacting the empire. His law on provincial governance stayed in force for centuries. The agrarian laws were effectively put in place thanks to installing a special commission and financed in such a way that they encountered little resistance. The leadership organisation Caesar recruited ensured that an enormous amount of work was done during his one year as consul. In conclusion, Caesar managed the two simultaneous passages, from business to group leader and enterprise leader, well. This second experience as general manager taught him, he could do this job well.

As consul, Caesar was again challenged by boundaries. Moreover, the consulship put Caesar in a position of shared leadership. While the other magistrates also had colleagues, in those cases, responsibilities were clearly defined and allocated. The consul was the only one for whom those clear boundaries did not exist. The two consuls shared the responsibility for governing the empire's military and administration. It was an invitation to accomplish goals through teamwork, which did happen sometimes. For example, Pompey and Crassus were twice consuls together and cooperated on passing laws. On other occasions, there was an agreement to distribute responsibilities—for example to command two separate armies in case of war. While the leadership pipeline concept does not really address shared leadership, it is becoming increasingly common in the twenty-first century, both in public and business administrations. For Caesar, shared leadership with a colleague imposed by the constitution proved daunting. Bibulus came from the opposing political faction, and he and Caesar had found it difficult to cooperate as colleagues in the past as aediles and praetors. Eager to keep things as they were, Bibulus was the opposite of the action-oriented Caesar. Again, the two failed to cooperate, and ten years later, they would inevitably find themselves on opposing sides of the civil war.

Regarding his other professional relationships, Caesar tried to convince the Senate through skilful argument. He devoted much effort towards designing an agrarian law that would cover all possible interests, yet little effort towards getting individual senators on board informally. Once again, his influencing proved insufficient, and the Senate failed to approve the bill. Caesar had learned from previous experiences; that is why he had first forged the coalition with two more powerful men before taking office. But even Pompey's and Crassus's networks were not enough to swing the opinion in the Senate. However, rather than improve his indirect leadership, Caesar compensated by utilising his strength in direct leadership. Unlike when he was a praetor, as consul, he had learned to switch strategies. His leadership organisation was ready to help him execute his ambitious legislation programme. Meanwhile, his colleague, Bibulus, was boycotting all proceedings, in effect leaving Caesar singly responsible—in his comfort zone. At the time, it was jokingly said that 59 was the year of the consulship of Julius and Caesar instead of Bibulus and Caesar. By the end of the year, Caesar had transitioned into his next leadership position.

3.5 What Leaders Can Learn from the Middle Stage of Caesar's Career

Caesar is most known for his conquest of Gaul and his time as a dictator. Yet, in terms of his career and leadership success, two periods discussed in this chapter were the most impactful: his governorship of Further Spain in 61 and his tenure as consul in 59. From day one, Caesar used his independence and the leeway granted by these roles to engage energetically in activity and innovation. Within a relatively short time, he made numerous important decisions; issued measures and laws that were strategically sound and addressed real issues in society, the economy and government; initiated changes that took the interests of different stakeholders into account; took the initiative to build an effective leadership organisation; seized on the opportunity to expand the empire; and pioneered new forms of communication. To accomplish all this, Caesar took advantage of the autonomy granted within the system. While staying within the boundaries of the constitution, he leveraged the power of the People against the senatorial majority that obstructed his plans.

Caesar provides an example of how a leader can compensate for a weakness by leveraging his strengths. Unable to convince the senatorial majority to accept his proposals, he compensated by forming the First Triumvirate and a leadership organisation that allowed him to mobilise the followers needed to get approval from the popular assembly. His strengths included leading both upwards (Pompey and Crassus) and downwards (Vatinius, Balbus and others). However, as we will see later when discussing crossing the Rubicon and Caesar's violent death, there is a limit to what a compensating strategy can bring. Despite the significant resources the triumvirate pooled, all three members were outsiders in some way due to their lack of influencing skills. The strategy worked for a time, but dark clouds were forming on the horizon.

When it comes to achieving performance objectives and building an effective organisation, Caesar scored highly on all counts during this period. There was one exception, however. Caesar ended the praetorship with a dented reputation after failing to deliver on expectations. His creditors even doubted that he ever would succeed in his goals and tried to stop him from leaving for his provincial command. Caesar's high performance in Spain, however, turned the tables, and he was soon after elected consul. Before the consular election, Cato had schemed to assign Caesar command of an insignificant province to thwart any opportunity for Caesar to stand out through exceptional performance. As consul, Caesar reinforced his reputation to the point that no one doubted that he merited a more substantial assignment. So, the decision was reversed, and Caesar was appointed to lead the Gallic provinces. Given how many were elbowing each other for the chance to follow Caesar to Gaul as an officer, supplier or business owner, his reputation as a people manager had clearly grown. Caesar actively worked on strengthening his visibility during this time. He managed to project a positive brand and reputation by communicating and taking credit for his ideas and achievements.

Caesar had the tendency to make the memory of a disappointing performance quickly go away by over-performing at the next opportunity. Such tendency was already apparent in his early career, when he sought opportunities to accomplish something remarkable after his lawyer experience. This made sense to keep a good reputation and it certainly enhanced his career chances in the Roman meritocracy. Recency counts. The more recent an achievement or a failure, the higher its value in performance and potential evaluations. However, it seems that Caesar was mainly driven by frustration and a search for excellence. It stopped him from pausing to reflect on what happened and use it for his leadership development.

Caesar's example shows that leaders can progress quickly through the ranks by following the existing career system, provided they use each position to their advantage. With one exception, Caesar proactively sought opportunities to contribute in a way that exceeded the expectations of each role. At the same time, he made sure that his accomplishments were visible and known.

Once the air became thinner, Caesar faced strong competition and even a power struggle. His courage and tenacity as well as a strong belief in his vision of government kept him going despite setbacks. He tried different ways to gain the upper hand until he found the combination that worked for him when he became consul: sound proposals, a coalition with powerful supporters and an organisation of his own to mobilise followers. In the long-standing competition between Cato and Caesar, the balance of power finally shifted in favour of the latter once he left for Gaul. It was here that Caesar would renew the triumvirate in a similar alliance of joint interests. This time, Cato, not for want of trying, failed to frustrate their plans, leaving Caesar free to pursue his objectives in Gaul. His organisation of followers, the alliance with two influential individuals who could provide him with resources and continuous publication of his accomplishments in Gaul eventually gave Caesar the edge over Cato, despite being absent from Rome. Cato did still hold considerable sway over a majority in the Senate. Yet his support base lacked the organisation of Caesar's followers and the triumvirate's glue of concrete joint interests. Moreover, arguing on moral grounds alone would not cut it in a context that demanded decisive action. When civil war broke out, the competition between Caesar and Cato flared up once more. It was no surprise that both would find themselves on opposing sides.

Bibliography

Greek and Roman Sources

Appian, *Roman History. The Civil Wars*, Book I–II.
Cicero, M. T., *Letters to Atticus; Letters to His Friends; Orations*.
Dio, L. C., *Roman History*. Book 36–38.
Plutarch, *Lives of Cato the Younger, Caesar, Crassus, Pompey*.
Sallustius Crispus, G., *The Conspiracy of Catiline*.
Suetonius Tranquillus, G., *Life of Julius Caesar*.

Modern Works

Badian, E. (1983). *Publicans and sinners: Private Enterprise in the Service of the Roman Republic*. Cornell University Press.
Benferhat, Y. (2017). Des hommes à tout faire dans l'entourage de César. *Dialogues d'histoire ancienne. Supplément, 17.*, Conseillers et ambassadeurs dans l'Antiquité, 373–385.
Broughton, T.R.S. 1952, The magistrates of the Roman Republic. Vol. II (99 B.C.–31 B.C.), : American Philological Association.
Charan, R., Drotter, S., & Noel, J. (2001). *The leadership pipeline. How to build the leadership powered company*. Jossey-Bass.
Connelly, B. S., & McAbee, S. T. (2024). Reputations at work: Origins and outcomes of shared person perceptions. *Annual Review of Organizational Psychology and Organizational Behavior, 11*(1), 251–278.
Crook, J. A., Lintott, A., & Rawson, E. (Eds.). (1994). *The Cambridge ancient history* (The last age of the Roman Republic, 146–43 B.C.) (Vol. IX, 2nd ed.). Cambridge University Press.
Drogula, F. K. (2019). *Cato the younger. Life and death at the end of the Roman Republic*. Oxford University Press.
Gelzer, M. (2008). *Caesar. Der Politiker und Staatsmann*. Franz Steiner Verlag.
Griffin, M. (Ed.). (2009). *A companion to Julius Caesar*. Wiley-Blackwell.
Gruen, E. S. (1995). *The last generation of the Roman Republic*. University of California Press.
Hölkeskamp, K.-J. (Ed.). (2009). *Eine politische Kultur (in) der Krise? Die "letzte Generation" der römischen Republik*. De Gruyter.
Hölkeskamp, K.-J. (2010). *Reconstructing the Roman Republic: An ancient political culture and modern research*. Princeton University Press.
KDVI. https://kdvi.com/tools/
Meier, C. (1997). *Caesar*. DTV.

Morstein-Marx, R. (2021). *Julius Caesar and the Roman people.* Cambridge University Press.

Richardson, J. S. (1996). *The romans in Spain.* Blackwell.

Syme, R. (1964). *Sallust.* University of California Press.

Vanderbroeck, P. J. J. (1987). *Popular leadership and collective behavior ca. 80–50 BC.* J.C. Gieben.

Vanderbroeck, P. (2010, March). When in Rome…Lessons on executive pay from Ancient Rome. *Financial World*, pp. 33–34.

Vanderbroeck, P. (2012). Crises: Ancient and modern. Understanding an ancient Roman crisis can help us move beyond our own. *Management & Organizational History, 7*(2), 113–131.

4

Proving His Mettle: The Conquest of Gaul

> …. *Standing alone outside his general's tent, smartly dressed in his military attire, he watched the dignitaries arrive one by one, some on horseback, some in a litter, some in a carriage. As the procession continued, a haze of dust hung in the air, kicked up by the incessant movement of so many arrivals. It was a mixed cohort of friends and allies, former adversaries and indebted senators seeking favour. Some conversations he looked forward to, for he valued generosity and forgiveness. Others promised to renew old friendships. Others, however, would surely leave him longing for straightforward conversations with his men…*
> (This quote is fictional and created by the author for illustrative purposes.)

Having completed his year as consul, and with four legions under his command, Caesar left Rome in 58 on the road to attaining his greatest achievement. No Roman before or since had ever added so much land to the empire in such a short time. He intended to amass both greatness and wealth. He also wanted to maintain his newly acquired status of being equal with Pompey and Crassus in the triumvirate. But even Caesar could not foresee the extent of what he was about to accomplish. He was 42 years old, and although he had reached the top rung of the Roman career ladder, retirement was the furthest thing from his mind. However, like any expatriate manager today, Caesar needed to keep in touch with Rome, where decisions were made about what lay ahead after his return.

This chapter delves into the period of 58–50 BC, a time when Caesar, as a general, conquered Gaul and spent significant time in the saddle (Fig. 4.1). Rather than exploring the intricacies of the war, this narrative homes in on the

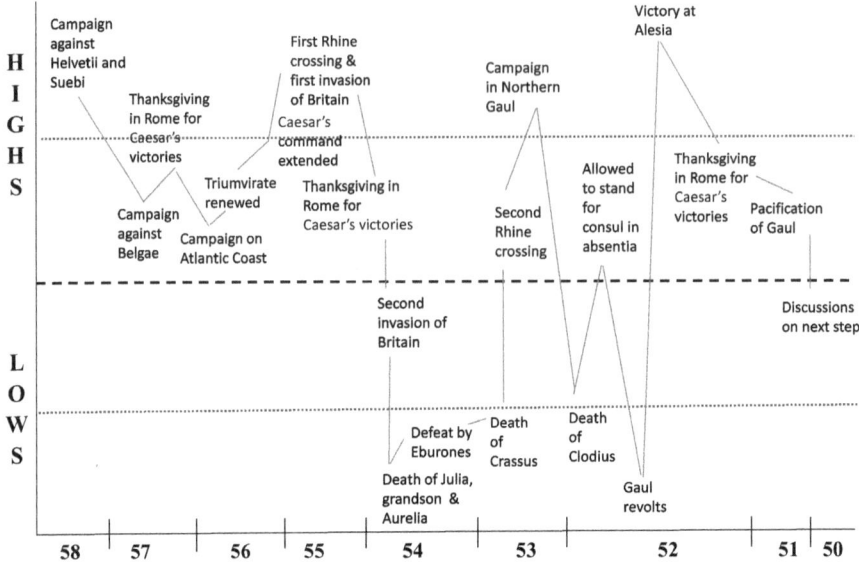

Fig. 4.1 Caesar's leadership timeline: Highs and Lows 58–50 BC. Author's own illustration

events and behaviours that shaped Caesar's career and leadership. Salient questions at this juncture include: What were the pivotal factors that led to Caesar's triumphs? How did he navigate and overcome setbacks? How did he wield his influence over events occurring and opinions held by those in Rome, even during his absence? And how did his brand and reputation develop during his time away?

4.1 Life Abroad

For nine years Caesar was away from Rome, carrying out his duties as governor of three provinces: Gallia Cisalpina (Northern Italy), Gallia Transalpina (modern Provence in Southern France) and Illyricum (modern Croatia). Although he often spent the winter in northern Italy, he did not travel to Rome. Legally, he could not enter the city without relinquishing his military command. However, during these winter months, when the fighting stopped, his close relatives could visit him: his new wife, Calpurnia; his daughter, Julia, who had recently married Pompey; his close friend and lover, Servilia; and his mother, Aurelia. He also maintained extensive correspondence with colleagues, friends and family.

Politically and personally, 54 was an annus horribilis for Caesar. In addition to the muted results of the second expedition to Britain, his beloved daughter, Julia, who had become a staunch ally over the years and with whom he was very close, died while giving birth to Caesar's first and only grandchild. Julia was 22 when she died; her baby died a few days later. She had been married to Pompey for five years and was instrumental in smoothing out the relationship between her father and her husband, two ambitious and influential figures in their own rights. Caesar, busy campaigning in Britain, could not attend the funeral. His wife, Calpurnia, would have to represent him. Nevertheless, he managed to be present from afar. He promised to organise gladiatorial games and a feast in his daughter's honour upon his return. Once again, this was innovative. Fighting (often) to the death in a gladiatorial arena was a traditional way of honouring a deceased man, but Caesar did it for a woman—for the first time. As with an earlier innovation—giving a speech at his young wife's, Cornelia's, funeral—it was an opportunity for image-building. But Caesar's desire to pay tribute to the important women in his life was genuine. In the same year, Caesar lost his mother, Aurelia, another critical female supporter of his. Caesar did not speak or write about his grief for his loved ones; rather, he seemed to have internalised such feelings. He must have felt very alone so far away. Adding to all this, next came the defeat of his army by the Eburones in northern Gaul in the winter of 54.

Caesar's wealth grew significantly during this period. He sold entire tribes into slavery and his army plundered several conquered cities. He also seized the rich offerings from Gallic temples, which was seen as controversial by some in Rome. He was also a shareowner in some of the trading and supply companies accompanying his armies in the wake of his conquests, a business venture that was common among Roman military leaders at the time. Interestingly, the value of the spoils that Caesar, his officers and soldiers pumped into Rome caused the price of gold to fall, a clear indication of the scale of his wealth accumulation. From 54 onwards, Caesar had to wage war almost constantly to conquer all of Gaul, which finally happened in 51. After that, he could concentrate on returning to Rome and assuming a new role in service of the Republic.

4.2   Caesar's Achievements in Gaul and in Rome

During his nine years as governor of his three provinces, Caesar faced three simultaneous challenges: conquering Gaul, integrating the new territories and their inhabitants into the empire and maintaining his position as one of Rome's pre-eminent leaders while away (Fig. 4.2).

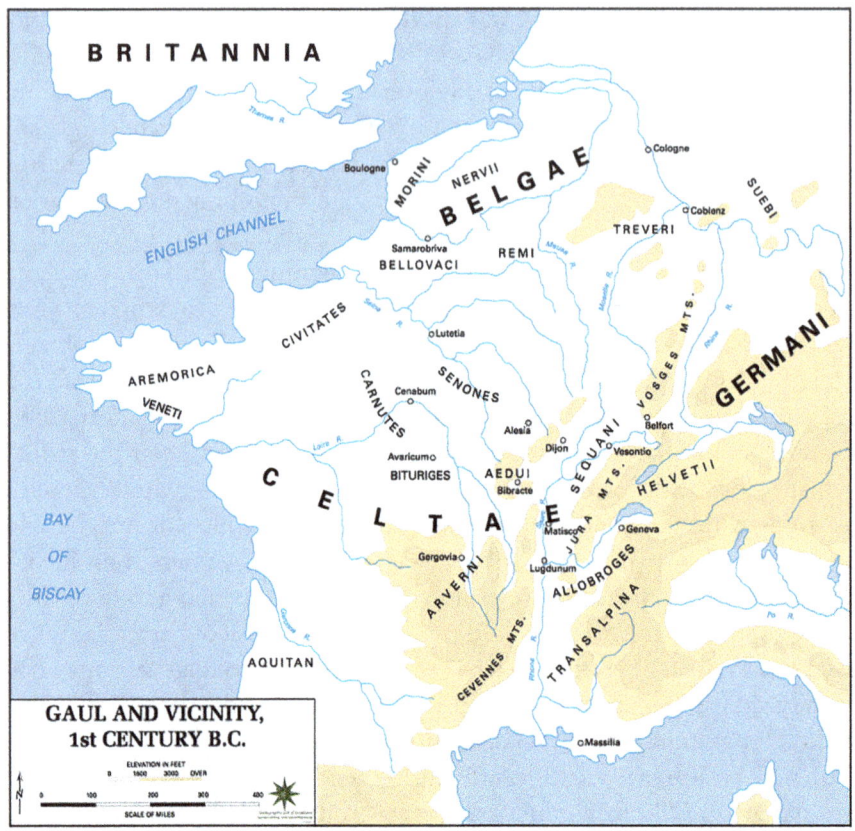

Fig. 4.2 Gaul in 58 BC. By The Department of History, United States Military Academy. Public Domain. https://commons.wikimedia.org/w/index.php?curid=621367

4.2.1 Winning the War

The Helvetii, a Celtic tribe, had crossed the Rhine into present-day Switzerland under pressure from other tribes. Their aim was to migrate towards the Atlantic coast in search of safer lands. They asked Caesar for permission to take the shortest route through the Roman province of Transalpine Gaul. However, Caesar, as governor of the province, refused. Strategically, he swiftly deployed a legion under Titus Labienus, his second in command, across the Alps from Italy to Geneva on the northern edge of the province, effectively blocking the Helvetii's passage. The Helvetii now took a northern route across the Jura mountains, through the land just north of the Roman province of Transalpina and inhabited by the Aedui, a Gallic tribe allied with Rome. The

Senate had previously instructed governors of the province of Transalpine Gaul to protect their allies as long as it was in the Republic's interest. Accordingly, Caesar felt authorised to act outside the province's borders. After all, he had done exactly the same thing in Spain three years earlier and was awarded a triumph. Caesar thus quickly moved his three remaining legions across the Alps into Gaul.

With the Helvetii ravaging their territory, the Aedui appealed to Caesar for help. Eager to thwart the invaders before they could enter the Roman province, Caesar surprised them as they crossed the Saône. After defeating their rear guard on the left bank, Caesar shocked them again by erecting a bridge and marching his army across—all in a single day. Negotiations followed. The Helvetii offered to withdraw in peace wherever Caesar directed them to go, as long as they could remain in Gaul. Caesar refused. The tribe set off again on their trek, with the Roman legions in pursuit. Near the town of Bibactre both sides took up arms. The Roman javelin, the *pilum,* proved its worth in this battle. Difficult to remove once stuck, it forced the adversary to toss off his shield, having become unwieldy. After heavy fighting, the remnants of the Helvetii fled north into the territory of the Lingones. In turn, Caesar sent envoys to this Gallic tribe, instructing them not to provide the Helvetii with food or refuge.

The Helvetii, having lost many warriors and short on supplies, eventually surrendered. Caesar, having successfully removed the threat, sent the Helvetii home, commanding the Allobroges, whose territory they had to cross, to provide food for the defeated Helvetii. This marked a significant victory for Caesar, his greatest to date. It was the first time he had fought and won such a large and decisive battle. Never before had he commanded an army of this size. Moreover, how he countered the Helvetii became the hallmark of his conquest of Gaul: rather than battlefield tactics, his victory resulted from using a combination of speed, surprise, technology and logistical planning. Caesar's actions were not without precedent. Not long before, an invasion by other Germanic tribes had threatened Roman territories. They defeated several Roman armies until Caesar's uncle, Marius, finally gained the upper hand. Caesar was aware of this recent history and did not want to prove himself inferior to his uncle.

Therefore, driven by a sense of urgency and determination, Caesar knew he had to confront yet another menace from across the Rhine. The Suebi, a Germanic tribe, had recently crossed the Rhine, acting as mercenaries in a conflict between Gallic tribes. Instead of returning, they settled in Gaul. Rome had recently acknowledged their presence and established friendly relations. Now, however, several Gallic tribes, including Rome's allies, the Aedui, specifically asked Caesar for protection from the Suebi, who were encroaching upon their lands and inviting other Germans across the Rhine to join them. Caesar saw this as a strategic opportunity, while remaining within the boundaries of his responsibilities as governor. Caesar went against the Suebi for the same reasons why he wanted to stop the Helvetii: a duty to respond to an ally's request for assistance and the determination to do whatever necessary to protect Roman provinces. Caesar thus marched his army towards the Suebi.

Caesar began negotiations. He proposed to the Suebian king, Ariovistus, that they meet at a place halfway between where their two armies were stationed. The Germanic leader hesitated, not seeing the point of meeting. Caesar then sent another message saying that to maintain peaceful relations with Rome, he should stop allowing more Germanic tribes to cross the Rhine and stop putting pressure on the Aedui, Rome's allies. King Ariovistus stubbornly replied that he treated his defeated enemies as the Romans treated theirs. In short: the Romans should mind their own business. Besides, the king had another grievance: since the Romans had arrived, the Aedui had stopped paying the tribute they owed the Suebi. He seemed to be saying that if everyone would just honour their agreements, then there would be no need for conflict. Yet the message was clear that if Caesar wanted to fight, then he knew where to find him.

Both armies now moved towards each other, in preparation for battle. Caesar hurried to be the first to occupy Vesontio (now Besançon), north of the Jura mountains. This city was rich in food and other supplies that his army would need. Notably, Caesar had to overcome challenges, namely, his army's fears and sense of demotivation (something that will be described later in the chapter when analysing Caesar's leadership). He left Vesontio and ordered his army to march on Ariovistus' base. When the latter heard that Caesar was near, he sent envoys and called for a meeting. Caesar agreed to Ariovistus' demand that each would be accompanied by ten men on horseback. Caesar's cavalry consisted entirely of Gauls from allied tribes. Not fully trusting them, he decided to bring along mounted soldiers from his loyal Tenth Legion. Caesar was about to meet a leader who was in many ways his peer: an ambitious and victorious leader of a proud and conquering nation, aware of the expectations placed upon him by his followers: Box 4.1.

Box 4.1 Caesar Confronts Ariovistus

Let us, then, imagine the meeting between them. The conference took place in present-day Alsace, the north-eastern corner of France. Each commander dismounted and walked up a hill in the middle of a vast plain, accompanied only by their interpreters, as they did not share a common language. From the top of the hill, the two men could see the plain stretching out in gentle undulations. To the west, in the distance, rose the dark walls of the Vosges. To the east, beyond the rolling countryside, lay the Rhine, dividing Gaul from Germania. It was summer, so the area was a patchwork of lush forests and bright green meadows. From their vantage points, each could observe the other's forces and detect a possible ambush. Their bodyguards waited under the hill.

Caesar would have wanted to impress Ariovistus, dressed in his general's outfit: a metal breastplate, a bronze helmet decorated with feathers and images, and a dark red cloak. Ariovistus, also keen to appear martial and regal, wore colourful woollen trousers and a tunic; he had long hair and a beard. He wore a leather breastplate and a feathered helmet. Both men were unarmed. After exchanging formalities, they began to negotiate.

According to Caesar's own account in *De Bello Gallico* (*Commentaries on the War in Gaul*) I-44-45, their dialogue unfolded as follows (author's translation): Box 4.2.

Box 4.2 The Discussion Between Caesar and Ariovistus

Caesar:
  Rome has given you the rare honour of being called 'friend'. We have acknowledged you as the leader of your tribe. At the same time, the Aedui are allies of Rome and must not be harmed. Therefore, I repeat our demands: stop harassing the Aedui and their allies, and stop any migration from across the Rhine.
Ariovistus:
  We came to Gaul at the invitation of the Gauls. Later they attacked us. We conquered them, and the law of war gives us the right to tax our defeated enemies. Friendship with the Romans should be mutually beneficial. If the Romans now prevent us from receiving the taxes we are entitled to, we can do without the friendship. We have taken a piece of Gaul, as the Romans did for their province. Besides, we were here first. So please take your army back and you will find me a generous friend and ally.
Caesar:
  I beg to differ. We, the Romans, set foot in Gaul long before you. And neither I nor the Roman people are in the habit of abandoning our allies.

At that moment, a scuffle broke out between Roman and Germanic horsemen. Thus interrupted, the two leaders broke off their conversation, descended the hill and rode back to their respective camps. The next day, Ariovistus invited Caesar to continue the talks. Caesar preferred to do so through intermediaries. He sent Procillus, a Gaul with Roman citizenship who worked for Caesar as an interpreter, and Mettius, who had conducted business with the Suebi. Suspicious, Ariovistus imprisoned both men for violating the rules of engagement.

The standoff then escalated into a full-blown conflict, beginning with a series of cavalry skirmishes. Ariovistus attempted to cut off Caesar's supply route, which the latter thwarted by building an additional fortified camp. The two armies then manoeuvred until Caesar moved his army towards the enemy's camp near the Rhine. Ariovistus decided to fight. The Suebi placed their wagons in a semicircle around their army. Their women stood on top of the wagons and urged their men into battle. The Roman soldiers fought at close quarters, preventing any distance between the armies. This rendered it difficult for their enemies to use their long swords and spears effectively. The Romans gained the upper hand and the Suebi fled towards the river; many did not make it across or were killed by the Roman cavalry.

With the Suebi and Helvetii vanquished, Caesar camped his legions in Gaul for the winter under Labienus' command. Meanwhile, Caesar crossed the Alps to conduct business as governor in northern Italy and to meet with visitors from Rome. In 57, Caesar heard that the Belgian tribes felt threatened by the presence of Roman legions in Gaul. In response, they had formed an alliance and began a military campaign to expel the Romans. Caesar returned to Gaul and marched his army, reinforced by two additional legions, north. The Nervii hidden in the Ardennes Forest attacked the legions by surprise. The Romans were hard-pressed until Caesar himself entered the fray, sword in hand, urging his officers and soldiers to carry on fighting. The arrival of two additional legions, which had been delayed, finally turned the tide in the Romans' favour. Next, Caesar turned against the fortified capital of the Atuatuci. Employing siege engines, the Romans forced the city to surrender and a cease-fire was agreed. The night after the truce, however, the Atuatuci attacked the Romans, but in vain. Unlike the Nervians, who had been treated leniently after their defeat, the Atuatuci faced Caesar's wrath for breaking their word. Caesar's soldiers were ordered to plunder the city, and the population was sold to the slave traders accompanying the army. Soon after, Caesar received news that the Gauls on the Atlantic coast had pledged allegiance to Rome. Rather hastily, as we shall see, Caesar declared that the whole of Gaul had finally been pacified after two years of war.

After a winter break from fighting, Caesar was informed that the Veneti, a seafaring tribe on the Atlantic coast, had refused to give the Romans the agreed-upon amount of grain and had even taken the Roman officers who came to collect it hostage. Other tribes in the north joined the Veneti, and the Britons sent troops across the Channel in support. In the spring of 56, Caesar directed his army to the coast and had ships built at the mouth of the Loire. Attacking the Veneti at sea, the Roman ships were at a disadvantage. Low-built and dependent on oarsmen for propulsion, they had to contend with the tall Gallic sailing ships. However, as in the past, Roman technology secured an advantage. The Romans had developed a technique for cutting enemy ships' ropes and pulling down their masts. Immobilised and surrounded by several Roman ships, like orcas around a whale, the ships were easy prey. The Veneti surrendered. In line with his policy of 'one strike meets with clemency; two strikes with wrath', the Veneti's leaders, after breaking their oath of allegiance the previous year, were executed and the rest sold into slavery. Caesar let his army plunder and massacre at will.

The following year, 55, two Germanic tribes crossed the Rhine. Fearing for Gaul's stability, Caesar attacked and defeated them. Immediately afterwards, Caesar secured the Rhine border with a punitive expedition across the river. Caesar's army built a wooden bridge in ten days—a true technological feat. The Germans quickly burned their villages and fled into the vast forests. Eighteen days later, the Romans crossed the Rhine again, destroying the bridge behind them to deny its use by the enemy. Caesar decided to undertake a similar expedition to Britain to secure the Atlantic frontier. However, when the Romans tried to dock their ships, the Britons put up stiff resistance along the south coast's cliffs and beaches. Furthermore, a storm destroyed some of the ships after Caesar's army had finally established a bridgehead. The expedition ended in a draw and the Romans withdrew to the continent.

Feeling that the job was not yet done, Caesar undertook an even more extensive expedition into Britain in the spring of 54. Again, his efforts proved to be a tough fight. The Romans managed to push the Britons back across the Thames, but without achieving a complete victory. After spending most of the summer on the island, Caesar retreated to the continent for the winter. Due to poor harvests, Caesar had to disperse his legions into winter quarters across Gaul to find enough food. Gallic tribes from the north saw this as an opportunity and attacked the Roman forts. In a locale not far from today's Maastricht, the Eburones ambushed and wiped out one and a half legions in a major defeat. Caesar, who had not yet left for Italy as usual, took command and relieved the besieged forts. In 53, he brought in more troops from Italy and attacked the enemy tribes one by one. This time he showed no mercy, wreaking havoc and destruction. With the Gauls receiving support from across the Rhine, Caesar undertook a second punitive expedition into Germania, again building a wooden bridge, modelled on the previous one.

Then came the year 52. Spending the winter in Italy, Caesar was taken by surprise. One Gallic tribe, seizing their last chance for independence, decided to rise up against the Romans. The Carnutes killed all the Roman citizens in their capital, including the manager of the army's grain supply. Inspired by the Carnutes' success, the Arverni, one of the most prominent tribes, joined in. They elected a 30-year-old nobleman, Vercingetorix, as their leader; he had long been anti-Roman and had assiduously studied Roman battlefield tactics. Soon many other tribes were swept up in this revolt against Roman rule. Where before only a few tribes had coordinated their actions, now all were united under Vercingetorix as their supreme commander. What is more, this time the Gauls had a strategy: instead of meeting the superior Roman army on the battlefield, the Gauls would prevent the Romans from amassing their forces and cut off their supply lines.

The Gauls' first action was to attack Narbonne, the capital of the Roman province of Transalpine Gaul. The Gauls set out before the end of winter, hoping to take the Romans by surprise while their legions were spread out in winter camps across Gaul. As soon as he heard the news, Caesar rushed across the Alps from Italy into the province, raising troops along the way. Force-marching his soldiers through the snow-covered Cevennes mountains north of the province, he fell upon the Arverni in their homeland. Caesar laid waste to their land, forcing Vercingetorix to turn back to save his tribe. Caesar, one step ahead, retreated over the mountains. Marching non-stop several days and nights, he reached one of the winter camps and joined the two legions encamped there.

What followed was a war of manoeuvres in which the Gauls used scorched earth tactics to deprive the Romans of supplies. They also plundered and captured many of the Roman merchants throughout Gaul. Caesar moved around to gather his legions in different places to concentrate his army. On several occasions the two adversaries met in serious sieges or light skirmishes. Both had their victories and defeats. Caesar finally managed to gather his army. Lacking cavalry, however, he called in mercenary Germanic contingents from across the Rhine. Now he could push Vercingetorix back. The decisive conflict occurred at Alesia in central Gaul. Vercingetorix retreated to the fortified city to await a relief army. Meanwhile, Caesar surrounded the city with fortifications, facing inwards towards the city and outwards towards the expected Gallic army. The relief army's arrival took longer than expected, and Alesia ran out of food, so they sent their elderly, women and children out of the city towards the Romans. When Caesar refused to let them pass, they turned back, but Vercingetorix refused to open the gates. The refugees were left to perish in the no-man's-land.

When the relief army finally arrived, several attempts were made to breach the Roman fortifications from both sides. The Gauls almost broke through, and Caesar himself went to critical points on the front line to urge his troops to stay in the fight. Finally, a surprise Roman cavalry sortie hit the Gauls from behind, forcing them to abandon their last attack. Vercingetorix was compelled to surrender. Many prisoners were sold into slavery, but Caesar let the members of the most powerful tribes, the Aedui, Rome's long-time allies, and the Arverni, Vercingetorix's tribe, go home as a sign of reconciliation.

Despite the main threat having been removed, Gaul was yet to be fully conquered. Caesar, not wanting to put his greatest achievement to date at risk, spent the winter in Gaul, fearing further revolts. The following year, 51, Caesar led several campaigns against tribes who had not yet given up the fight. At the end of the year, he went to his province in Transalpine Gaul to oversee matters there but did not cross into Italy for the winter.

4.2.2 Winning the Peace

Pushing two tribes back across the border was one thing; conquering Gaul was quite another. Caesar's official mission was not to conquer new lands, let alone to establish a new province. His assignment was instead to protect the provinces under his jurisdiction. In doing so, he was willing to be drawn into a series of conflicts with Gallic tribes. It was out of the question for Caesar to retreat after defeating the Helvetii and the Suebi; he was determined to ensure that no threat would ever again emanate from Gaul and that the new territory would add material value to the Republic. This would be done through tribute, trade and military support. He had done the same, on a much smaller scale, in Spain some ten years earlier. Caesar thus followed standard Roman practice after a conquest: leave the local infrastructure and leadership intact as much as possible. The Romans did not have the manpower to replace the existing administration with their own. Nor did they have the population to colonise new territories. From the outset, Caesar took steps to integrate Gaul more fully into the empire. In the winter of 57, he sent a legion and some cavalry to open the mountain passes in the Alps to merchants. Until then, traders passing through had to pay high tolls to local tribes.

Caesar developed individual relationships with the tribes and their leaders, following the practice that had served him well in Roman politics. He supported pro-Roman leaders in each tribe. Once or twice a year, he organised large conferences to which he invited leaders from different tribes to discuss issues, gain their allegiance and agree on how they could support him with troops and supplies. However, Caesar could not win the Gauls' collective hearts and minds over to Roman rule. Caesar did not fully appreciate the role of the Druids in Gallic society as a political and ideological factor, which added a layer of complexity to the situation. Although the Gauls were divided against one another as oft-warring tribes, they did share a common religion led by a priestly class. These Druids held significant influence, often settling disputes and advising leaders. Moreover, they had a network that spanned all tribes. As custodians of Gallic culture and tradition, the Druids thought the Romans threatened their existence. Roman religion in contrast was mostly self-organised; it lacked professional full-time priests. For this reason, Caesar underestimated the Druids' role and capability. It can hardly be a coincidence that the uprising, of which Vercingetorix became the leader, was started by the tribe of the Carnutes, in whose lands the great annual druidic assembly took place. Thanks to the Druids, Vercingetorix could convince the previously divided tribes that they had a common purpose to see Caesar's support network disintegrate. Even the Aedui, Rome's long-time allies whom Caesar had rescued from the Helvetii, eventually joined Vercingetorix.

The uprising under Vercingetorix almost unseated Caesar's power. Caesar realised that his previous policy had not worked. Whereas he would normally be very harsh with allies who had betrayed him, this time he made a distinction. He decided to show leniency towards the Aedui, because he realised that many of them had opposed betraying the alliance with Rome. This strategic decision showcased that Caesar was getting a better grasp of the political landscape. He also demonstrated leniency towards the Averni, Vercingetorix's tribe and important because of their size, hoping that they would be incorporated as part of Gaul's future.

Caesar (Fig. 4.3) somehow convinced the Gauls that it would be to their advantage to join Rome rather than fight its rule. After this, hardly any incident of rebellion occurred in Gaul. The Romans worked hard to suppress druidism after their conquest. Although the Gauls did fight on both sides in the civil war that followed, they did so as professional soldiers, not as part of an independence movement. For example, notably, during the civil war, which Caesar would be fighting next, battles raged across the entire empire, even involving local populations, except in Gaul. Caesar did not have time to turn the new territory into a province (that would happen under Augustus). However, once the fighting had finally stopped, he travelled around Gaul to build personal and positive relationships and to avoid any cause for further

Fig. 4.3 Bust of Julius Caesar. Staatliche Museen zu Berlin, Antikensammlung/ Johannes Laurentius, CC BY-SA 4.0, Inventarnummer: Sk 342. Reprinted under license

rebellion. He honoured the tribes and rewarded their leaders. He avoided imposing punitive taxes. In this way, he applied techniques that had worked well in Spain and acted in the spirit of his own law of good provincial governance.

4.2.3 Winning the Home Front

Caesar foresaw that, once abroad, it would be challenging to continue influencing decisions in Rome from afar. He observed how Pompey, stationed in the east, had to make multiple attempts to secure land for his veterans and approval for his arrangement of the eastern provinces. Ultimately, he had to rely on Caesar's support as consul to get it all done. Formally, as governor, Caesar reported to the Senate and the consuls in Rome. The central authority then decided what resources Caesar could dispose of, including the funding of legions, the number of officers and the renewal of his command.

After his consulship ended, Caesar spent the first few months of 58 in Rome, diligently and successfully trying to uphold his promises to the triumvirate by preventing any violations of the laws he had passed as consul. Publius

Clodius—the same one who had allegedly had an affair with Caesar's second wife Pompeia five years earlier—became a powerful tribune of the plebs in 58. One of his first acts was to prosecute Cicero for executing the Catilinarian conspirators—Roman citizens—without trial. Before a popular assembly, Clodius asked Caesar for his opinion on the matter. Caesar reminded everyone that he had opposed the execution at the time. Simultaneously, he declared that he preferred let bygones be bygones. Cicero left the city in voluntary exile before a decision was made. Caesar offered him a position on his staff in Gaul, but Cicero refused and sent his brother Quintus instead. Finally, two praetors began investigating whether Caesar's legislation as consul had followed due process. Caesar said that the Senate should decide and joined in on the discussions. The senators were lost thickly in debate. After three days, Caesar could no longer be bothered by it and left the city to formally assume his duties as governor. He left for Gaul upon hearing that the Helvetii were on the move towards Roman territory.

From Gaul, Caesar continued to work with Clodius, while Caesar's opponents attempted again to repeal Caesar's consular laws. They prosecuted Vatinius, Caesar's mid-level leader, who had been instrumental passing legislation through the popular assembly the previous year. Vatinius was accused of having done so illegally. He had followed Caesar to Gaul as a military officer and had now returned to stand trial as a result of these accusations. However, Clodius mobilised a group of people to sabotage the trial by destroying the jury's ballot boxes. The trial was never reconvened and Vatinius returned to Gaul unopposed.

During 58–56, Rome was torn by factionalism among the elite. This manifested itself in the courts and in violence in the city's streets, where leaders mobilised crowds against each other. It was not just a matter of career competition among individuals, but also of how to solve the pressing problems. Meanwhile, the conservative majority remained keen to roll back some of Caesar's legislation and, in particular, to remove him from his command in Gaul. The triumvirs were now clearly a class apart in terms of wealth and influence, resembling modern-day oligarchs. Caesar knew that his command depended on the continuation of this coalition so that the other two, Pompey and Crassus, could defend his interests in his absence. So, he invited them to a meeting at Luca, on the southern edge of his province in northern Italy.

The coalition was renewed based on the same formula of supporting each other's interests. Pompey and Crassus would be consuls again—as they had been in 70—to implement their plans. To raise the probability of being elected, the two would work in Rome to delay the elections until later in the year. This would allow Caesar's officers and soldiers, who were off duty during the winter months, to come to Rome to vote. The agreement was to extend Caesar's command for another five years and to grant state funding for additional legions. As for Crassus, he was eager to fight a 'real' war. He had defeated Spartacus' slave army in 71, but it was considered an 'unworthy' enemy. Therefore, he would get Syria as a province, expecting to fight Parthia; Pompey would get the two Spanish provinces and continue his position as troubleshooter by overseeing the city's grain supply. The triumvirate and its renewal were Caesar's idea. It fitted with his organisational philosophy. Particularly, its renewal strengthened the executive leadership. The first coalition placed Caesar in an executive role as consul first and as governor next. Its renewal gave all three triumvirs executive roles. Pompey and Crassus realised the triumvirs' plans during their joint consulate in 55, but not without difficulty. Cato the Younger once again led an opposition, but despite speeches, procedural obstructions and pushing and shoving in meetings, Pompey and Crassus prevailed.

As mentioned above, 54 was a difficult year for Caesar. As well as serious setbacks in Gaul, his support network in Rome disintegrated. Crassus left and was killed in battle against the Parthians in 53, reducing the triumvirate to a duumvirate. The triumvirate had been held together by common interests and a delicate balance of power. The inherent competition among these three ambitious individuals was kept in check, as no one could ever become more powerful than the other two. The balance became unstable after losing Crassus and the death of Julia, who had been a force of stability between Caesar and Pompey. What's more, whereas previously Caesar could count on his mother, wife and daughter to work for him behind the scenes in Rome, his wife Calpurnia was now the only survivor of this powerful female team.

In the late 50 s, Rome once again fell victim to civil unrest. Electoral corruption, political competition, riots and assassinations stifled the political process. This proved yet another opportunity for Pompey to become Rome's trouble-shooter. This time, however, he had the support of the senatorial majority, which gave him the recognition he had always craved as a relatively new member of the upper class. Cato the Younger and Bibulus, now Cato's son-in-law, led the conservative faction and struck a deal with Pompey. They stopped short of dictatorship and proposed that Pompey become consul in 52 without a colleague. With all the consular powers in one hand, they hoped Pompey could pacify the city. It was a double exception to the existing rules. First, constitutionally, a consul should have a colleague; secondly, there should be a ten-year interval between consulships, but Pompey had been consul in 55, only three years earlier. Pompey deployed soldiers to restore order in the city, and a crackdown by trial followed. However, these trials were biased towards convicting the enemies of Cato's conservative faction. Many were exiled and found their way to Caesar in Gaul.

Caesar maintained an organisation of mid-level leaders who worked on his behalf as magistrates and senators to influence decisions in Rome. He sometimes sent officers back to take up magisterial roles in Rome (e.g. Vatinius as praetor in 55 BC). During the winter months, when there was a lull in fighting, Caesar returned to the Roman provinces under his command, most often to the south of the Alps. There he oversaw his administrative duties as governor. This brought him closer to Rome and allowed him to hold discussions with senators and businessmen who travelled north to meet him. Candidates for office came to seek Caesar's financial support for their campaigns. Caesar also maintained a direct link with the business community, who had much to gain from his conquests as bankers, army suppliers and tax collectors. When he was further away, Caesar used a system of couriers to carry his extensive correspondence back and forth from Gaul to individuals in Rome. With two of his key aides, Oppius and Balbus, he had agreed on a system that allowed them to exchange coded messages. Letters were often accompanied by gifts of money or valuables. All this allowed Caesar to remain actively involved in Roman politics. Towards the end of his command in Gaul, when his return was imminent and the triumvirate had fallen apart, Caesar worked tirelessly to strengthen his leadership organisation in Rome.

For Caesar, as for any modern expatriate leader, the challenge was to ensure that his achievements were recognised at home, that he had sufficient support and that he would be remembered for his future career moves. After Caesar announced in late 57 that all of Gaul had been pacified, the Senate decreed a *supplicatio* in his honour, a festival to thank the gods for Caesar's victories. The Senate decided on an unprecedented duration of fifteen days for the celebration (the previous record was held by Pompey in 63). In 55, Caesar received another thanksgiving, after the Senate had discussed his report on Gaul and the spectacular expeditions to Germania and Britain. Finally, after Caesar's victory over Vercingetorix in 52, he received a third thanksgiving.

These public celebrations of Caesar's achievements contributed to his visibility among Rome's stakeholders. It helped Caesar to persuade the Senate to commit additional legions to the war in Gaul. Moreover, to maintain a permanent visibility—also in competition with other wealthy Romans—and to show his generosity, Caesar began investing some of his booty. He purchased land in Rome for future prestigious real estate projects, including a new marble voting enclosure on the Campus Martius for electoral assemblies, and a forum of his own crowned with a temple dedicated to his family's patron goddess Venus.

Caesar reported to Rome extensively from Gaul, reports that one can still read today in *De Bello Gallico*, a collection of his personal accounts of the war in Gaul. In these bulletins, Caesar was deliberately ambiguous as to whether he was waging a defensive war to protect Rome's interests or a war of conquest, for which he was not authorised. Confident of success, he chose to ask for forgiveness after the fact rather than asking for permission beforehand. After all, his mandate as governor in general and in the Gallic provinces in particular was not very precise. Decisive and ambitious as he was, he used this grey area to push the boundaries of his mission. Rome was still building its empire. The idea that Rome's future depended on the consistent and sustainable management of the empire, let alone the awareness that an organisational structure with adequate processes and systems was needed to make it work, had only begun to dawn on some members of Rome's elite. Caesar was one of the few who did, as he had shown as governor in Spain with his law on provincial government and his attitude to tax farmers.

4.3 Caesar's Leadership During the Gallic War

After this historical overview, let us now analyse Caesar's leadership behaviour from a modern perspective again. Salient questions at this point are: What competencies did Caesar use to meet his challenges? How did he apply them? Figure 4.4 summarises the evaluation of Caesar's leadership behaviours during this period.

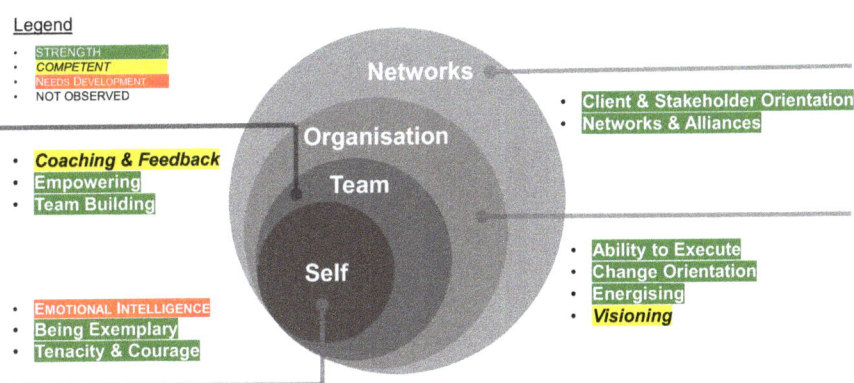

Fig. 4.4 Evaluation of Caesar's leadership behaviours as commander during the war in Gaul. Author's adaptation: Based on GELM by KDVI

4.3.1 Leading Self

Over the years in Gaul, Caesar proved an exemplary leader to his soldiers. He shared their simple food and tents, even in the most adverse conditions. The army was impressed by Caesar's stamina, as he was undeterred by his headaches (possibly migraines) and occasional epileptic seizures. Caesar often travelled by coach or litter, sleeping on the move or dictating letters and memos to a slave accompanying him, sometimes two at once to keep up with his dictation speed. The bravery he had shown as a soldier in his youth returned to the fore. On several occasions, he turned the tide of battle by visibly fighting in the front ranks. The legionaries felt that he was amassing wealth to enrich himself as well as to generously reward those who performed well.

Caesar continued to act in accordance with his value of clemency. He was capable of a great deal of violence and cruelty, but this was not his default mode of action. He had people executed, committing what we would now call genocide against the Eburones, sold entire tribes into slavery, sacked cities and cut people's hands off. Yet he allowed the Helvetii to return home in peace, ensuring they had enough food on the way. He pardoned the Aedui and the Arverni, despite theirs betraying his trust. If anything, Caesar was consistent: he was genuinely forgiving and eager to establish peaceful relations with all defeated adversaries after an initial conflict. After a second fight, however, he was quite unforgiving.

The success of Vercingetorix's revolt, six years after Caesar's arrival in Gaul, revealed a strategic miscalculation on Caesar's part. It was a testament to the fact that he had yet to win the hearts and minds of the people he had conquered. This unexpected turn of events, a blind spot in his leadership, hints at the need for further development of his Emotional Intelligence, a phenomenon that was observable previously. Caesar clearly was not determined to offer either the Helvetii or the Suebi a way out that would somehow take their interests into account. He went for win-lose outcomes and, luckily for Caesar, he came out winning. In Gaul, despite his efforts to build relationships with individual tribes and leaders, showing clemency and generosity, he failed to recognise the Gauls' readiness as a whole to be mobilised behind a common cause. He was oblivious to the Druids' persuasive power. Consequently, he was unable to craft a timely and compelling message to persuade the Gauls collectively to relinquish their independence and embrace Roman rule.

The war in Gaul is often seen, not least because of Caesar's writings, as a period of non-stop fighting and high-intensity action. But that's not the whole story. Military campaigns were high-stakes, exhausting, stressful and sometimes life-threatening. But the battles were also interspersed with periods of travel and preparation. Especially during the winter months, when the fighting stopped, Caesar could recharge back in Italy. Work was slower and less intense. He spent time with family and friends who came to visit. He had the time to read and write, to exercise or relax in Roman baths. In fact, this seasonal rhythm kept his energy levels high. It also made him resilient. Caesar did not dwell on defeat. In fact, given his speed of reaction, setbacks actually boosted his confidence and made him spring into action. His strong Tenacity was the result of his desire to efface the memory of failure by immediately overperforming afterwards. His extreme reaction towards the Eburones was motivated by his frustration about the severe defeat they had inflicted on his army.

4.3.2 Leading Teams

In his role as general, Caesar had a fantastic opportunity to demonstrate and develop his skills as an operational leader. Success on the battlefield was also due to Caesar's team of officers. Many of them were recruited by Caesar himself, a process that involved careful consideration of their skills, loyalty and potential. He also continued to draw on the pool of talent from the lower ranks of society, such as Vatinius, who helped him pass laws as a consul and then followed him to Rome as an officer. Chief among these men was Titus Labienus, the first of his family to become a senator. Furthermore, Caesar and Labienus had known each other for a long time. They were the same age and met as junior officers during a campaign against pirates in the 70 s. In the 60 s, they had worked together in Roman politics, supporting Pompey.

Labienus followed Caesar to Gaul. Having seen him at work, Caesar made him his second in command, a position that carried significant responsibilities and decision-making power. Labienus is credited with several victories and never suffered defeat as a commander. He was clearly Caesar's best right-hand man. During the winter, when Caesar was in Italy, he empowered Labienus to manage matters north of the Alps. Labienus was charged with preventing the Helvetii from crossing the Rhone gap near Geneva, while Caesar was recruiting additional legions in Italy. In the war against Vercingetorix, he was indispensable in preventing the Gauls from concentrating their forces. Despite centuries of warfare, the Romans never could develop a cavalry as a significant strategic weapon. It cost them dearly against Hannibal, for example. Labienus was the first to effectively integrate the mounted soldiers of Gallic allies and Germanic mercenaries into the Roman army. He was to Caesar what Joachim Murat was to Napoleon.

Caesar employed officers from upper-class backgrounds as a favour to people in his network or on their recommendation. Publius Crassus, Crassus' son, was Caesar's best officer next to Labienus. Crassus Jr. successfully led the campaign to conquer both western Gaul and the Atlantic coast. He then departed from Gaul and joined the ill-fated expedition against Parthia, where he died with his father. Cicero's younger brother, Quintus, performed admirably, notably holding his fort against the onslaught of Eburones' vastly superior force. After this, he left to serve under his older brother when Cicero became governor of a province in the east. Later in the war, Marc Antony joined Caesar. Although not all of Caesar's officers were of the same quality, most performed well in the Gallic campaign, forming strong bonds with Caesar and each other.

As well as empowering them, Caesar actively supported and protected his staff. Earlier we read of his support for Vatinius when he was put on trial in 58. Similarly, when Caesar's networker and former chief engineer, Balbus, was prosecuted in 56 for allegedly obtaining Roman citizenship illegally, Caesar and the other triumvirs hired Rome's best lawyer, Cicero, to defend him successfully. He also actively promoted his officers' careers, sending them back to Rome to stand for election and hold government office. Vatinius returned to become praetor; Marc Antony returned to be tribune of the plebs. As for Labienus, Caesar appointed him governor of Transalpine Gaul in 50 to gain additional experience in management.

Caesar relied on his colleagues in the triumvirate and the popular leader Clodius to successfully oversee things in Rome. In addition, Caesar used informal intermediaries such as the fixer-banker team comprised of Balbus and Oppius, who also handled his correspondence between Gaul and Rome. These intermediaries played crucial roles in maintaining the flow of information and resources, allowing Caesar to focus on his military and political strategies.

To help him manage the size and complexity of governing three provinces and waging a war of conquest in Gaul, Caesar surrounded himself with highly professional specialists, often men of high potential whom Caesar recruited early in their careers: engineers, secretaries for his correspondence and reporting, purchasing and supply managers, interpreters and financial specialists. One of these was Gaius Trebatius Testa. At the age of 30, on Cicero's recommendation, he became Caesar's chief legal adviser. He remained on Caesar's staff throughout his career, providing invaluable legal counsel and support. Under Augustus, he became one of Rome's leading legal scholars. Notably, how Caesar staffed and structured his team was not unusual. The state provided a general with a fully manned and equipped army, including an officer corps. A governor was given minimal staff for civil duties. However, Roman government officials were expected to hire additional staff and pay their wages from their own funds.

Motivating a team of officers to fight a battle is no small challenge, even for a talented leader like Caesar. One notable event occurred during the campaign against the Suebi in 58, which is insightful for Caesar's skill in Coaching & Feedback. After Ariovistus initially refused to talk, Caesar repositioned his army against the Suebi. Upon doing so, he found that the troops were lukewarm about following him. Such hesitancies began among his officers, especially those with little experience and who had joined to attain glory. They had heard stories from the merchants and the Gauls and were therefore gripped by fear of their Germanic enemy. They were also unsure whether the war was legitimate or an excuse to serve Caesar's ambitions. At this juncture, there was even talk of desertion. Caesar and the Roman historian Dio Cassius describe this episode in detail, including a long speech by Caesar (Box 4.3).

Box 4.3 Caesar Re-Motivates a Reluctant Army

Concerned that he might be unable to influence the soldiers' mood, Caesar gathered only his officers and centurions rather than the whole army. This amounted to about sixty men. The meeting occurred in the Gallic city of Vesontio (now Besançon), where the Romans had stopped to resupply. In this town, there would have been a hall large enough to assemble the officers and subalterns so that Caesar could address them privately. In his speech, he addressed, one by one, the various reasons why people were reluctant and why they should reconsider absconding.

First, Caesar reminded them that the negotiations were not yet over. He argued that Ariovistus would probably come to his senses and everything would end peacefully. Instead of sitting around wasting public money, Caesar said that, as officers, they should protect those, like the Aedui, with whom Rome was formally allied, while expanding the empire. If not, then they should not have come to Gaul in the first place. He also reminded them that most of them had volunteered to join him on this campaign. Contributing to the prosperity of the Republic benefits everyone, he continued. To those who claim that the campaign is none of their business and can only cause more trouble, Caesar replied that Rome did not become great by quitting now or leaving because of fear. Rome had, after all, grown from a small city into an empire by taking the fight to the enemy, not by waiting for the enemy to come to them. Rome's destiny and happiness, he exhorted, is to be free and prosperous only by ruling others; anything else would mean ruin and decline. Caesar then adds that such a goal can only be achieved if Rome is always ready to maintain a lasting peace, to engage in actual combat to avoid constant strife, to broaden alliances by promptly supporting allies when they ask for it, and to refrain from appeasing trouble-makers so they stop seeing any advantage in undermining Roman rule.

> Caesar dismisses the argument that this war was not explicitly approved by the Senate or the People by pointing out that most wars actually are unplanned. Besides, he contends, why would the People have agreed to an exceptional five-year rather than a two-year command and four legions if they did not expect any military conflict? Moreover, it was sensible that the command did not specify exactly who was to be fought because that would be too difficult to judge from such a distance. Ariovistus should be judged by his actions as well as his intentions. Moreover, Ariovistus' refusal to meet Caesar was not a personal slight. Rather, it was a sign of disrespect for the proconsul's role and Rome's authority.
>
> After all, there was nothing to fear: supplies were taken care of. Moreover, had they not just defeated the Helvetii with relative ease? Rome had defeated other Germanic armies before, such as the Cimbri and the Teutones in the days of Marius, and more recently Spartacus' slave army. This could be repeated, he urged. The Roman military was better equipped and had better tactics than the enemy. With all this, Caesar managed to turn the army's mood back in his favour. During the meeting, the centurions and junior officers immediately pledged their support and left to convince the soldiers under their command. Sensing the momentum, Caesar broke camp and set the army marching the next day.

These accounts give us a rare insight into how Caesar energised his followers and into his personal motivations.

In his speech, Caesar used a mixture of rational and emotional arguments: stating the facts of the current situation and the state of the army, appealing to the duty of the citizens of Rome, recalling past successes in similar situations to alleviate fears and pointing out the opportunity for material gain. He also argued that his actions were consistent with the mission and the means he had been given to accomplish it. No doubt Caesar used his rhetorical skills in full whilst making this speech. He had employed the same skills to sway the Senate to his point of view during the debate on conspirators' fate five years earlier. Now, however, there was no Cato to oppose him. This is a striking example of how Caesar motivated his troops through orders and persuasion, even in a military organisation with a top-down command structure. He was generous with rewards and recognition, both material and symbolic. Caesar's attention to logistics, for instance, ensuring there was enough food and other supplies, gave his men a sense of security and reflected their leader's empathy. He cared for his people by giving them time off after battle to relax and have fun. He kept his promises, which built the requisite trust to motivate his soldiers to follow him into battle.

4.3.3 Leading the Organisation

One compelling example (Box 4.4) gives us insight into how Caesar energised his army after a defeat. In 52, Caesar laid siege to the fortified city of Gergovia. Part of the army stormed the walls at their initiative, perceiving a weak spot. Their officers could not hold them back. The Gauls repelled the attack and, through a sortie from their city, inflicted considerable losses on the Romans. As a consequence, Caesar had to abandon the siege.

> **Box 4.4 An Example of Performance Management**
>
> How Caesar handled the situation is textbook performance management. He gathered the army together and addressed them. He first gave them his feedback: their defeat resulted from ignoring their officer's commands and reckless behaviour. At the same time, he commended them for their courage. He then reformulated his expectations: he expected them to show modesty, self-control and valour and to look beyond the obvious. Not wanting to leave them on a low note, he concluded by encouraging the soldiers to achieve better next time. To ensure they would regain their confidence, he led the army outside the camp and prepared them for battle several times. In line with their new strategy to avoid engaging the Romans in the open, the Gauls refused to respond. Caesar portrayed this to his troops as a sign of superiority. He could then march his troops away in a positive mood.

There is no evidence that Caesar developed his own vision for this venture into unconquered territory. He believed in the vision of his employer, the Republic, which was that Rome was destined for conquest, as he had impressed upon his officers at Vesontio. However, he did not devise a specific strategy to achieve this vision. In fairness to Caesar, it was only during his consulship that he discovered which provinces he would be given, leaving him little time to develop a strategy. Initially, Gaul was a similar but much bigger job than Caesar's governorship in Spain. His plan was to find similar opportunities for military action and material reward beyond the borders of his provinces. Yet as events unfolded, the campaign's scope expanded significantly. Caesar seized the opportunities that presented themselves and pushed the boundaries of his initial plan. He adapted to changing circumstances with agility and executed a strategy that to this day is a model for military strategists.

The legitimacy of Caesar's actions in Gaul has been debated by his contemporaries and ever since. Having been given vague objectives, he did not overstep any boundaries in the first year. However, he may have interpreted things to his advantage. The threat from the Helvetii was real, and he had to do what was necessary to protect the Roman province. Going after Ariovistus was preemptive and at the request of Rome's Gallic allies, the Aedui. In fact, the Suebi crossing the Rhine looked a great deal like the invasion of the Germanic tribes in Marius' time, an event that had menaced not only the provinces but also Rome itself. Keeping the legions in Gaul for the winter after eliminating the Germanic threat, rather than retreating into Roman territory, was stretching Caesar's objectives as governor. It is understandable that the Belgae saw it as a provocation. Admittedly, going after the Belgae in 57 was asking for forgiveness rather than permission. But Caesar knew that both the Senate and the People of Rome were quite forgiving of generals who had pushed boundaries to secure a victory. After all, Rome's destiny was conquest. The thanksgiving they granted him proved his point.

Caesar developed his strategy as he went, from campaign to campaign. His initial approach was Spain 2.0, removing threats to the Roman provinces while giving himself opportunities for military glory. After two years, he thought the job was completed and declared victory. The following year, 56, he began to see he had been wrong. In 54–52, his army suffered several setbacks and defeats as the Gallic tribes began adapting and cooperating. Eventually he prevailed through speed, logistics and technology. He secured the borders of newly acquired territories by sending the Helvetii home and crossing the Rhine and Channel twice to deter future invaders. In his final years, he learned through hardship that he needed to implement more than just a Spain 2.0. As a result, he offered the Gauls incentives to align them more closely with the Roman Empire, paving the way for full integration by his successor.

4.3.4 Leading Stakeholders and Networks

During this period, Caesar had to influence two main groups of stakeholders: the Senate and the People of Rome on the one hand, and the Gauls on the other. In addition to his coalition with Crassus and Pompey and his organisation of mid-level leaders in Rome, Caesar exerted influence through his letters, financial support and envoys to individuals in Rome. People often travelled from Rome to northern Italy during the winter to meet him. His network in Rome remained strong, and he gained visibility through the thanksgivings and his building plans. He applied what he had learned from his mother, Aurelia, about deploying informal power.

And then there were Caesar's *Commentaries on the Gallic War*, or *De Bello Gallico* for short. Each year, during the winter break, he wrote down the previous' year's events. Much later these were compiled into one volume and published to cement Caesar's legacy for posterity. During the war, he communicated through dispatches, a customary way for Roman generals to report to the Senate on events. Some of these reports, short versions of the later Commentaries, may have been read out loud to informal gatherings of citizens. Caesar's reports had a different style. He gives the impression of objectivity by referring to himself in the third person. His Latin is concise, grammatically correct and uncomplicated. These dispatches were clearly intended for a wider audience. Caesar can be called the inventor of embedded journalism because of his style and how he disseminated news. It fitted with his policy of transparency, as he had done by creating an audit trail for provincial governance and by introducing daily public reports of Senate meetings and popular assemblies, when he was consul. He showed that transparency was vital to him; no doubt he expected that he had more to gain than to lose from openness. It also positively affected Caesar's reputation as a leader. Interestingly, it did so despite, or perhaps because of, the fact that he not only boasted of victories but also addressed challenges and gave ample praise for the achievements of his legionaries and officers.

4.4 Caesar's Career Development During the Gallic War

Proconsul of three provinces at the same time was Caesar's first position with a longer tenure. In fact, starting at five years and extending for a further five, it was the longest position he held in his entire career. Previous positions had been much shorter, lasting little more than a year. Career development at this stage of Caesar's career involved getting his assignment extended after the first five years, preparing for the next move towards the end of his assignment and securing a favourable opinion from those deciding on his future position. All this had to be done from afar, as he was prevented from entering Rome as a military commander. Meanwhile, the scope of his responsibilities grew with the addition of legions and territories.

Why did Caesar want to extend his command from five to ten years? Most historians argue it was a desire for conquest and material gain. Caesar may have hoped for more such opportunities, despite the extension being planned when it seemed that things in Gaul had calmed down and he could claim victory. Indeed, in 56, he had thus far been successful on the battlefield, but the main financial windfall was yet to come. Some claim that Caesar sought to retain his immunity and be protected from prosecution for irregularities as consul. While there was a risk of this later, after his network of key supporters had thinned out, he had little to fear during the first five years. He was immensely popular, and the triumvirs and Clodius effectively protected him from political danger.

Career decisions are often made for very personal reasons. So, let us look at the alternative to staying on. Caesar could have returned home with glory and wealth. But he could not assume another magistracy for a while. The Romans, always concerned about individual power, had decreed a mandatory ten-year interval between consulships, except in times of crisis. What was left was to retire early and enjoy life on a luxurious country estate, as some victorious generals did. Or he could become an influential senator, laden with prestige. The former would be boring for a Caesar in his forties. The latter meant returning to the rhetorical debates with Cato and his followers, for which he lacked the patience and conviction. Finally, Caesar believed in the primacy of the executive over the Senate. Caesar simply had the time of his life in Gaul. That, more than anything else, was likely to be the driving force behind his decision to stay. Certainly, Gaul offered opportunities for growth to feed his ambition. But just as importantly, he could enjoy achieving tangible results, making quick decisions, taking risks and being appreciated by his followers.

To win an extension of his command to complete the job in Gaul, Caesar used the same tactic that had served him well as consul: renewing the coalition of mutual support and benefit among the three triumvirs. The regular reports he sent from Gaul throughout the nine years in command and the three thanksgivings he secured gave the Romans the impression that he was excelling. He influenced decision-makers through a constant flow of correspondence, face-to-face meetings during the winter in northern Italy, giving generous support for those in financial need and an informal organisation of partisans and officials in the city. This enabled him to thwart several attempts to recall him from Gaul and to gain support for his future career.

What would make sense for Caesar's career after Gaul? He had already reached the highest position, consul. He would be 50 at the end of his term. Moreover, early retirement was far from Caesar's mind. Professional advancement in Rome was more than just moving up the hierarchy of the magistracies. It also meant contributing to the Republic when not holding a magistracy: as a governor, as a senator or as an orator in the courts and popular assemblies. Ultimately, and this was the crucial point for Caesar, it was about gaining prestige (*dignitas*) through high performance for the common good, that is, the Republic. The hierarchy certainly counted and offered prestige. At its core, however, the Roman Republic was a meritocracy; rising to the top in the eyes of others was ultimately about merit. Hierarchically, becoming governor of the Gallic provinces after the consulate was a step down. More important, in the eyes of the Romans, was the opportunity—and duty—to contribute. And contribute Caesar did. Caesar passed the law on stricter control of provincial administration in 59, before he got the big ticket of three provincial commands that led to the conquest of Gaul. Thus, he limited his own opportunity for enrichment and exploitation of the empire. It is a telling example of choosing to do the right thing for the Republic as opposed to the right thing for himself. Come to think of it, previously, Caesar served three times in a provincial administration. There is no evidence of him having ever engaged in provincial exploitation. Caesar did loot and plunder, but always across the border of the empire.

Cicero, in a plea in defence of Lucius Murena, a consul-elect accused of electoral corruption in 63, expressed the Roman view of career success as follows (author's translation):

> The highest esteem [*dignitas*] belongs to those who excel in military glory.
> They are expected to defend and strengthen the state and the empire.
> They also add the most value because their competence and willingness to put themselves in danger allow us [*as citizens*] to benefit from both public and private affairs.

Only the worthiest to be offered the opportunity to contribute to the Republic were elected by the People for office. That the actual outcome of elections was increasingly a matter of political machinations or even corruption is a different matter. In the Roman belief system, the Republic was a meritocracy. The logical step for Caesar, therefore, not wanting to pause and ever in search of *dignitas*, would be another magistracy—obviously not a position below the consulship—or perhaps a Pompey-style special command to solve a big problem.

Caesar expressed his desire to run for the consulship a second time. To be elected consul more than once was extremely rare and highly prestigious; Crassus had been consul twice, Pompey thrice. Caesar certainly wanted to match that number. He asked for permission to stand in absentia, and he had made a similar request for his first consulship in 60. Then it was to combine his triumph with the election, ultimately thwarted by Cato the Younger, as recounted in the previous chapter. This time it was to enable Caesar to finish his command and leave Gaul and his three provinces in good order. By moving from governor to consul without interruption, Caesar could enjoy immunity from prosecution. Political opponents, led by Cato the Younger, were working to depose him in Gaul. Caesar had pushed boundaries and may have in fact overstepped them; a case could therefore be made for his prosecution, although the chances of that actually happening were slim as Morstein-Marx in his biography explains. A conviction would end in exile and exclude Caesar from the next position of leadership. The institutional and ideological conflict over which institution—the Senate or the executive—held the primary role in the Republic, which Caesar had fought before leaving for Gaul, had resurfaced. The fight over the exception to stand for election in absentia was also part of this power struggle. This time, however, there was no more triumvirate. Crassus was dead and Cato managed to draw Pompey increasingly over to the side of the conservative majority in the Senate, leaving Caesar isolated. At first the exception was granted, but then other machinations led to it being withdrawn. A civil war would thus decide Caesar's next career move.

Caesar remained true to his brand as a generous and forgiving leader. He demonstrated this to his soldiers, the Gauls, the citizens of Rome and the senators who visited him during the winter months. Caesar forged a formidable reputation through his triumphs on the battlefield and his leadership, which in turn propelled his army to extraordinary feats. The three thanksgivings, as well as his own regular war reports, bolstered his brand and reputation in Rome. Discharged soldiers and officers returned with tales of their general. The perception of a capable leader positioned Caesar in a strong way. He could rely on an army willing to follow their general who was a winner. In Rome, the People were happy to see him stand for election as consul, and, in 52, they granted him the exception of standing for election without being physically present at the polls. As fears of civil war escalated in 50, the business community advocated for a peaceful resolution that would not exclude Caesar.

Let us now turn our attention to the *Leadership Pipeline* and scrutinise this stage in Caesar's career through that prism (Fig. 4.5). Governor of three provinces was Caesar's second 'business manager' role. He had undertaken a similar task in Spain three years earlier, albeit on a smaller scale. This role necessitated a transition to supervising managers in government and the army. There was a modest administration to oversee, along with town councils and local chiefs in each province. Over time, managing leaders of conquered tribes was added to the role. As a general, Caesar also commanded an officer corps that expanded with his army. Navigating this passage requires a manager to evolve into a strategic and full-time leader, with limited time for individual contributions. Once again, Caesar demonstrated his adeptness at these transitions. As a general, he did not just command battles; he crafted a strategy that evolved from defending Roman territory to conquering new lands as

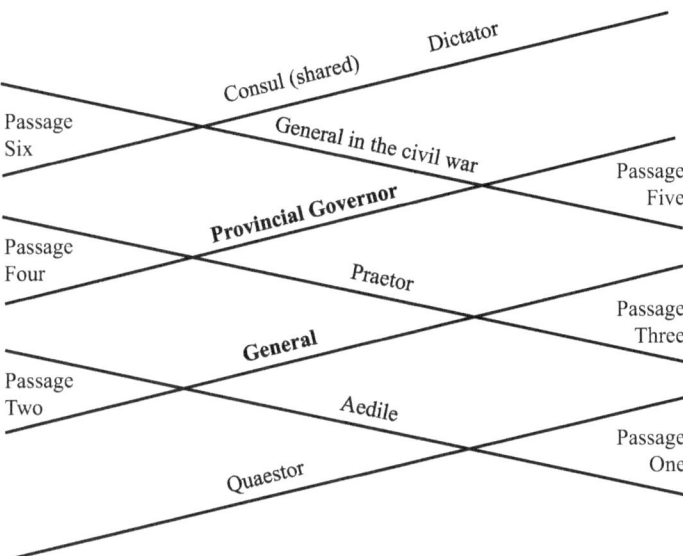

Fig. 4.5 Julius Caesar's career passages in the Roman Career System during his assignment in Gaul. Author's adaptation: based on Charan et al. (2001)

circumstances and opportunities unfolded. In devising and implementing this strategy, Caesar relied on his most talented officers, Labienus and Publius Crassus. However, there were several significant setbacks in bringing the strategy to a successful conclusion. Occasionally, Caesar had to descend to the operational level and fight on the battlefield. These were not instances of micromanagement, but rather necessary interventions to reverse critical situations.

Another transition for a new business manager is to demonstrate a forward-looking, profit-oriented perspective. Caesar exhibited this on several occasions, including securing road links for merchants and deterring future invasions from Britain and from across the Rhine. At the end of his mission, he introduced measures to facilitate incorporating the new territories into the empire through taxation and forging relationships with the local elites. Caesar leveraged the autonomy that came with his position effectively. In Gaul, Caesar found himself back in his comfort zone of clear boundaries and direct authority.

However, a key difference from his previous position in Spain was that Caesar was now at the pinnacle of the Roman Republic. Remaining at this level required constant involvement in events in Rome, while having no formal authority beyond his provinces' boundaries. The Leadership Pipeline concept unfortunately hardly deals with indirect leadership from afar at a senior level. Influencing skills are needed to be effective in 'virtual' indirect leadership. In the early years he was deft at this. In particular, his cooperation within the triumvirate and with Clodius protected the legacy of his laws, prevented an early transfer and secured an extension of his command. Then Caesar began to lose critical individuals in his support network on the home front.

In 54, Julia, the glue between him and Pompey, died. The triumvirate broke up when Crassus fell in 53. In 52, Clodius, a highly influential and independent politician, was killed. These were significant blows to Caesar's support network and his influence in Rome. He tried to compensate by strengthening his direct relationships with other and more junior magistrates like Curio and Mark Antony so that they could act on his behalf. What did not help was that Caesar did not travel to northern Italy for the last two winters (52–50). He stayed north of the Alps to ensure peace after the cessation of hostilities. As a result, he could not meet personally with visitors from Rome, as he had done in most previous winters. Securing his next career step became a challenge that proved too difficult to overcome, as the next chapter will explain.

4.5 What Leaders Can Learn from Caesar's Assignment in Gaul

When examining the period of 58–50, one cannot help but be captivated by Caesar's monumental achievements in Gaul. However, we should remember that he also shouldered the formal responsibility of governing three neighbouring provinces and the informal duty of influencing decisions in Rome to maintain his leadership position. In this context, the magnitude of Caesar's achievement cannot be underestimated. Gaul stands as the most significant territorial conquest ever accomplished by a Roman general, propelling Greco-Roman civilisation some 1000 km north into the heart of Europe, thereby altering the course of world history.

The lessons of the war in Gaul for modern leaders lie less in Caesar's military exploits per se than in how he got there. His success was not just a result of his individual competencies but was also due to building an effective team of officers and specialists. He empowered them to take on crucial tasks and valued their input, often choosing them for their talent rather than their background. As a result, he could successfully draw on the full spectrum of movement, logistics, technology and innovation. His soldiers and officers followed him with enthusiasm, brought along by his vision of doing great things for Rome. He instilled in them a sense of pride and achievement, while being sensitive to their concerns, needs and motivations. He willingly gave negative and positive feedback where it was deserved and needed. Caesar stayed true to his values. He held no grudges against defeated enemies, and he aligned his interests with those of the Roman people, which he imparted to his followers.

Caesar was quick to make decisions and put them into action with breathtaking speed. He was also quick to declare victory, not fully aware of what might be brewing beneath the surface. An important value, vital to his success in creating a following, was holding no hard feelings against a defeated opponent. His blind spot was not realising that others, namely the Gauls, might still have unfulfilled desires even though they had agreed to end the conflict. His desire for clear boundaries led him to believe that the transition from conflict to peace was crossing a hard boundary. For others, however, the line was much softer, especially from an emotional point of view. But he was quick to adapt. After Vercingetorix, he realised that he had to strengthen his strategy to win the Gauls' hearts and minds. He drew on his experience of two stints in provincial government in Spain and his observations of what was happening in other provinces.

In some ways, his collective influence from a distance in Rome was more successful. Earlier we had concluded that influencing was a weakness. As consul, Caesar could compensate through an organisation designed to mobilise followers. From Gaul, he remained virtually present in Rome thanks to his relentless communication through news coverage, correspondence and conversations with visitors. He built and maintained his leadership brand and created a positive reputation. He managed to remain influential at the highest level of decision-making in the Republic. This resulted largely from his work through coalitions and intermediaries, a variation on the approach that had worked well for him as consul. Julia, his daughter, and networkers like Balbus and Oppius worked on his behalf. So did leaders and influencers such as the triumvirs, Clodius and Cicero. Seeing themselves as peers, they probably advised him about how to proceed. When those who could stand up to him died, Caesar was left alone, working through more junior people who may not have given him the feedback he needed. Nor did not having the opportunity to meet face-to-face with visitors from Rome during the last two winters help. The same may have happened in Gaul, where he was always absent during the winters before the final uprising. He depended on others to inform him about what was happening. Without such assistance, he was oblivious to undercurrents that could make followers less loyal and stakeholders less willing to cooperate. Inadequate and ineffective feedback from his subordinates may have caused him to be blindsided by the great revolt.

Caesar showed how a mission can be implemented effectively in terms of personal energy. The seasonal rhythm of higher and lower work intensity suited him well and maintained his resilience. Professionally, this period was the high point of Caesar's career. He loved what he was doing. However, he lost his most important allies and suffered the loss of family members, who were exceedingly dear to him. At the end of this period in Caesar's career, he must have felt a profound sense of loneliness, both professionally and personally. He was about to enter the final phase of his life, which was to be yet another eventful stage.

Bibliography

Greek and Roman Sources

Appian, *Roman History. The Civil Wars*, Book I–II.
Caesar, G. J., *Commentaries on the Gallic War*.
Cicero, M. T., *Letters to Atticus; Letters to His Friends; Orations*.
Dio, L. C., *Roman History*. Book 38–40.
Plutarch, *Lives of Antony, Cato the Younger, Caesar, Crassus, Pompey*.
Suetonius Tranquillus, G., *Life of Julius Caesar*.

Modern Works

Badian, E. (1983). *Publicans and sinners: Private Enterprise in the Service of the Roman Republic*. Cornell University Press.
Charan, R., Drotter, S., & Noel, J. (2001). *The leadership pipeline. How to build the leadership powered company*. Jossey-Bass.
Connelly, B. S., & McAbee, S. T. (2024). Reputations at work: Origins and outcomes of shared person perceptions. *Annual Review of Organizational Psychology and Organizational Behavior, 11*(1), 251–278.
Crook, J. A., Lintott, A., & Rawson, E. (Eds.). (1994). *The Cambridge ancient history* (The last age of the Roman Republic, 146–43 B.C.) (Vol. IX, 2nd ed.). Cambridge University Press.
Gelzer, M. (2008). *Caesar. Der Politiker und Staatsmann*. Franz Steiner Verlag.
Griffin, M. (Ed.). (2009). *A companion to Julius Caesar*. Wiley-Blackwell.
Gruen, E. S. (1995). *The last generation of the Roman Republic*. University of California Press.
KDVI. https://kdvi.com/tools/
Meier, C. (1997). *Caesar*. DTV.

Morstein-Marx, R. (2021). *Julius Caesar and the Roman people*. Cambridge University Press.

Strassler, R. B., & Raaflaub, K. A. (Eds.). (2018). *The landmark Julius Caesar, Webessays*. Pantheon Books. Accessed January 26, 2023, from www.landmark-caesar.com

Vanderbroeck, P. J. J. (1987). *Popular leadership and collective behavior ca. 80–50 BC*. J.C. Gieben.

Vanderbroeck, P. (2012). Crises: Ancient and modern. Understanding an ancient Roman crisis can help us move beyond our own. *Management & Organizational History, 7*(2), 113–131.

5

No Turning Back: How Followers Can Push a Leader into Crossing the Rubicon

> *… Reclined upon the opulent sheets of this foreign palace, he pondered the extraordinary encounter he had just experienced. It demanded courage and cunning to navigate enemy territory under the shroud of night and outsmart his legionaries. Her appearance was a paradox of royal poise and vulnerability. Undeniably, the young woman had leadership potential and a fantastic sense of humour for that. Her intelligence, ambition and sense of power reminded him of his mother, who—as a woman—was barred from official office in Rome. Here, things were different, though. 'Tomorrow I'll make her Queen' were his last thoughts before falling asleep …*

(This quote is fictional and created by the author for illustrative purposes.)

During the final stage of his career, Caesar found himself in a unique and complex situation, occupying two distinct leadership positions: one as a military leader in Rome's civil war and the other as the sole leader of Rome and its empire. These roles, with their stark differences, offer distinct learning opportunities for modern leaders. To better understand Caesar's leadership in these two roles, it is beneficial to dedicate a separate chapter to each. The next chapter will delve into Caesar's non-military leadership when he finally reached his most powerful and senior position. The current chapter will explicate Caesar as a general. After crossing the Rubicon, Caesar's role transformed into that of a military leader in a civil war. Within months, he seamlessly merged this task with his governmental responsibilities. Having emerged victorious in the civil war in 45, he continued to steer the government until his untimely demise in 44.

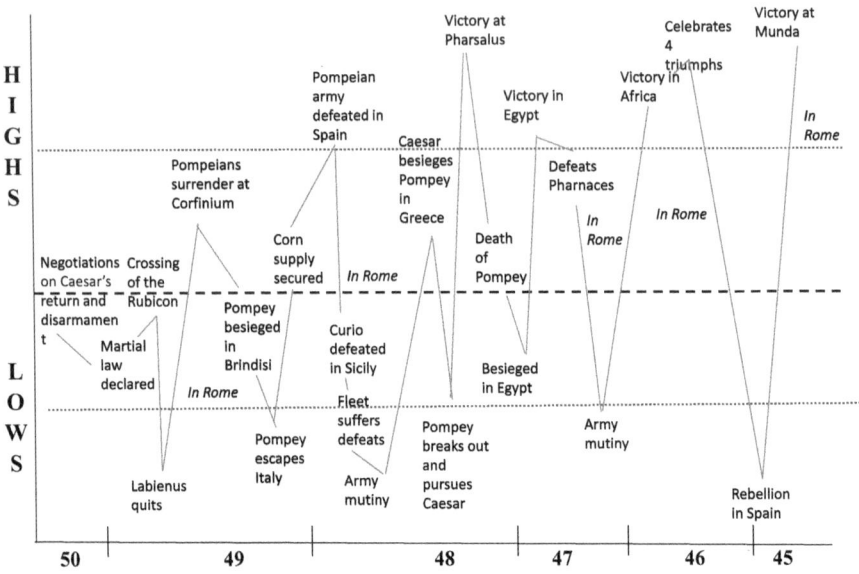

Fig. 5.1 Caesar's leadership timeline: highs and lows 50–45 BC. Author's own illustration

This chapter will outline the key events of and Caesar's achievements during the civil war (Fig. 5.1) to permit a thorough analysis of Caesar's leadership behaviours and detail his career progression as a military leader. Crossing the Rubicon was such a critical inflexion point in Caesar's career that it deserves special attention. Starting from the premise that Caesar would have preferred to avoid it, the description concentrates on what Caesar did to prevent it. While explaining the other challenge—winning the civil war—military details will be reviewed only as far as they elucidate Caesar's leadership style. Some of this chapter's driving questions include What were the keys to Caesar's success? How did he overcome setbacks? How did his brand and reputation develop now that his enemies were Roman citizens—the effective result of having crossed the Rubicon?

5.1 Caesar's Challenges and Achievements in the Civil War

5.1.1 Preventing a Civil War

During the years preceding the civil war, that is in the late 50 s, Roman political circles feverishly attempted to find a solution to growing political tensions and avoid letting them escalate into violent conflict. In the years before, the senatorial establishment had seen its power wane as the triumvirs stood well above their peers in wealth and influence, and the popular leader Clodius reigned over the People. In 54, Julia died; Crassus in 53. The next year, in early 52, Clodius was assassinated; meanwhile, Caesar was preoccupied with the revolt of Vercingetorix in Gaul. Caesar's opponents sensed an opportunity to restore the Senate's primacy. Under the leadership of Cato the Younger—who else?—they devised a two-pronged strategy to play the two remaining magnates against each other.

First, the *optimates* faction persuaded Pompey to distance himself from Caesar in exchange for gaining recognition from the upper class, into which Pompey was still not fully accepted. (The Pompeii were a rich rural family and Pompey's father was the first to enter the Senate in Rome.) They did this by granting Pompey yet another opportunity to show himself as Rome's foremost trouble-shooter, this time by restoring order in the city, which at the time was engulfed in political violence and crime. Simultaneously, they aimed to pull Caesar down from his position of power by preventing him from assuming another leadership role and, ideally, having him exiled. Although the odds were against them, Caesar's opponents hoped to achieve the latter by prosecuting him for alleged illegal acts during his consulate and in Gaul.

As his assignment in Gaul was ending, Caesar felt his career was far from over; after all, he was only in his late forties. Nor is there any indication that he sought a position of absolute power. He did not have a fundamentally different view of the Roman Republic's future, except for his belief in the primacy of the executive over the Senate. However, he believed that his performance entitled him to a position of the highest importance so that he could continue to perform great deeds on the Republic's behalf. He perceived himself as bound by a commitment to his family to restore its former lustre. He also was aware that his standing, his brand as a leader, depended on delivering on the commitments he had made to his followers, notably his soldiers and officers. Caesar remembered well how difficult it had been for Pompey and other generals in the 60 s to get land distribution for their veterans approved and how they depended on other executives to get it done—all the more reason to vie for an executive position.

Therefore, Caesar proposed to stand for the consulship for the year 48 and to do so in absentia during the elections planned for the summer of 49. In that way, so Caesar argued, he could complete the pacification of Gaul in good order whilst still running for the consulship. The need to stay behind in Gaul was not merely an excuse. The popular assembly after all accepted Caesar's proposal when he was busy suppressing the Gauls' great revolt in 52. Getting the job done in Gaul and getting it done right was of strategic importance. There was also another, more hidden reason for running in absentia.

Caesar knew that prosecution might be waiting for him in Rome. Attending the elections in person meant entering the city and losing his governorship and, thereby, his immunity. Caesar was quite aware that he had crossed legal boundaries by ignoring his consul colleague Bibulus' objections and overstepping the formal limits of his authority as a governor in Gaul. Yet he also believed that his record had been cleared in light of his achievements. Why else should the Senate, which included his political adversaries, have granted him big thanksgivings on three occasions? Whereas the chances of being convicted were in all slim, Caesar did not want to risk it or felt that he had more important things to do. He could not allow another surprise like Vercingetorix to happen. Finally, Caesar was probably expecting to be awarded a triumph for his conquest of Gaul. He once had to choose between a triumph and standing for election. Although he never said so, he probably did not want to be put in that situation again.

By 52, Caesar's interests were still being served, and the Catonian strategy had yet to bear fruit. Legislation allowing Caesar to stand in absentia was passed during Pompey's consulship. Simultaneously, Pompey secured a 5-year extension to his own governorship of the two Spanish provinces. This renewed the mutual alliance that the triumvirs had agreed upon at the Luca conference in 56. In the same year, Caesar was honoured with his third thanksgiving for his triumph over Vercingetorix. Cato's bid for the consulship was unsuccessful. Whereas neither Caesar nor Pompey wanted to be in a subordinate position to the other, their working relationship was still intact. They both recognised that, all things considered, the Republic, with its expanding empire, was big enough for both of them.

After failing to prevent Caesar from being permitted to stand in absentia, Cato and his allies devised a new plan. During the following year, 51, they started working on getting Caesar recalled from Gaul earlier. This was a strategic move to bring Caesar back to Rome so that he could be prosecuted. Caesar, meanwhile, feeling that his interests were now too dependent on Pompey, worked to broaden his support base in Rome.

When Clodius was killed in 52, several members of his entourage joined Caesar. Marc Antony went to Gaul to serve in Caesar's army. Gaius Scribonius Curio stayed in Rome to further his political career. Both differed significantly from the many social upstarts aligned with Caesar. Antony and Curio were young, bright, brash, boisterous sons of the elite with a rebellious stance against the establishment and its conventions. To Caesar, they looked like younger versions of himself, so he had much time for them. A fashionable dresser like Caesar, Curio had the requisite ambition to become Clodius' successor and rebuild his former leader's power base among the urban population. He was also ambitious enough to become an independent actor next to Caesar and Pompey. Curio had fallen into debt from the games and theatre he had financed to support his political career. Caesar bailed him out, just as Crassus had done for him early in his own career.

During the year 50, the Catonians increased their efforts to get Caesar recalled. Curio, as tribune of the plebs, managed to prevent it. Curio, who was a bit of a loose cannon, sought to antagonise Pompey through speeches and interventions more than Caesar would have liked him to do. While Curio was trying to pull Caesar to his side, the Catonians did the same with Pompey. Pompey felt that the balance of power was shifting to his disfavour. Pompey's weak spot—influencing internal politics in Rome—emerged. Extremely successful outside Rome on the battlefield, on the sea, in logistics and state organisation, he lacked Caesar's influence on the People, a weakness that became more apparent now that Caesar could leverage Curio's popularity. Pompey never built an organisation as strong as Caesar's to mobilise the popular assembly in his favour. Concerned, he began to support the view that Caesar had been granted too many exceptions and that he should either finish his command or be required to stand for election in person.

Starting December, the situation rapidly escalated. At the end of his tenure, Curio passed a motion in the Senate that Caesar and Pompey both discharge their armies. This compromise, intended to reduce the rising tension, was approved almost unanimously, indicating that a silent majority wanted anything but civil war. Meanwhile, the business community was lobbying for a peaceful resolution. Frustrated, the anti-Caesarian consuls then assigned Pompey two legions to defend the city. Once his tribunate ended, Curio travelled to Caesar, urging him to start a war. Marc Antony, sent back from Gaul to replace Curio, became tribune of the plebs in 49 and launched himself in defence of Caesar and in critique of Pompey.

Caesar sent Curio back to Rome with a letter to the Senate. The letter stated that Caesar was willing to accept Curio's compromise proposal. If his offer was not accepted, then Caesar would not give up without a fight. The letter, once read out by Marc Antony, prompted the Catonians to pass a motion for Caesar to relinquish his command or be declared a public enemy. Marc Antony and his colleague tribune Cassius Longinus vetoed this proposal. The Senate ignored them and delivered an ultimatum to Caesar instead. When the ultimatum expired, the Senate decreed martial law on 7 January 49, authorising all magistrates to take whatever steps necessary to preserve the state's safety. Pompey was assigned to raising an army to execute the decision. Marc Antony, Cassius Longinus and Curio fled Rome during the night. Disguised as slaves and travelling by hired carriage, they reached Caesar in

Ravenna. Caesar persisted, just as he had done when disregarding Sulla's ultimatum to divorce his wife about 25 years earlier. On 10 January, he crossed the Rubicon after uttering the famous dictum: 'Let the die be cast'.

The library of publications about who was 'right', politically and legally, is as extensive as the one about Caesar's assassination, which means it is impossible to find a clear answer. Or, perhaps more precisely, each party was both right and wrong. For example: crossing the Rubicon was unlawful because Caesar was forbidden to bring an army into Roman territory; doing so would also violate the senatorial order to relinquish his command. Yet, that order was itself unlawful as it ignored the tribunes' veto. Therefore, ascertaining the reasons why the situation resulted in war should be sought elsewhere.

By the end of the 50 s, the followership of Pompey and Caesar diverged considerably. Pompey had always recruited members of the elite establishment as military officers and political supporters, hoping for acceptance in their ranks. That same establishment used this proclivity to seduce Pompey into a leadership role over the very social class he had been working so hard to join. When he realised, that he was losing out against Caesar, he allowed himself to be coerced into joining the uncompromising position of Caesar's adversaries from which there was no turning back. Cato and his supporters were fed up with the pre-eminence of both Caesar and Pompey. For some, like Cato, the reasoning was ideological. Cato wished to restore the collective rule by the Senate. For others, feeling entitled to their status and upbringing, the magnates' power and influence blocked their career advancement and opportunities to enhance their prestige. Multiple consulships and commands that lasted 5 or 10 years (rather than the traditional one or two) had been concentrating too much power and opportunity in the hands of a few individuals over the past decade. Crassus and Clodius were already out of the way; now Caesar must be removed, and Pompey would be next. The latter needed his followers' support to maintain his leadership status and gain acceptance from the upper class. That support depended on him meeting their expectations regarding career opportunities and political power. He could not ignore their wishes. Soon, those same followers would cause Pompey's downfall by pushing him into battle with Caesar and doing so on unfavourable terms.

Caesar's followership relied on social and political outsiders. The Roman elite, meritocratic as it may have been, was anything but inclusive. For outsiders, it required much talent and hard work to reach the top, let alone be accepted as a social peer. Individuals like Cicero and Pompey proved this point well. A career under Caesar's wing was more promising for the socially mobile. In addition, there were those who, like Caesar and Clodius, had the People's interests in mind out of ambition and political conviction. These followers, driven by their desire for social mobility and their belief in Caesar's cause, were crucial to his leadership. Caesar needed their support to maintain his leadership status. In turn, that support depended on him meeting the expectations of providing career opportunities for his junior leaders and officers and land for his veterans. He could not ignore their wishes. Later in this chapter, when we discuss Caesar's leadership behaviours towards his followers, we will showcase some essential individual followers and how their motivation influenced Caesar's decision to escalate the conflict.

Neither Caesar's nor Pompey's followers having something to gain from the other side fuelled polarisation. A compromise would only make both lose what they would stand to gain from not giving in. Things also came to a head because the two top leaders were only indirectly involved in debates and negotiations. Many discussions were held in the background; notably Cicero talked to both. Despite these efforts neither party was willing to budge. Holding a provincial command with military authority, Caesar and Pompey were both prevented from entering the city. Although Pompey was nearby in the city's outskirts, he could therefore not participate in the critical meetings of the Senate or address the People. Die-hards and hardliners from each side acted as proxies; any information that got back to the leaders was undoubtedly biased, as was the feedback and advice they received from their followers.

The failed rapprochement was not for lack of contact between Pompey and Caesar. The lines of communication never broke down. Even after Caesar crossed the Rubicon, there was continuous contact between the two. Both leaders proposed to each other new concepts, compromises and concessions, many of which could potentially resolve the stalemate and cool the conflict. Yet neither side believed that such proposals were genuine. The lack of trust prevented an agreement from materialising. Caesar and Pompey never meeting each other in person at this point did not help. Hence, both were dependent on their followers for advice and counsel. The tragedy of this critical historical crossroad was that few followers believed they had anything to gain from the other side; thus, they convinced their respective leaders the same applied to them.

5.1.2 Winning the Civil War

After outlawing Caesar, the Senate passed several decrees in quick succession. They removed Caesar from his governorship and revoked the privilege to stand for consul in absentia. The Senate charged Pompey with levying troops and allocated funds from the treasury for that purpose. A few days later, the news that Caesar had crossed the Rubicon reached the city. The Senate decided to accelerate its recruitment of soldiers and agreed to send an embassy to Caesar. When, on 17 January, news arrived that Caesar had conquered several cities, Pompey proposed to the Senate that they should evacuate Rome, taking the treasury with them. Not having enough troops at the ready, Pompey, opting for a defence in depth, withdrew to a point where he could match Caesar's forces in battle. Possibly, he may have followed the advice of Labienus, who knew very well what Caesar's swiftness was capable of.

Indeed, often convinced that celerity was of the essence, Caesar struck at the heart of Italy with the single legion he had at his disposal rather than waiting for reinforcements from across the Alps. Instead of encountering resistance, he was met with open gates, allowing him to swiftly advance down the Adriatic coast. Pompey was hindered by entitled nobles who had been looking for a fight from the start. One was Domitius Ahenobarbus, a Catonian. He collected troops to block Caesar's advance at Corfinium, north of Rome. Caesar surrounded the city, and Domitius' forces compelled their general to surrender without a fight. Caesar offered safe passage to all who wanted to leave, even allowing them to take their personal belongings. Domitius and his fellow senators left for Pompey with Caesar's permission to take the public funds with them. Most of the rank-and-file joined Caesar's army.

This was an opportunity for Caesar to demonstrate that he was serious about leniency. At Corfinium, in Rome and Italy as a whole, Caesar minimised violence and destruction and showed clemency to adversaries. He wanted to make it perfectly clear that he was not Sulla and that such violence should not be expected from him. It was a great relief to Italy's inhabitants, rich and poor alike. He encouraged members of the Roman upper classes to abstain from the conflict. About 40% of the senators remained in Rome, either to join Caesar's cause or adopt a neutral position.

Meanwhile, Pompey managed to withdraw to the port of Brindisi. Caesar caught up with him but could not break through the defences. In March, Pompey, his followers and the soldiers he had mobilised in Italy were evacuated in an orderly fashion across the Adriatic (to what is now Albania) under his strong fleet's protection. Pompey's navy stood under the command of Caesar's eternal adversary, Bibulus. Caesar turned around and went to Rome to address matters there. He also sent troops to Sardinia and Sicily to protect Rome's corn supply. Next, he concentrated on Spain, where Pompey had a strong army of seven legions who from that position could imperil Caesar's rear, once he began moving against Pompey's forces in the East.

In April, Caesar left for Spain. On his way through southern France, he passed through the independent Greek port of Massilia (Marseille). Well fortified and with a strong fleet, its inhabitants had chosen Pompey's side. Domitius Ahenobarbus, whom Caesar had let go free a few months earlier in Corfinium, led the city's defence. Caesar decided first to eliminate this obstacle while sending part of his army to Spain. After 2 months, the city still held out. In Spain, Caesar's lieutenants encountered trouble after crossing the Pyrenees. Caesar decided to leave the siege to Trebonius and Brutus and manage matters in Spain himself. After taking command in Spain, Caesar was able to turn the tables. After a series of skirmishes and manoeuvres, Caesar blocked his enemies, putting them in a position where they were deprived of food and resources. They surrendered. With few casualties on both sides, Caesar had reconquered Spain. The leaders were let go to join Pompey in Greece. The legionaries were given the choice of staying in Spain as decommissioned soldiers or joining Caesar's army. Massilia still had not fallen. On his way back to Italy, Caesar retook command of the siege and finally forced the city to surrender.

While Caesar was occupied in Spain, Curio crossed from Sicily to Africa with a few legions, he soon found himself in a precarious situation. Several Pompeian lieutenants, along with King Juba of Numidia, a neighbouring kingdom allied with Rome, controlled the province. In a dramatic turn of events, Curio's expedition ended in failure. His army was defeated, and he perished on the battlefield. Caesar mourned his death.

Through December, Caesar stayed in Rome. In January, he left for the coast to sail with his army across the Adriatic in pursuit of Pompey. Caesar managed to transport part of the army into Greece. The rest remained blocked in Brindisi due to wintery weather and patrolling enemy ships. Meanwhile, Pompey had been recruiting and training troops; he was also waiting for Scipio to join him with an army from Syria. Caesar caught up with Pompey on the coast near Dyrrachium (modern Durrës in Albania). Although short of resources and outnumbered, Caesar laid siege to Pompey's army by building fortifications, blocking their access to the land.

After enduring a gruelling siege and engaging in negotiations, Pompey's forces successfully sortied and routed Caesar's army. Despite personally engaging in the battle, Caesar could not stop his army from fleeing the battlefield. Luckily for Caesar, the Pompeians did not pursue the Caesareans. Simultaneously, Caesar directed part of his army eastwards to prevent Scipio from joining with Pompey. After rejecting a peace proposal from Caesar, Scipio defeated the Caesareans and the two Pompeian armies merged.

Caesar had to withdraw quickly so he could stock up on food and materials and allow his troops to rest. Happy to have Caesar on the run, Pompey wanted to continue his strategy to deprive Caesar of resources. Pompey, however, was surrounded by a large group of nobles with a strong sense of entitlement. They had accompanied the army with all their pomp and circumstance; each had brought a luxurious and comfortable tent to stay and slaves to attend to their needs. They were eager to return to Rome, resume their careers and get their hand back on the helm of the Republic. Rather than focusing on the battle at hand, they had been discussing who should stand for election in the next few years and who should replace the magistrates currently aligned with Caesar. For far too long, they had put the state's power in the hands of a single individual. It was high time to return to collective leadership by the Senate. Pompey was a necessary evil, their instrument, to be discarded immediately after use. So, they urged him to seek a decisive battle, the more so because his army more than doubled Caesar's.

The two armies met on the fields of Pharsalus in northern Greece in August 48. Although outnumbered by two to one, Caesar's army was more experienced and accustomed to fighting together. As for Pompey's army, his was a collection of Romans and auxiliary troops from various provinces; they had little to no experience in joint combat. Given the former's advantage, Caesar managed to gain the upper hand by disarming Pompey's key strength: his large cavalry, led by Labienus. When they attacked and reached the Caesarean lines, a group of hidden legionaries on foot jumped up in surprise, aiming their spears at the cavalrymen's unprotected faces. Although numerous, these troopers were mostly made up of inexperienced youth from Italy. Taken off guard and scared, they turned around and fled, exposing Pompey's left flank. Caesar's experienced cohorts could now roll the Pompeians up from their left side. Caesar then sent heralds around who shouted to the Roman soldiers that they had nothing to fear should they stop fighting. Soon, the Pompeians broke ranks, allowing the Caesareans to pass and pursue the allied contingents fleeing the battlefield. After the battle, Caesar found Pompey's letters of correspondence in his tent. As a gesture of pacification, he burned all the letters without reading them. These would have contained much intelligence about who was or was considering joining Pompey.

Caesar pursued Pompey to Egypt, only to discover he had been murdered. Egypt was caught up in a civil war between Cleopatra and her brother, Ptolemy XIII. The latter's party had killed Pompey, hoping to find favour with Caesar. This backfired: Caesar was saddened and infuriated. He respected and appreciated Pompey a lot. This was unworthy death for a general and Caesar would have preferred for Pompey to surrender to him. Moreover, Caesar needed to secure Egypt and stabilise the situation, for Egypt was a strategic supplier to Rome regarding corn and other materials. Caesar decided in favour of Cleopatra and restored her to the throne. As a result, Ptolemy's army besieged

Caesar and his small force in the royal palace of Alexandria. The siege was destructive; the great library went up in flames, and after months of fighting, a relief force finally arrived for Caesar, giving him the upper hand in early 47 BC. At this point, two and a half years after the Rubicon, Caesar had won the civil war strategically. His armies held about three-quarters of the empire's territory, including the wealthiest half. In addition to Italy's political centre, he controlled most of the wealth, manpower and food. Therefore, he knew he could relax for a while. Caesar stayed on for another 6 months in Egypt to help Cleopatra establish a stable regime and to enjoy time with her.

Caesar's sojourn in Egypt was interrupted by an invasion in Asia Minor led by Pharnaces, the Crimean king, who saw an opportunity in the Romans' internal conflicts. Pharnaces defeated the two legions under Caesar's officer, Calvinus, prompting Caesar to take matters into his own hands once more. This resulted in Caesar's famous rapid victory at Zela, which he concluded with the mother of all victory speeches: *veni, vidi, vici* ('I came, I saw, I conquered').

Meanwhile, the remnants of Pompey's army regrouped in Africa under Scipio, Pompey's second in command. Other escapees from Pharsalus, Labienus and Cato among them, joined him there. Caesar, after addressing matters in Rome, turned his attention to Scipio, which seemed to be the final point of resistance. But first, in Italy, he had to confront a mutiny staged by some legions who were reluctant to sail to Africa.

After Caesar disembarked on the African coast with a relatively small force, Labienus and his cavalry immediately attacked. Mauled, Caesar's army escaped by a hair into their fortified camp. Here, Caesar awaited reinforcements from Sicily. Scipio and his army later joined Labienus, seeking a final engagement with Caesar. They were supported by King Juba and had 60 war elephants at their disposal; these animals often had a frightening effect on the adversary on the battlefield. Caesar's expeditionary force had scant provisions with the enemy controlling the province. Occupying one port, Caesar had supplies shipped in from Sicily and Italy. He also sent emissaries around to local towns to wrest them from Scipio. Because the Pompeiians had extracted a large tribute from the province, some towns were willing to switch sides and send food and troops to Caesar. It appears that Caesar's law against extorting the provinces, passed under his consulship in 59, made him popular among the province's inhabitants. Thus, Scipio's military strength started to suffer from these men's desertion. Caesar had a few elephants transported from Italy so his soldiers could be trained how to handle them on the battlefield. Finally, the two armies engaged at Thapsus in modern Tunisia. Caesar's soldiers spontaneously attacked without orders from their general. Still, they managed to scare off the elephants and put the enemy to flight.

Caesar's army was showing fatigue. Keeping discipline was a challenge for the general; they had attacked Scipio without waiting for a signal. After the battle, his professional troops, frustrated and tired of the war, gave no quarter. Caesar was unable to restrain his troops and his clemency towards his surrendered adversaries failed this time. This prompted Caesar to decommission and settle a number of his experienced soldiers in new colonies before leaving Africa. He also believed he had fought the last battles of the civil war and therefore would no longer need as many soldiers. On this occasion, too, he burned the letters of the Pompeian commander, Scipio, without reading it. Meanwhile, Scipio died on the run and Cato committed suicide before Caesar could get to him. Only Labienus escaped. The local support for the Pompeiians collapsed. Caesar showed mercy on the local Romans who surrendered. He reorganised the province, and the towns loyal to Scipio were taxed more severely.

Caesar returned to Rome in June 46, hoping to finally deal with the aftermath of the civil war. However, his visit was short-lived. The news that Pompey's two sons, together with Labienus, had managed to recruit an army in Spain took Caesar by surprise. The governor, Cassius Longinus, whom Caesar had put in place, had created a mess. Cassius had been Mark Antony's colleague in January 49 and fled with him and Curio to Caesar. The latter put Cassius in charge of Hispania Ulterior because he had been quaestor there earlier. Perhaps unbeknownst to Caesar, he had already built up a bad reputation as an extortioner during that time. Caesar had made a wrong choice. Cassius was so indebted that he again resorted to extortion to the point that locals attempted to assassinate him. He also got into a row with some of his legions and their officers, who mutinied, almost leading to a local civil war. Caesar sent Lepidus, who had helped him greatly in governing Rome, to Spain to rectify it. Lepidus prevented an internal conflict within the Roman army stationed there but did little to undo the damage Cassius had caused. Caesar then dispatched Trebonius to replace Cassius, but it was too late.

In November, Caesar left for Spain. The second Spanish campaign was not only a surprise but also proved a more significant challenge than in 49. Caesar met an enemy with a strong army recruited from Spanish cities and Roman troops stationed there. After several weeks of skirmishes and putting towns under siege, the two armies finally came to arms at Munda in March 45. It would be one of Caesar's most brutal battles. He had to fight with relatively inexperienced and newly levied soldiers, after having demobilised several legions. The Pompeian troops in Spain, who had surrendered to Caesar in the civil war's early days, knew that they could no longer count on Caesar's leniency, as they had now risen against him for a second time. Caesar had to engage himself personally in the battle once more to remotivate his troops, who were giving way to the enemy. He even jumped off his horse to join the mêlée. The battle's success hung in the air for a long time until the Caesareans finally gained the advantage. Labienus fell on the battlefield and Pompey's oldest son lost his life while trying to flee. Only Sextus, Pompey's youngest son, escaped to fight another day.

After the battle, it became apparent that the Pompeiians had mustered considerable support in Spain. Caesar therefore would have to conquer several fortified towns, which resisted despite the Pompeiian leaders being dead or on the run. Hispalis (modern-day Seville), the capital of Further Spain, was one of the rebelling cities. Caesar's *Commentaries on the Spanish War*, the account of the civil war on the peninsula, conclude with his speech to Hispalis' inhabitants. Based on Caesar's description and what we know about the city then, the following picture emerges: Box 5.1.

Box 5.1 A Quite Different Speech from *Veni, Vidi, Vici*

Once the fighting stopped, Caesar, accompanied by a retinue of soldiers and staff, travelled to Hispalis along the Guadalquivir River from Gades (modern-day Cadiz). The river connected the fertile lands of southern Spain and the Atlantic close to the Strait of Gibraltar, offering a promise of its future wealth within the Roman Empire. But now the port of Hispalis, typically bustling with traffic and barges loading and unloading, was unusually calm with Roman soldiers keeping guard. During this trip, Caesar would likely have had mixed feelings. He was likely proud that he had won yet another battle and relieved that he had yet again dodged death. Additionally, he would have been mournful about the loss of life and the blood spilt and thankful that he had now put what looked like the final, *final* end to the fratricidal conflict. But he also would have been thoroughly perplexed about how he could have possibly missed that this revolt had been brewing. More than that, he was deeply disappointed and saddened that the city he was about to enter, which was so dear to him having served twice in the province's government and in which he had invested so much, had joined the uprising.

Caesar entered the city through the new walls that he himself ordered to be erected after evicting the Pompeiians for the first time 4 years earlier. These same walls had kept Caesar's troops out during the past months. Soon, Caesar noticed a temple, statues, Latin inscriptions, decorations and other signs of Romanisation that had begun to leave its mark on the city. On horseback, draped in his bright red general's cloak and adorned with a shiny helmet and breast plate, the defeated population, mourning their dead, received him in silence. It was a short distance to the town centre in this city of 10,000 to 15,000 inhabitants, a mixture of Iberians, Roman immigrants and veterans. Emotionally worked up, Caesar expressed his feelings to the locals. He ordered a platform to be built in the town square and called an assembly of the population. The people gathered, full of anxiety and afraid of Caesar's legionaries lining the forum. There was no need for Caesar to announce the outcome of the battle of Munda and the subsequent subjugation of the remaining pockets of resistance. So, he went straight in and spoke from the heart.

Caesar expressed his dismay at the behaviour of the Spaniards who had risen against him. Caesar reminded them that when he worked in the provincial administration as quaestor and praetor and then later as consul, he had done a lot to serve the province's interest. He had reduced taxes and defended their interests in Rome. Caesar spoke of his utter surprise that the Spaniards had seemingly forgotten all the good things he had done for them. He asked, why did they always quarrel among each other and always find reasons to revolt? By now, they were well acquainted with Roman law. Still, they plotted to murder Cassius, the governor, in broad daylight in the forum. They had given refuge to Pompey's sons and joined his uprising. 'Was it worth it?' Caesar added, 'You never won, did you? And be that as it may, how on earth could you think that you could win against the might of Rome even if I, Caesar, would have perished?'

Caesar stayed in Spain to reorganise the province, distinguishing between loyal and rebellious towns. By establishing colonies of veterans and settlers from Rome, he hoped to end any future attempts at rebellion. The civil war was over (Fig. 5.2).

Fig. 5.2 Rome and its empire in 40 BC, after the death of Julius Caesar. By Tataryn77 - Own work, Public Domain. https://commons.wikimedia.org/w/index.php?curid=11154814

5.2 Caesar's Leadership During the Civil War

After this historical overview, now let us analyse Caesar's leadership behaviour from a modern perspective again. What competencies did Caesar use to meet his challenges? How did he apply them? Figure 5.3 summarises the evaluation of Caesar's leadership behaviours during this period, notably as a military commander.

5.2.1 Leading Self

It is both interesting and telling that the same thing happened to Caesar at the end of the war in Gaul and the end of the civil war, or more accurately when Caesar thought the war was over. In both cases, Caesar was caught off guard by a major uprising. After defeating the Pompeiians in Africa, he knew there were some areas of resistance in different places in the empire, but nothing that should have stopped him from returning home to finally oversee matters of statecraft and leave the mopping up to subordinates. Pompey's sons, however, could leverage their father's excellent reputation and network; after all Pompey had governed the two Spanish provinces for 5 years before Caesar defeated the former's army in Spain in 49. As he had demonstrated by reorganising the provinces and new territories in the East, Pompey was at least as good at governing provinces as Caesar. The context and the reasons for the uprisings in Gaul and Spain differed. Still, for Caesar's leadership, it is essential to note that he failed to detect the dissatisfaction brewing in the locals' collective minds. In both scenarios, Caesar emerged victorious, but only with incredible difficulty. Emotional Intelligence therefore remained a development need for Caesar.

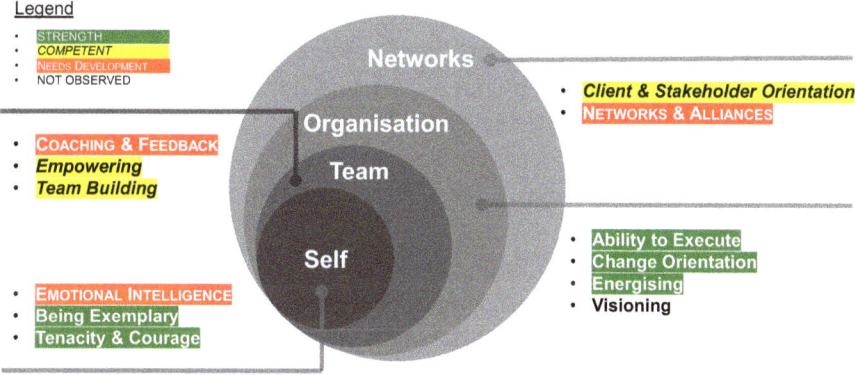

Fig. 5.3 Evaluation of Caesar's leadership behaviours as general during the civil war according to the GELM. Author's adaptation: Based on GELM by KDVI

Caesar's clemency made him stand out as a leader. This forgiving and compromising attitude was a substantial value that Caesar consistently applied throughout his career. During this war, he had plenty of opportunities to do so, clearly distinguishing himself from the leaders in the previous civil war and the Pompeiians. His officers and troops did not always understand this. On some occasions, for example, after Thapsus, Caesar could not contain his followers' wrath. Still, because his leadership behaviour generally was in line with his values and because he tenaciously pursued against odds and setbacks, Being Exemplary and showing Tenacity & Courage are rated as strengths.

5.2.2 Leading Teams

Caesar initiated the civil war without the two key players on his team of senior officers, who had played pivotal roles in conquering Gaul. One of them, the Young Crassus, had departed a few years earlier. The second, Labienus, sided with Caesar's enemy immediately after the Rubicon. Although their departure still left Caesar with tactically capable officers who could secure a victory in a battle, they lacked the strategic acumen necessary to ensure a campaign's success. A campaign necessitated meticulous planning, deft manoeuvring and the ability to overcome logistical challenges in addition to winning battles. As a result, Caesar found himself having to revise his plans and step in for his subordinates on several occasions: in Spain, both in 49 and in 45; at the siege in Massilia in 49; in Asia Minor and Italy in 47; in Africa in 46. Only Vatinius consistently achieved success. Prior to crossing the Rubicon, Caesar had found himself depending on relatively junior politicians like Curio, Antony and Cassius to advocate for his interests with the Senate and the People. In retrospect, it becomes apparent that engaging more seasoned and less confrontational intermediaries could have been a more prudent strategy.

The life-and-death situation of the civil war required a considerable effort from Caesar to motivate his team members and his army as a whole. An essential group among Caesar's followers joined him out of mutual interests, not because of a shared purpose. It has already been mentioned that Caesar recruited relatively more officers outside the senatorial elite than Pompey; he enlisted scions of families from all over Italy, often men who had only recently been naturalised after the Italian war, and foreigners like Balbus. Their loyalty depended on their individual interests being met. For this reason, Caesar let himself be influenced to take an uncompromising attitude and ultimately cross the Rubicon. Two individuals, who ultimately turned their backs on Caesar when they saw he did not deliver on meeting their ambitions, are a case in point. Labienus (Box 5.2) and Trebonius (Box 5.3) exemplify the self-interested individuals whom Caesar wished to retain by crossing the Rubicon.

> **Box 5.2 Shifting Loyalties: Labienus**
>
> Labienus had a successful career as a military officer under Caesar and was quite ambitious. Caesar became aware that he needed to help develop Labienus' career. Therefore, in the year 50, he nominated him as his successor as governor in one of Caesar's provinces. Labienus feared he would never move beyond being number two in Caesar's camp. Hoping for an army of his own and believing that switching to work with Pompey would tip the balance in his favour, Labienus joined the other camp. This was a mistake. Labienus would never get the level of responsibility under Pompey that he had under Caesar. In Pompey's entourage, there were too many people who politically and socially outranked him. Labienus' defection was a significant loss for Caesar, for until the civil war's end, it was Labienus who would put up the most staunch and effective resistance to Caesar. Publicly, Caesar showed no hard feelings; he allowed Labienus to take all his possessions with him and also a group of Gallic cavalrymen. After Labienus perished on the battlefield of Munda, Caesar also granted him an honourable funeral.

> **Box 5.3 Shifting Loyalties: Trebonius**
>
> Gaius Trebonius' career resembled Vatinius': he was the first among his family to become senator; he passed legislation on behalf of the triumvirs as tribune of the plebs, which was followed by a successful career as a military officer under Caesar and interspersed with government positions in Rome. In 49, when Massilia's siege took longer than expected, Caesar left Trebonius in charge, while Caesar had to leave for Spain. Trebonius could not finish the job, so Caesar had to take over on his way back from Spain. In 47, Caesar sent him to Further Spain to replace Cassius Longinus, who had made a mess out of his governorship. If Trebonius had any hopes for glory in the province, he was soon disappointed. The Roman army's disaffection under Cassius grew into a revolt and an alliance with the Pompeiians. They kicked Trebonius out, and Caesar had to travel to Spain to take over yet once again. After being disempowered twice, Trebonius must have felt that his career had plateaued. Caesar allowed Trebonius to become his replacement consul together with Fabius Maximus, whereas Trebonius felt entitled to a full consulship. On top of that, Fabius, who had fought successfully with Caesar in Spain, was granted a triumph, which Trebonius considered an affront. Finally, Caesar offered Trebonius another position as governor in Asia; however, that was not a promotion. Frustrated by his unattained ambitions and feeling unappreciated, Trebonius joined the plot against Caesar.

Mark Antony and Curio, two upper-class men like Caesar, belong to a different category. In addition to career ambitions, they shared Caesar's organisational concept. In 50 and 49, they acted as mid-level leaders on behalf of Caesar in Rome. Caesar, moreover, identified with Antony and Curio as junior versions of himself. This applied particularly to Curio, whom Caesar saw as the next generation. After crossing the Rubicon, Caesar wanted to provide Curio similar opportunities to prove himself, just as he himself had received early in his career. Therefore, he gave him a military command. Yet Caesar overestimated Curio, for the latter had less military experience compared to Caesar at the time of his first military command.

Moreover, whereas Caesar sprung into action after conducting a swift analysis, Curio was impulsive—and it cost him his life in Africa. With Curio gone, Caesar put much faith in Mark Antony, even if he was far from successful in military and government matters. However, Antony was anything but untalented; he did manage to become one of Caesar's successors later on. Before the Rubicon's crossing, Curio and Antony, having started their careers under the uncompromising Clodius, equally persuaded Caesar to reject a compromise.

Caesar had come a long way, thanks to delivering on his followers' expectations. Standing at the Rubicon in 49, he was not faced with the choice between a civil war, with the possible result of one-man rule, and peace. Caesar did not aspire to supreme power. On the one hand, he could resign from his offices and, with that, completely lose his own (*dignitas*) and the Julii's prestige, plus the ability to support his assistants. Or, on the other hand, he could instigate a civil war. Caesar must have realised that his followers—the people who had served him in Gaul and Rome and several malcontents and opportunists—still expected a lot from him. Caesar's supporters would have pressured him not to give in to his opponents. After all, they had nothing to expect from a settlement with the *optimates*.

To sum up: on the shores of the Rubicon, Caesar did the best he could to build a team from the officers he had at his disposal. He empowered his subordinates by enabling them to reach various levels of success, and he was tolerant of mistakes and failures. The fact that not every delegation was successful mainly resulted from Caesar insufficiently developing his people, which, admittedly, was no small challenge given that Caesar's supervision often occurred from a distance. Possibly, Caesar did too little to curb unhealthy competition among his subordinates, who were vying for position and attention. Moreover, failing to coach individuals through their frustration made retaining talent difficult.

5.2.3 Leading Organisations

From a military strategy perspective, Caesar's approach to the civil war was top-notch. Before the Rubicon's crossing, Caesar had had some time to think through 'what if' scenarios. He had consciously left his main army north of the Alps, thereby denying his adversaries any arguments that he was looking for a fight. He also took the risk of starting the war from a position of weakness. This left him with the element of surprise, though, when he swiftly took action after a compromise proved impossible. Attacking Italy first with a small force could have ended the war there if Pompey had not escaped to Greece. Unable to pursue, Caesar covered his rear by eliminating Pompey's army in Spain. Once he had gathered some ships, he crossed into Greece to take the battle to Pompey, who was building up his army's strength. After Pharsalus, Caesar's needed to systematically conquer the provinces still in the enemy's hands. Caesar's capacity to change strategies as things developed or when events did not go to plan was impressive. In Africa, friend and foe alike were surprised that Caesar did not pursue his usual strategy of speed and surprise. After meeting with an unusual adversary, who fielded a superior cavalry and war elephants, Caesar decided it was better to take time to prepare, stock up on supplies and train the soldiers in new tactics. His only mistake was to besiege Pompey in Dyrrachium while being outnumbered. If Pompey had pursued him after breaking the siege, this book might have been about Pompey.

Throughout the civil war, Caesar had to energise and remotivate his army several times. Often, he used speech to do so—the first instance when he was on the verge of crossing the Rubicon. When, in early 49, the Senate declared martial law and Caesar a public enemy, the two tribunes of the plebs, Mark Antony and Cassius Longinus (who had been lobbying on behalf of Caesar) and Curio fled Rome to avoid arrest. They ditched their togas and hid themselves, disguised as slaves, in a hired carriage in which they made it to safety to Caesar's camp. The news from Rome that the Senate had declared Caesar an outlaw did not come as a surprise.

Caesar had planned for the eventuality, as we can read in Appian's and Caesar's own account of the civil war. Caesar did not miss the opportunity to show his army the three men in their sorry condition. He said to his soldiers that they, too, had now been stigmatised as public enemies despite all they had done for Rome. Moreover, these three distinguished men, who had stood up for them, had been chased from Rome in such unworthy conditions. He argued that the Senate had passed an illegal decree by ignoring the tribunes' constitutional right to veto. Secondly, traditionally, the declaration of martial law would only be passed after something violent or dangerous to the city had happened. In the current scenario, this was not the case; Caesar was still in his province, and no violence had been committed. Next, he recalled the great successes the army had achieved alongside him. He asked his soldiers to defend his honour and his reputation. The army affirmed that they would indeed do so. Later, Caesar said that he had crossed the Rubicon to protect himself, restore the rights of the tribunes of the plebs and free the People from the domination of a small clique. Claiming to protect the rights of the tribunes, who traditionally were chosen to protect the People's rights in the Roman system of checks and balances, was consistent with Caesar's political position as a *popularis*, which he held throughout his career.

Overall, Caesar now had to overcome more formidable motivational challenges than when he was in Gaul. In late 49, while returning from Spain and Massilia, Caesar faced a mutiny by his troops in northern Italy, in Placentia. The legions had not been paid since the outbreak of the civil war, and they were frustrated about Caesar's clemency, which forbade them to plunder. Caesar asked for their patience in his speech, reminding them they had reaped great rewards in Gaul under his command and had taken an oath to follow him throughout the entire war. He asked them to finish the job. The soldiers' mood did not change, however, until Caesar announced he would send them home immediately. Fear of going home empty-handed and hurt pride made them change their minds; the soldiers thus stayed on. Next, Caesar ordered some disciplinary measures and had 12 of the mutiny's 120 ringleaders executed. Interestingly, when it became known that one soldier had been falsely accused of participating in the mutiny by his superior, Caesar freed him and had the officer executed instead. Caesar thus gave a clear message that he was careful not to pass arbitrary judgement.

In 48, after Pompey's successful breakout at Dyrrachium, Caesar addressed his soldiers. He took responsibility for what had happened and forgave them for breaking ranks. He reminded them of the successes they had garnered since the beginning of the civil war and that they had overcome setbacks. These should give them confidence for the next battle, Caesar reasoned. In turn, the soldiers were relieved by Caesar's moderate approach. They thus took the initiative to retake an oath that they would not leave the field of battle before the end. Soon after, before the battle at Pharsalus, Caesar delivered a speech to his army, reminding them of their recent oath to him and that the soldiers they were about to fight against had been defeated before and that Caesar's attempts to reach a cease-fire had been turned down. He also asked them to remember their experience with him as a caring and generous leader. Moreover, Caesar argued, they faced relatively inexperienced Roman troops and allied troops from other nations who did not have the same capabilities as Caesar's army, which was primarily Roman. He asked them to spare the Italians but slaughter the allies to frighten the allied troops further.

In 47, on his return from Egypt, Caesar was confronted by mutinying troops in Italy. However, his subordinates could not handle it, so the army marched to Rome and Caesar met them on the outskirts. He addressed them as 'citizens', indicating that they were now no longer soldiers as far as he was concerned. The prospect of being sent home and others taking the full glory of the victories and the spoils of the upcoming campaign in Africa had a similar effect as in Placentia; the soldiers thus changed their minds. In addition, Caesar laid out his plans for land distribution, which, unlike Sulla, he would do without expropriation. He took few disciplinary measures, but just as he had done with reluctant followers in the first year of the Gallic Wars, he immediately gave the troops new marching orders and sent them to Africa.

In 46, when two legions who had recently mutinied arrived in Africa, he decided to set an example. He had taken good note of who the ringleaders had been. One had even chartered a vessel to transport his slaves and livestock rather than troops for Caesar from Sicily. There was no execution this time, but five ringleaders and officers were publicly dismissed and discharged dishonourably. Their possessions were confiscated, and they were put on a ship to Italy. Caesar sensed that the years of fighting and travelling had taken a toll on his men, and this was validated by their lack of discipline in the ensuing battle of Thapsus. After his victory, Caesar retired these legions and settled the veterans in colonies.

On balance, we see here that Caesar, except for the conflict's very beginning, failed to weld his army followership together in a shared vision. There was no joint purpose, other than continuing to participate in a successful venture that had served everybody's interests during the war in Gaul and anger at being outlawed rather than honoured for their exploits. Instead, at this point, theirs was a transactional relationship that led to victory, but one that could break down quickly if the contract's terms were unmet.

5.2.4 Leading Stakeholders and Networks

How Caesar managed relationships with stakeholders (the Roman citizenry, the Senate, the business community, and the subjects in the provinces) during the civil war will be discussed in more detail in the next chapter. It is important now, however, to remind readers that Caesar failed to keep and rebuild his alliance with Pompey that had served him so well thus far.

5.3 Caesar's Career Development During the Civil War

This chapter concentrates on the position of a military leader, an operational leadership job similar to the one Caesar had just completed in Gaul. However, this new endeavour was on a grander scale, spanning the vast Mediterranean. Furthermore, he had to combine the position of general in the civil war with government leadership at a much higher level of complexity than he did as

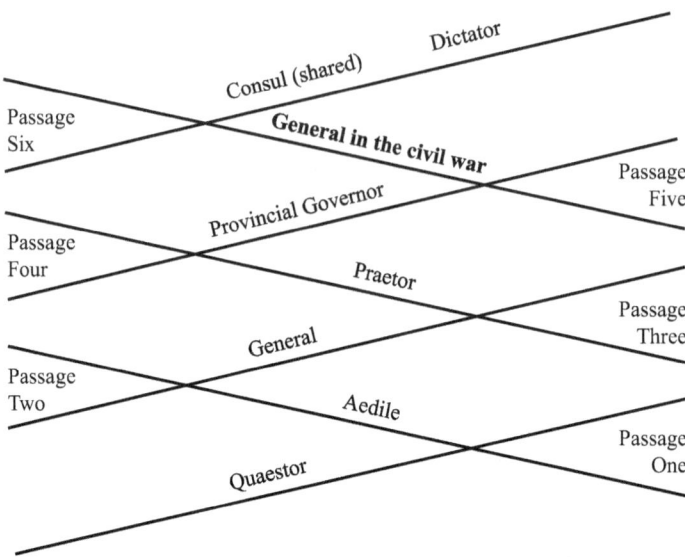

Fig. 5.4 Julius Caesar's career passage in the Roman Career System during the civil war. Author's adaptation: Based on Charan et al. (2001)

governor of three provinces. Finally, Caesar faced a formidable foe, one with greater resources and capabilities than Gallic or Germanic tribes could field.

When the Senate ordered him to resign from his position, Caesar's career reached a crossroads that called for a clear decision: 'Lead, follow, or get out of the way'. In Caesar's case, 'get out of the way' offered only unattractive options. There was no alternative organisation he could join, nor was pursuing a business career his kind of thing. Voluntary exile was too much for his pride. Nor was he in for early retirement. 'Follow' would mean stepping down and potentially putting himself at the mercy of a lawsuit, which he expected his adversaries and competitors to initiate as soon as he entered Rome. So, Caesar decided to 'lead', meaning taking the initiative to turn the momentum of change into his advantage.

During this period, Caesar solidified his brand as a generous leader to his soldiers and a forgiving leader to his adversaries. His reputation, that of an almost invincible general, had only continued to grow throughout his military career, and he had deftly reinforced his standing by the four triumphs he celebrated in 46 and 45. In the weeks leading up to his death, he began preparations to lead the largest Roman army ever against Parthia. It was widely anticipated that he would return with similar victories.

From the perspective of the *Leadership Pipeline*, Caesar's military leadership in the civil war resembled his role in Gaul as a 'business manager' (Fig. 5.4). He was equally successful in managing an officer corps, developing and implementing strategies and maintaining a forward-looking perspective. With no one to report to, Caesar was in his comfort zone, operating within clear boundaries and direct authority.

5.4 What Leaders Can Learn from Caesar as a Military Leader During the Civil War

Caesar was not the first to literally cross the Rubicon, nor the only one to do so with an army. Yet, he was the first to cross both literally and metaphorically. More precisely, Caesar was the only one to have turned the literal crossing into a metaphor. The fact that this event took on metaphorical dimensions reflects Caesar's decision's impact on world history. Ever since 49 BC, crossing the Rubicon has become the archetype of a point of no return. But, of course, for someone like Caesar, that was not enough. He also accompanied the infamous crossing with one of the most iconic phrases that that became part of his legacy: '*Alea iacta est*', or 'Let the die be cast'. This showed Caesar's considerable self-awareness as a risk-taker.

Caesar, as a general, continued employing the same successful behaviours that he had applied in Gaul. His military strategy combined tactics on the battlefield, manoeuvres and logistics. His trademark speed of decision-making and movement was put to expedient use when he dashed from the Rubicon into Italy. But in Dyrrachium, he learned that precipitation only sometimes worked to his advantage. Subsequently, he became more circumspect in his actions. Caesar motivated his troops by offering them a perspective grounded in glory and military gain. When things became difficult and motivation waned, he reminded them of past successes and how, as a leader, he had delivered on his commitments. Rather than passing the blame, he took ownership for failure. He punished his men for their lack of discipline while maintaining a sense of fairness and leniency. Towards his enemies, he continued to behave according to his core value, clemency. His brand as a fair and generous leader and his reputation of success contributed to a strong bond with his followers. Combined, these attributes made it easier for the defeated Pompeiians to join his army.

Moreover, Caesar felt bound to his promise of restoring his family's fortune, but in 49 he was not done yet. In addition, he was convinced that he, as any elite member of Roman society, was called upon to gain prestige through great deeds on behalf of the Republic. Such great acts also included protecting the People's rights. Caesar believed that no one else was better placed to ensure this. Hence, he reasoned, staying in a leadership position after successfully conquering Gaul was a win-win for the Republic. Interestingly, not one of his followers dared to or seemed to have an interest in explaining that that could also be perceived as being one step away from enacting one-man rule, as his adversaries did. Rather, Caesar had a far greater purpose than merely pursuing a self-interested career. As such, he missed the fact that the feedback and advice he received from his direct followers was biased by their self-interest. Caesar's entourage undoubtedly triggered his pride and unwillingness to lose face in the situation. They also knew quite well that delivering on commitments was a significant personal value for their leader. To counter wayward influences from followers, organisational psychologist Lynn Offermann recommends leaders to stimulate dissent and cultivate truth telling. Boxes 5.4 and 5.5 look into the dynamics of this crucial episode.

Box 5.4 The Real Reason Why Caesar Crossed the Rubicon

Let us look again at what made crossing the Rubicon happen. The 'mixed' constitution of the Roman Republic contained built-in checks and balances. Yet, as a state, the Republic lacked a constitutional court or a similar institution (provided it is politically neutral) that could have arbitrated who had the law on their side in this fraught, high-stakes dispute between very powerful men. If the Republic were a corporation, we would be observing a conflict between opposing views within the executive leadership, a divergence of opinions that the supervisory board would normally arbitrate. However, in this case, the overlap between executive leadership and a supervisory board—magistrates sitting on the Senate—made the latter subject to bias. Alternatively, it would have been possible to ask the shareholders, that is, the People, for their view, but that had already been done. They had previously agreed to Caesar's being awarded the in absentia exception. However, putting the matter before the People again was a risk that Caesar's enemies did not want to take. The People certainly would have leaned towards the one who, at that moment, had most recently bestowed so much honour and wealth onto Rome. Absent a conflict resolution mechanism, it was therefore left to the individuals involved. This was an accident waiting to happen. Both parties were locked into political allegiances and ideologies as well as in a competition for power. They interpreted events, decisions and rules in their own favour and pushed boundaries accordingly.

Therefore, the single most important factor that led to Rome's civil war rather than a peaceful resolution was the followers' role in influencing their leaders' behaviour. Different groups saw their vital interests endangered in the polarising situation: careers and retirement for Caesar's officers and soldiers, public order for Rome's citizens, trade routes' stability and property protection for the business community, and power and influence for the Senate. In this kind of crisis, followers often pressure their leaders to take action quickly to mitigate their anxiety and reduce uncertainty. Crossing the Rubicon, therefore, became a stark example of how followers can convince or seduce leaders to make a decision they do not really want, leading to dramatic consequences. Even while at the top of an organisation, a leader's agency can be reduced when one gets entangled by forces much weaker than oneself, like the strings with which the islanders of Lilliput immobilised Jonathan Swift's Gulliver.

> **Box 5.5 And What He Could Have Done to Prevent It**
>
> It bears questioning, therefore, what Caesar could have done to prevent this escalation into irreversible violence. To answer this line of enquiry, it can help to take another look at the larger picture. The triumvirate had always been a coalition based on mutual interests rather than a joint purpose. Caesar twice had taken the lead in building and renewing the alliance between the three mighty men. However, on each occasion, he could have taken it beyond solidifying unity through mutual interests and instead formulated a shared purpose to pursue. After Crassus was gone, Caesar missed the opportunity to draw Pompey into such a common vision when they renewed their cooperation as a duo. As a result, Pompey kept pursuing his personal goal of gaining social acceptance. Once the coalition with Caesar had achieved its goals, Pompey was open to accepting what he perceived as a better deal from the establishment.

The other thing Caesar could have done was to reduce his dependency on information and advice from his followers. Although he was in touch with intermediaries such as Cicero through correspondence, he based his decision on indirect information and its interpretation by the people around him. It was a shame that he never talked to Pompey directly. Other than individual pride, nothing prevented them from meeting another time on neutral ground, as they had done in 56 in Luca, which was the last time they discussed face-to-face.

Finally, the last throes of the civil war provide another lesson. Caesar had difficulty sensing collective undercurrents. Before the civil war ignited, he underestimated how far the Senate would go to follow those who stood against him. Similarly, he was clueless that things were turning again for the worse in Spain when he thought the war was over. When news started reaching him from Spain, he completely missed obvious signs of trouble. (It seems that the same thing happened regarding the build-up of Pompeiian forces in Africa when he was in Egypt with Cleopatra.) Having some people further down in the organisation to keep him apprised of changing currents would have been helpful for Caesar. Or perhaps he did and disregarded their feedback. After all, Balbus, his close collaborator, hailed from southern Spain and could have done just that. Instead, Caesar tried to manage the situation too long through Lepidus and Trebonius. More importantly, it remained a blind spot for Caesar, as becomes clear from his speech in Hispalis, which was discussed before. He was perplexed that the Spaniards thought they had a fighting chance against Rome. Rationally, Caesar of course had a point. Emotionally, it is a different matter: clearly, Caesar was either unwilling or unable to put himself in their sandals and search for the root causes for their revolt.

Having won the war after the final battle in Spain, Caesar could now fully concentrate on his second responsibility: leading Rome and its empire. This will be the subject of the next chapter.

Bibliography

Greek and Roman Sources

Appian, *Roman history. The civil wars*, Book I–II.
Caesar, G. J., *Commentaries on the civil war, the Alexandrian war, the African war and the Spanish war*.
Cicero, M. T., *Letters to Atticus; Letters to his friends; Orations*.
Dio, L. C., *Roman history*. Book 41–45.
Plutarch, *Lives of Antony, Brutus, Cato the Younger, Caesar, Pompey*.
Suetonius Tranquillus, G., *Life of Julius Caesar*.

Modern Works

Badian, E. (1983). *Publicans and Sinners: Private enterprise in the service of the roman republic*. Cornell University Press.
Benferhat, Y. (2017). Des hommes à tout faire dans l'entourage de César. *Dialogues d'histoire ancienne. Supplément*, 17, Conseillers et ambassadeurs dans l'Antiquité (pp. 373–385).
Broughton, T. R. S. (1952). *The magistrates of the Roman Republic* (Vol. II) (99 B.C.–31 B.C.). American Philological Association.
Charan, R., Drotter, S., & Noel, J. (2001). *The leadership pipeline. How to build the leadership powered company*. Jossey-Bass.
Connelly, B. S., & McAbee, S. T. (2024). Reputations at work: Origins and outcomes of shared person perceptions. *Annual Review of Organizational Psychology and Organizational Behavior, 11*(1), 251–278.
Crook, J. A., Lintott, A., & Rawson, E. (Eds) (1994). *The Cambridge ancient history* (2nd Edn, Volume IX). *The last age of the Roman Republic, 146–43 B.C.* Cambridge University Press.
Drogula, F. K. (2019). *Cato the Younger. Life and death at the end of the Roman Republic*. Oxford University Press.
Gelzer, M. (2008). *Caesar. Der Politiker und Staatsmann*. Franz Steiner Verlag.
Griffin, M. (Ed.). (2009). *A companion to Julius Caesar*. Wiley-Blackwell.
Gruen, E. S. (1995). *The last generation of the Roman Republic*. University of California Press.

Hölkeskamp, K.-J. (Ed.). (2009). *Eine politische Kultur (in) der Krise? Die "letzte Generation" der römischen Republik*. De Gruyter.

Hölkeskamp, K.-J. (2010). *Reconstructing the Roman Republic: An ancient political culture and modern research*. Princeton University Press.

KDVI. https://kdvi.com/tools/

Meier, C. (1997). *Caesar*. DTV.

Morstein-Marx, R. (2021). *Julius Caesar and the Roman people*. Cambridge University Press.

Offermann, L. R. (2004). When followers become toxic. *Harvard Business Review*, January, 54–60.

Pauli, A. F. (1958). Letters of Caesar and Cicero to each other. *The Classical World, 51*(5 (Feb)), 128–132.

Richardson, J. S. (1996). *The Romans in Spain*. Blackwell.

Strassler, R. B., Raaflaub, K. A. (Eds) (2018). *The landmark Julius Caesar*, Webessays. www.landmarkcaesar.com. Accessed 26/01/2023. Pantheon Books.

Syme, R. (1939). *The Roman revolution*. Oxford University Press.

Vanderbroeck, P. (2012). Crises: Ancient and modern. Understanding an ancient Roman crisis can help us move beyond our own. *Management and Organizational History, 7*(2), 113–131.

Vanderbroeck, P. (2014). *Leadership strategies for women: Lessons from four queens on leadership and career development*. Springer.

Yavetz, Z. (1983). *Julius Caesar and his public image*. Cornell University Press.

6

Alone at the Top: Chairman and CEO

> ... *Putting on a smile, ready to greet his fellow senators, he entered the temple where the meeting was to occur. He wanted to get it over with quickly, eager to return to preparing for his next war. Exchanging greetings, the group of senators surrounded him. The first stab he felt was a sharp pain in the back. Surprised more than shocked, he tried to wheel around when the next stab hit him in the side and then the next and the next. Looking at the sombre faces around him, he was flabbergasted. 'Why on earth ...?' were his final thoughts ...*
> (This quote is fictional and created by the author for illustrative purposes.)

In the final chapter of Caesar's career, we will examine how he reached the pinnacle of his organisation, maintained and exercised his power and met his sudden and violent end. By setting foot on the Rubicon's southern bank, Caesar had not only crossed the boundary between peace and war but had also made a career transition. It would catalyse a several-years-long 'shoot-out' that—if history bore a lesson—would end with one-man rule, at least for a while. Thus far, Caesar's highest position in the Roman state had been consul, which he shared with Bibulus. Holding all state powers in one hand would be new to Caesar. Moreover, it propelled Caesar into a level of complexity he had not managed before. Whereas his biggest job thus far, taking command in Gaul, had covered a large geographical area, he would now control the entire Mediterranean. Admittedly, taking command in Gaul went beyond leading military operations; it included integrating and reorganising a new territory as well as governing three existing provinces. Still, assuming one-man rule of Rome and its empire was a responsibility of an entirely different order.

Jumping ahead to this chapter's conclusion, we'll see that Caesar was not ready for this. More precisely, despite all his talents and competencies, his leadership hadn't developed to meet the level required for the role. He could only realise part of his potential while having absolute power. Nonetheless, brilliant as he was, he would leave a legacy that has an impact still today.

In examining this final chapter of his career, we describe how Caesar fared when he finally arrived at power's apex. This chapter starts in April 49 BC when Caesar first arrived in Rome and started exercising political power. It was 3 months after crossing the Rubicon and the beginning of the hostilities in the civil war. The chapter then continues its analysis from the final battle of the civil war in 45 BC until the Ides of March in 44 BC. This chapter, therefore, covers Caesar's behaviour as the leader of the Roman Republic, most of the time running parallel with his military command (Fig. 6.1). In the years between 49 and 44 BC, Caesar's geographical authority steadily grew with every piece of territory lost by his adversaries. When the war ended, Caesar was nominated dictator for an unlimited time period. This formalised his de facto one-man rule, a novelty for the Roman Republic's constitution. Neither having to share power with a colleague nor having the Senate to report to was the equivalent of being both Chairman and CEO in today's terms.

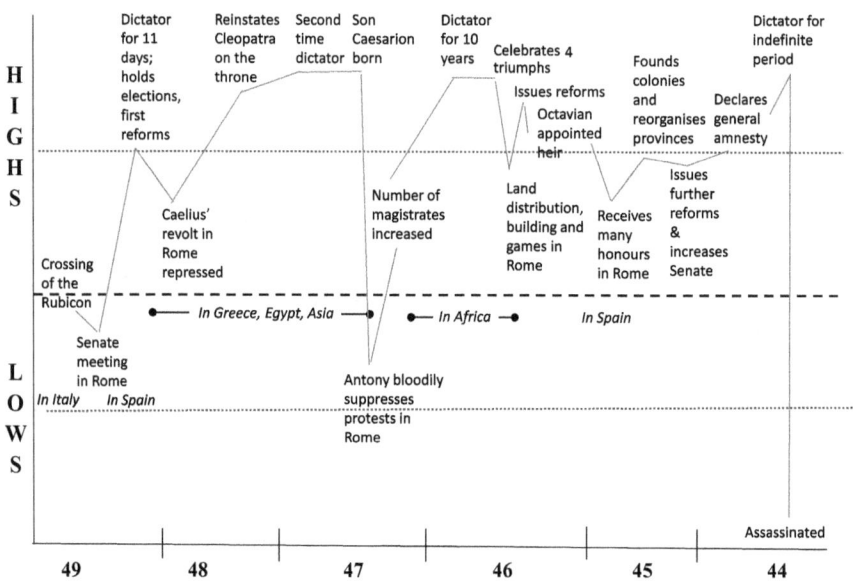

Fig. 6.1 Caesar's leadership timeline: highs and lows 49-44 BC. Author's own illustration

6.1 The Final Stretch to the Top

Up to and including Caesar's assassination, both the Senate and the general public were deeply divided on whether Caesar was right to traverse the Rubicon. Within weeks after the crossing, Caesar's adversaries, including most public officials and about half the Senate, left Rome and Italy to form what they claimed to be a government in exile. The citizens, who had the power to pass laws and elect magistrates, some magistrates and one-third of the Senate stayed behind. Thus, it was unclear which was actually the legitimate government; one could argue both ways. Caesar therefore had to seek formal, legitimate authority to remain in power and swing the balance of who was entitled to govern Rome in his favour. He thus faced the tremendous task of waging a full-scale war while simultaneously governing Rome and its empire.

While Caesar was securing Italy between January and April of 49, he was favourably received wherever he went. His leniency and forgiveness towards Pompeian commanders and soldiers, coupled with his disciplined approach of eschewing looting and property confiscation, quickly turned public opinion in his favour. As Cicero wrote to his friend Atticus on 1 March 49 (translation by Loeb Classical Library): 'They [the people in Italy] fear the man [Pompey] they used to trust and love the man [Caesar] they used to dread.'

In April 49, Caesar paid a short visit to Rome, his first of five during the civil war. At that point, Caesar's power rested in his army and their loyalty. His formal leadership authority was limited to the provinces at the other bank of the Rubicon. He first tried to secure his legitimacy by governing through the Senate, requesting a meeting of the senators who had stayed in Rome. He was careful to remain within constitutional boundaries by meeting outside the city's boundaries; he was not allowed to enter Rome while under arms. However, the Senate agreed to meet at this request. At the gathering, he presented his viewpoint and invited the Senate to govern the state jointly with him. The Senate deliberated for 3 days, finally agreeing to send envoys to Pompey to negotiate. However, no one volunteered to go, for Pompey had decreed that anyone who stayed behind was considered an outlaw. Caesar had to find other ways to come to an agreement.

Caesar voiced the same message in a speech to the People. Hoping to gain legitimacy through positive actions, he promised to ensure the corn supply, even if Pompey had cut Rome off from Egypt and Africa, both important food exporters. The People's reaction, wary of previous unkept promises made by politicians, was lukewarm.

Yet Caesar needed cash to finance his war machine. Thus, he decided to empty the state treasury. Previously, the Senate had authorised Pompey to seize all public and temple treasures to finance the war effort. Most of the funds were still there because the Pompeiians had fled Rome with haste and panic. One of the tribunes of the plebs who had stayed in Rome, however, opposed Caesar, trying to bar him from taking the treasury. This tribune, when threatened, backed down. In this instance, Caesar arguably used force illegitimately. He crossed an unambiguous boundary despite previous efforts to work through formal channels. Instead, he could have asked the remainder of the Senate to grant his request. Still, already fed up with the slow decision-making, impatience got the better of him, creating a tense atmosphere. Frustrated that he could not get anywhere with the Senate and conscious of the threat to his back, Caesar left Rome to pry Spain away from Pompey, leaving Mark Antony in Italy to keep order.

In December 49, Caesar returned victorious from Spain and paid Rome a second visit. This time, he changed tack. He first ensured he received formal and absolute authority. The praetor, Aemilius Lepidus, the highest magistrate present in Rome (the two consuls were with Pompey), appointed Caesar dictator by agreement of the popular assembly. Caesar used these emergency powers to hold the annual elections for magistrates and religious officials. Thus, after filling the vacancies, public administration could function again. Caesar stood for the consulship and was elected with P. Servilius Isauricus as his colleague for the year 48. For Caesar, the dictatorship also provided an effective exception to the rule that combining civil authority in Rome with a military command was unconstitutional when Rome was not at war with an external enemy. True to form, Caesar abdicated the dictatorship after only 11 days. He had shown he could be as speedy in civil as he was in military leadership. Interestingly, however, he was swift when having sole power, but not when collaboration was required. In April, he had not progressed very far in persuading the Senate to act. Caesar may have made a note to himself in this moment. Less than 11 months after crossing the Rubicon, he formally took over the government.

Caesar spent the whole year of 48 away from Rome, waging war in Greece and Egypt. Finding Pompey dead and Egypt plunged into civil war, Caesar, as a consul and formal representative of Rome, intervened in Egypt by taking Cleopatra's side and reinstating her on the throne. During his absence, the annual elections took place, a sign of political stability in Rome. Caesar was nominated dictator for the second time and for the entire year of 47. He received Marc Antony as his deputy. The latter was to manage matters in Italy during Caesar's absence. Typically, a dictatorship was legal for a maximum of

6 months only; thus, the 1-year period granted to Caesar was an exception—but not unprecedented since Sulla had held the office for 2 years.

In August, Caesar returned to Rome and made it clear that he had lost confidence in Antony, who failed to maintain order without considerable loss of life. Caesar then arranged the elections for the new year (46 BC), and then ensured that the offices went to his partisans. He also stepped down from the dictatorship to be re-elected consul for the third time, with Aemilius Lepidus as his colleague. This, too, was an exception to the law, which required a 10-year interval between consulships. Again, however, this was not unprecedented since the same allowance had been granted to Pompey in 52. In December, Caesar left for Africa to deal with the Pompeiian forces there and returned victorious in mid-46, when he again received the dictatorship, this time with Aemilius Lepidus as deputy. This nomination was for 10 years, again not unprecedented, because Sulla's dictatorship had been formally indefinite. Caesar used his powers to begin stabilising and organising Rome and its empire after the civil war.

Soon after his return from Africa, Caesar celebrated four triumphs in a row. The first, for the war in Gaul, had been postponed back in 49 due to the civil war (Box 6.1). The subsequent three concerned more recent victories: Egypt (47), Asia Minor (47, the *veni vidi vici* one), and Africa (46). Although the latter conquered another Roman army, it involved defeating a foreign king and therefore qualified as a triumph.

> **Box 6.1 A Triumph, At Last**
>
> To get an idea of what this meant, it is helpful to picture how the first triumph for Gaul unfolded. The participants in the procession assembled early in the morning in the open space of the Campus Martius. From there, they proceeded very slowly to the Forum through the crowds lining the streets or watching in awe and fascination from their windows in the multistorey apartment blocks. The visual spectacle was overwhelming. Captives were paraded in chains, the most prominent being Vercingetorix, whom Caesar had kept imprisoned for this occasion. Vercingetorix, the Gallic chieftain, was on his way to being strangled in public to the delight of the Roman people as the ultimate proof of Roman conquest. War chariots that once belonged to the defeated Britons rumbled down the streets, as well as carts full of spoils of war: weaponry, objects made of gold and silver, coins, statues and precious curiosities and artefacts. Attendants carried boards with the numbers of cities conquered, enemies slain and treasures collected. Paintings and models displayed Rome's military prowess by visualising the war's most meaningful events. Musicians played their instruments. Flowers were strewn along the path. Senators and magistrates, all of Rome's elite, walked along, clearly visible in their official togas.

> Then, it was Caesar's turn: standing on a four-horse chariot accompanied by a public slave. He wore a purple toga to signify victory and divine favour. The toga also effectively proclaimed that his military authority had ended and that he had returned to Rome as a citizen. A laurel wreath covered his head, and his hands held a laurel branch and a sceptre. In front of him walked the lictors, his honorific bodyguard, this time carrying fasces decorated with laurels. His officers and soldiers, with whom he had shared hardships in the field, followed behind.
> Caesar must have relished this moment of public accomplishment. Driven to re-establish his family's fame, the spectacle around him was irrefutable proof that he had achieved all that he had wanted to be: the best of the best. His first and only triumph taken from him by Cato's scheming back in 60 after returning from Spain, Caesar was now about to start the first of four triumphs that would honour his victories in the next few weeks. He finally surpassed Pompey the Great, always his benchmark, who had celebrated three. As Caesar's chariot started moving, he could see the parade ahead of him entering the city like a gigantic snake wriggling itself into its lair. He could hear the music and the city coming alive with the jubilant crowd's loud cheers. Behind him, his soldiers sang songs and shouted hurrahs. The long procession culminated in Caesar's ascension to the Capitol to perform a sacrifice in the temple of Jupiter.

In addition to the four triumphs, Caesar organised large festivities in the city and gave his soldiers a hefty pay-out. At the end of the year, he was elected consul for the fourth time while remaining dictator. Caesar left in November 46 and returned for his fifth and final visit to Rome in October 45.

When his victory was becoming apparent, the Senate and some officials started bestowing honour after honour upon Caesar. The Roman historian Dio Cassius even found it too tiresome to list all of them. Some honours were traditional and others unprecedented. Caesar refused to accept them all because he felt that some made him look too much like a king, which would violate the Roman constitution. There has been much discussion among historians, ancient and modern alike, about whether these honours were to pay tribute to Caesar or confer royal status, or whether they were intended to trick him into accepting, thereby creating the grounds by which to eliminate him. Some historians have questioned that whether Caesar refused some because he indeed found them excessive or if it was more of a humble brag. In any case, the many actors' motivations are unclear to us today due to a lack of trusted sources. Moreover, it must have been murky to Caesar's contemporaries, too. Suffice it to say that those who wanted to take issue with Caesar for seizing absolute power would have had ample evidence. Similarly, those who hoped to see Caesar as an exceptional person deserving of extraordinary honours while staying loyal to the constitution did so. Without question, bestowing honours resulted from competition between different individuals and groups who outdid themselves to curry favour with the power that was. Finally, the Senate may have decided on some tributes to project an image of involvement and autonomy towards a top leader who had amassed so much power. (Quite likely, a similar desire prompts some modern supervisory boards to reward their star CEO with stellar compensation packages.) Either way, Caesar was challenged by finding the right balance between not appearing too eager to accept the honours and not appearing ungrateful in refusing them.

While establishing himself at the top, Caesar passed many laws and decrees and oversaw the election of public officials. After an initial period during which he had difficulties staying within constitutional boundaries, he implemented his decisions using constitutional methods: edicts, senatorial decisions and laws passed by the popular assembly. Caesar also made it clear that working within the bounds of legality was important to him. Yet he did benefit from constitutional innovations and exceptions, such as dictatorships beyond 6 months. That some perceived him as an autocrat, therefore, is understandable. Then, during the last months, after he had won his final battle at Munda, Caesar's power base grew rapidly. Caesar planned his next project, a 3-year campaign to contain Parthia, the Middle Eastern kingdom that threatened Rome's borders. Notably, the People voted Caesar to lead this campaign. Meanwhile, they granted Caesar the right to nominate all magistrates in Rome and the provinces for the campaign's duration. Plus, a few months before his death, Caesar accepted the title of dictator for an unlimited period. The title imbued him with absolute power as long as he wished. Combined, this effectively strained the Republic's constitution, which was based on annual elections and power sharing. During the 5 years of the civil war, Caesar crept increasingly close to that final moment, where—in modern corporate terms—he was both the top operational leader and the head of the supervisory body, that is, the Senate, which was supposed to control top management.

Sixty senators conspired against Caesar and knifed him to death on the Ides of March 44. The formal reason was that Caesar was on his way to becoming a king, which was constitutionally and traditionally forbidden in the Republic. For some, it was the key motivation. For other conspirators, it hid more personal reasons, such as personal resentments, stolen pride, envy and frustrated career ambitions. This dramatic event will be covered more in detail later because the reasons why it happened say much about Caesar's leadership.

Regarding Caesar's personal life, Dio Cassius tells us that Caesar, even in his later years, was acutely conscious of his appearance. After celebrating his four triumphs, he always covered his head with a laurel wreath. He continued wearing his loose-fitting toga and took to wearing high, red shoes as a fashion statement. When the civil war started, Caesar was again childless after losing Julia. Although he had been married to Calpurnia since 59, they had no children together, and then she became his widow in 44. Their union was an arranged marriage in which Calpurnia took the role of a loyal wife. It seems that she tolerated Caesar's infidelities. If anything, they spent little time together. Soon after their wedding, Caesar left for Gaul. Apart from Calpurnia taking occasional trips to northern Italy, they would not have spent time together until Caesar traversed the Rubicon 9 years later. In the remaining time of Caesar's life, he spent the equivalent of only 1 year out of 5 in Rome.

In parallel to his marriage to Calpurnia, Caesar's love affair with Servilia continued. The romance was well known but did not negatively impact Caesar's standing or reputation. Servilia, interestingly, is the mother of Brutus, who joined Pompey, then was pardoned by Caesar and given a provincial governorship only to become the leader of Caesar's assassination. Servilia had always stayed loyal to Caesar while trying to protect her son from harm. In the aftermath of Caesar's murder, she became more active in protecting her son. She was also involved in political meetings and used her network to influence matters in the years following Caesar's death. Servilia was a well-connected, capable woman who did what she could to actively influence politics despite women being barred from public office, similar to Caesar's mother, Aurelia, and his daughter, Julia.

For the last 4 years of his life, Caesar had a love affair with Cleopatra once their working relationship became a personal one. They spent more than 6 months together in Egypt and enjoyed a cruise on the Nile. Although Caesar was formally Cleopatra's boss, they formed a dual-career couple, something unheard of for Romans, except in business. They also had a son together, Caesarion, born mid-47, Caesar's second child after Julia. Cleopatra visited Rome twice with their son to conduct business with Caesar and the Roman government. Caesar was a prolific letter-writer and, most probably while travelling, he maintained his private relationships through correspondence. Meanwhile, during these final 5 years of his life, his most intimate relationships were with Servilia and Cleopatra, two capable, assertive, influential women.

After Caesar's death, a series of civil wars broke out, from which Octavian (later, Augustus), ultimately emerged victorious in 31 BC. Politically, it marked the Roman Republic's end and the start of the monarchy and the Roman Empire.

6.2 Caesar's Vision and Achievements

At first, in the aftermath of the first bloodless confrontation in March 49 at Corfinium, Caesar articulated his aims in front of his soldiers and those of his adversaries, who had just surrendered. In his memoir of the civil war, Caesar recorded these goals: (1) to restore his personal reputation, (2) to reinstate the powers of the plebs and (3) to reclaim his own independence and that of the Roman people, which a small clique, namely the oligarchy, had usurped. These were constitutional, personal and, in fact, conservative terms. Over time, it started dawning upon Caesar that this conflict was about more than himself and restoring what was lost. About 1 year later, in Greece before his final confrontation with Pompey, he, therefore, formulated his vision for the future, which he also wrote down in that same memoir, *Commentaries on the Civil War*. Once the civil war ended, he claimed, he would establish *order in Italy, peace in the provinces and prosperity in the empire* (3.57. Author's translation, italics added). This section will now review to what extent Caesar realised this vision during the last 5 years of his career.

6.2.1 Establishing Order in Italy: Winning the Peace

Whereas Caesar knew perfectly well that the die he cast by crossing the Rubicon would start a conflict, he attempted to minimise violence from the outset. He knew that winning the war made little sense without winning the peace. He experienced several civil conflicts during his lifetime, none of which had created lasting peace. When Caesar was a teenager, Cinna, Marius and Sulla, one after the other, took power in Rome. All three tried to win the peace by crushing their enemies, confiscating their properties and reducing the civil rights of their and others' offspring. Catilina's failed coup in 63 was bathed in blood, whereas many senators were against using such violence to restore order. Notably, Caesar had taken a conciliatory stance in these conflicts. The short-lived political peace that these crackdowns established proved Caesar right. In each case, violent political conflict had swiftly flared up as politicians sought retribution or capitalised on the ill will that had been created.

Caesar remained convinced that lasting peace could only be possible through pardon and reconciliation. Whereas Pompey declared that anyone not with him was against him, Caesar professed that anyone who was not against him was with him or at least neutral. He continued his amnesty policy for those who fought on the other side during the civil war, culminating in a general amnesty for political opponents and their families and protecting their possessions. In addition, he took measures to right past wrongs; he recalled exiles and restored the political rights of the descendants of the victims of Sulla's purges. Today, we know that following an internal conflict or a painful restructuring, members of the same organisation must work together again without hard feelings. Otherwise, the organisation is doomed to failure. Finally, Caesar granted citizenship to all Italian inhabitants north of the Po River. No doubt, all this would also reinforce his political support base.

Caesar continued to offer to parley with Pompey during the civil war. He communicated his vision to the Pompeiians, inviting them to join him in this vision, although he never received a positive reply. Pompey did send offers in return, however. Whether either party genuinely wanted to vie for peace or whether this was mere propaganda or simply a way to sow division in the enemy camp is debatable. In any case, Caesar's actions were consistent with his forgiving attitude towards the defeated Romans. At the very least, it demonstrates that he wanted to minimise violence to secure lasting peace after the war. As Robert Morstein-Marx in his biography of Caesar shows, the loss of life among the elite and soldiers was substantially less than it had been during the civil wars of the 80 s. Caesar genuinely wanted to make a difference by his restraint.

Social and political unrest in the Roman capital marked the years leading up to Caesar crossing the Rubicon. Most among Rome's governing circles had concluded that reforms were needed for the Roman state to have a stable and sustainable future. There was broad agreement about what needed improvement in the Republic. In two speeches, in 52 (*Pro Milone*) and 46 (*Pro Marcello*), Cicero gave Pompey and Caesar respectively similar advice. Cicero proposed that each reform jurisdiction, strengthen the credit system, ensure population growth and ensure public and moral order.

Caesar realised that peace depended on social and economic circumstances. During his first and second visits to Rome, both in 49, Caesar took immediate measures to stabilise the situation. He decided on a process to ensure that the money, which was being hoarded because of civil strife, started flowing again: capping the amount of cash people could hold onto and arbitration between debtors and creditors. Land and immovables, which had lost value because their owners were fighting in the war or had fled—were honoured at pre-war worth for debt repayment. Together, these measures' purpose was to increase credit availability to bolster the economy and curb speculation and deflation.

While Caesar was away fighting Pompey in Greece in 48, the praetor Caelius Rufus seized the moment to promote his political standing. He was unhappy that Caesar had assigned his colleague Trebonius more prestigious responsibilities; he thus tried to sabotage Trebonius wherever possible. Ultimately, Caelius proposed measures for debt relief that exceeded Caesar's. Caelius' proposals favoured creditors and poorer tenants in Rome's housing estates. They led to the very turmoil that Caesar's consul-colleague Servilius Isauricus—whom Caesar had left in charge of the city—had difficulty controlling. The Senate and other magistrates cracked down on Caelius, who left the city to start an armed revolt and free slaves. Caesar's troops, stationed in Italy, crushed the uprising.

During the latter half of the civil war, when Caesar could spend more time in Rome, he launched a flurry of legislative activities and other measures. He distributed loot and plunder from his victories to veterans and the poorest citizens. He and the state invested in building, land distribution and colonies to ensure an income for decommissioned soldiers and poorer citizens. He ordered a census, which lowered the number of free corn recipients by 50%. Reducing the number of free corn recipients incentivised those who had been removed from the list to accept land outside the city.

Moreover, the recipients of free land who had returned to the city were excluded from future corn distributions. He offered premiums for large families to compensate for the loss of life on the battlefield. He also increased the middle class; for example, medical doctors and teachers from abroad who were willing to relocate to Rome received citizenship. Furthermore, the debt issue repeatedly came to the fore. Caesar had to intervene, arbitrating between debtors and creditors and re-establishing credit flow. Caesar also passed a law against displaying private wealth to reduce social tension.

Regarding public order, he commanded large ranchers in Italy to limit the number of their slaves to two-thirds of their staff. This was intended to prevent future slave revolts such as Spartacus', which Caesar had witnessed himself, or using slaves for political unrest, as Caelius had attempted in 48. He also banned professional associations (*collegia*), which had often served as the core organisation of mass movements and riots.

Caesar restructured the Republic like Sulla had done before him, hoping to improve its government and prevent a future civil war. Whereas he took great pains to distance himself from Sulla when it came to the bloodshed that Sulla generated, he learned politically from this previous dictator. Once victorious in the civil war, Sulla reformed the Republic's political system to remove the elements causing political tension and conflict. According to Sulla, the checks and balances established by the founding fathers had evolved into a system that could not resolve political opposition; he also claimed they led to too much competition for holding offices. Disagreements could only be resolved by violent conflict and repression, culminating in the civil war he had just fought.

Caesar agreed with Sulla's analysis. He also concurred with part of his solution: to increase the number of magistrates and senators to keep pace with the city's and the empire's growth. Therefore, he increased the number of magistrates several times during his final years, which helped to reduce competition and satisfy his followers' ambitions. His successor, Augustus, expanded this further into an imperial civil service. Sulla had increased the Senate from 300 to 600 members; Caesar enlarged it further to 900 and replaced those who had fallen in the war.

Caesar's reforms, particularly his decision to alter the Senate's composition by incorporating newcomers from Italy and beyond, significantly impacted the traditional oligarchy. This move, which aligned with his belief that the Republic should recruit its elite from a broader geographical base, diluted the traditional oligarchy's political influence. Politically, this made sense, considering that the Italian peninsula had recently become fully Romanised. Caesar also ensured that the growing number of senators matched the increased number of magistracies, a detail Sulla had overlooked that led to more competition and electoral turmoil.

However, Caesar disagreed with Sulla on how to reform institutional equilibrium. Sulla shifted the balance of power to the Senate and removed the tribunes of the plebs' right to veto. Caesar witnessed how this right was quickly restored after Sulla's death and that Sulla's reforms did little to reduce political conflict or engender an effective governance system. In addition, throughout his career, Caesar's experiences of trying to work with the Senate had only disappointed and frustrated him. Therefore, Caesar was convinced that the balance of power should shift to the executive. Working repeatedly with Bibulus taught him that a system comprising at least two individuals sharing the same magistracy created frequent collegiate disputes and could obstruct effective governance. Shared leadership only worked well if magistrates were not from opposing factions and collaborated well, as Pompey and Crassus had demonstrated twice as consuls. If not, the government worked better under a single leader. For evidence, one only needed to look at Pompey's brief but effective period as consul without a colleague, his special command to run the corn supply or Caesar and Pompey's provincial commands. Following the formation of his belief in the executive's primacy (and blaming the system rather than his lack of skills in cooperation and influencing), Caesar started considering a solution, which would not be an autocracy, let alone a monarchy. This brings us to the question of what *dictator perpetuum*, often translated as dictator 'for life', really signifies. Caesar accepted this office in the weeks before his death, a decision that both his assassins and many scholars saw and continue to see as proof of his desire to become king.

A recent archaeological find in Privernum near Rome sheds light on this question. It concerns a copy of the *fasti consulares*, a tablet hung up in public that displays the consuls' names in chronological order. The list was supposed to be updated yearly after the elections. In this case, it also contains Caesar's succession of dictatorships, his deputies and their replacements. Notably, the inscription mentions that Caesar had assigned Lepidus as his deputy (magister equitum) and provided replacements for Lepidus when he was away governing a province. It says that Caesar was designated dictator *in perpetuum*. I follow Morstein-Marx's view that how *perpetuus* is used and specified in these *fasti* cannot mean 'for life'. It deserves a different translation. Instead, I would argue the better translation would be an assignment for an indefinite period, equivalent to our modern permanent employment contract. In contrast, the standard for all other magistracies and governorships was fixed-term. Hence, Caesar's dictatorship was not until he died (like a monarch) but until he stepped down or until he retired (as Sulla did incidentally).

This concept of an indefinite dictatorship was a significant departure from the traditional Roman political system, indicating Caesar's contemplation of introducing a more centralised and enduring form of leadership in the shape of an additional magistracy hierarchically positioned above the consuls. Instead of resorting to the dictatorship sporadically in times of crisis, Caesar appeared to envision this office as a permanent fixture in the *cursus honorum*. This new office would be held by one individual with full decision-making powers and supported by a deputy, the *magister equitum*. Drawing from his own experiences, he believed that the expanding empire, with all its complexity, necessitated a leader with unrestricted authority and for whom continuous deliberations with colleagues would not hinder or frustrate efficient governance.

Caesar's thinking about the dictator as a permanent office should also be viewed in relation to the consuls' changed role. From the start, supreme command of the armed forces was an essential responsibility of theirs. However, Rome became so powerful that it was no longer existentially threatened by a foreign invasion. In the year before Caesar's birth, his uncle Marius, as consul, repulsed the last such danger from the Cimbri and Teutones in Northern Italy. Henceforth, wars were regional and waged by provincial commanders. During Caesar's time, the consuls were mainly concerned with matters in Rome and their military role remained dormant. Francesco Pina Polo fittingly labels this professional differentiation as a shift from the consul-general to the consul-politician. With the military responsibility practically gone, the consuls had less to do with the empire despite its growing importance to the Republic. Unless they could count on support from Pompey's and Crassus's wealth and military resources, or maintain a firm grip on the People (Caesar), the consuls would become increasingly dependent on the Senate, hence weakening the executive branch. Caesar observed that this was not working. It contradicted his belief in the primacy of the executive rather than the legislative. It was another reason why—in my view—Caesar wanted to introduce a kind of super-consul, comparable to a CEO in corporate terms or a presidential system in political terms.

Caesar conjured this idea in haste while preparing to depart for Parthia in 44. He had not yet thoroughly thought it through, let alone taken the time to explain it to his followers. It is, for example, unclear whether Caesar saw the indefinite period only applying to himself until he had completed his vision or whether he believed that this office should normally be held longer than the other annual magistracies.

Additionally, the question of the dictator's immunity after leaving office had not yet been addressed. Caesar, notably, was not against answering for his actions. On the contrary, in his speeches before the Senate and the People, as quoted by Dio Cassius, he specifically mentions that his accountability distinguishes him from the previous civil war leaders Sulla, Marius and Cinna. Moreover, he claimed, his record shows he does not want to be a tyrant. Caesar goes even further, saying that whatever he does for the Republic, he does as consul and dictator. But if he wrongs someone, he does so as a private citizen, implying that he would not be immune to prosecution. Referring to Sulla was cheeky: after stepping down as dictator, Sulla did, in fact, publicly announce that he was willing to be held accountable now that he was a private citizen. However, no one dared to do so for fear of his partisans and veterans. Caesar no doubt banked on being similarly protected. Still, throughout his career, Caesar reported back to the Senate and the People through speeches and his writings. He was in favour of transparency, to which the introduction of the publication of the Senate and popular assembly's proceedings—his first decision as a consul—attests. He explained, for example, that a tax hike was necessary to keep the army happy. Of course, he gave his reports a positive flavour but, then again, what executive doesn't?

Caesar left too much room for interpretation, offering his assassins, who claimed to be tyrannicides, the opportunity to argue that his aim was autocracy. The institutional innovation of making the dictator a permanent magistracy got mixed up with Caesar's arrangements to ensure Rome's stability while he was away fighting the Parthians. Concerned about turmoil caused by elections, he decided on another constitutional innovation to assign the public officials, customarily elected yearly, for 3 years in advance: *bricolage institutionnel*, 'amateurish institutional restructuring' as Jean-Louis Ferrary aptly puts it. Octavian-Augustus took his cue from Caesar and, after another civil war, did establish an autocracy while astutely avoiding the laden term of dictator.

Caesar succeeded in establishing order in both Rome and throughout Italy, which was undone by his violent death. Tensions flared up, and civil wars followed. Nevertheless, Caesars's measures were considered sensible by many. There was broad consensus among all stakeholders that his decisions and reforms should stay in force and be implemented. For instance, Octavian-Augustus built on Caesar's precedent to retain power and maintain order. He regulated senatorial careers and made the elite's career successes dependent on their loyalty to the emperor. He ensured the senators' ambitions were sufficiently satisfied by increasing the number of magistracies further. He also created opportunities for upward mobility among the lower strata of society. In Rome, Augustus effectively dismantled popular influence. Simultaneously, he met the plebs' needs through regularly supplying bread and circuses. Regarding the latter, he mimicked Caesar's strategy for garnering popularity. What Augustus did not do was emulate Caesar's principle of no hard feelings: the civil wars Augustus participated in were marked by a murderous purge of his adversaries.

6.2.2 Establishing Peace in the Provinces: Safeguarding the Empire's Security and Stability

The Romans developed a practice of governing the conquered territories of their growing empire through *provinciae*. In addition to being a source of tax revenue and resources, the provinces contributed to the Roman economy by trade. Caesar had governed provinces in Gaul and Spain during his career, and by the end of his career, he had visited most provinces in the empire.

Caesar implemented significant provincial reforms, building on his experience governing Spain and Gaul. He aimed to improve administration, reduce corruption and enhance economic development. He reorganised the provinces' taxation by making the system fairer, less exploitative and thus more sustainable. For example, after securing victory at Munda in 45, Caesar dwelled in Spain for 2 months to reorganise the two Iberian provinces. Caesar founded colonies for veterans and Rome's inhabitants (Fig. 6.2). These also served as military strongpoints. He established new city constitutions, modelled on the Roman constitution, with a local senate, magistrates and a small

Fig. 6.2 Foundation charter of a colony founded by Caesar in Spain (Urso). Inscription on bronze which stipulates the governance of the colony. Museo Arqueológico Nacional, Madrid. Inv. 18,630; imagen 18,630-ID001. Foto: Raúl Fernández Ruiz. Reprinted under licence

civil service. He also specified that freed slaves had the right to stand for election to the municipal council. Such measures sped up the Iberian Peninsula's Romanisation. His cherished collaborator Balbus, who hailed from Gades in Spain, will have given Caesar advice in these matters.

Passing through Southern France on his way back to Rome, Caesar made similar provisions there, for instance, offering citizenship to wealthy inhabitants. In other provinces such as Sicily, he issued Latin rights, a reduced form of Roman citizenship and a stepping stone towards full citizenship. With these measures, plus founding colonies in several provinces, Caesar catalysed the empire's Romanisation, not unlike the Hellenisation of the Middle East following Alexander's conquest. He didn't take this lightly. After discovering that some of his staff were selling Roman citizenship in Sicily, he ensured that the practice would be corrected. He then revoked citizenship for those who had purchased it. Moreover, building on the law on provincial governance he had passed during his consulship, Caesar limited the tenure of Roman governors of provinces to 1 or 2 years. This curtailed opportunities for exploitation. Finally, he also secured the empire's borders, securing it against incursions.

Octavian-Augustus later followed Caesar's lead in reforming the provincial administration. He increased and professionalised the administration, founded colonies of veterans and citizens and stimulated cultural and economic integration.

6.2.3 Establishing Prosperity in the Empire: Creating a Sustainable Future

Throughout his 5-year leadership of the Republic, Caesar implemented several measures to stimulate the empire's growth and integration. These measures—such as offering Roman citizenship to some people in the empire's cities, founding colonies, distributing land, reforming taxes and improving administration—all contributed to economic integration and stimulus. Caesar's economic interventions to combat deflation and facilitate credit flow not only quelled unrest but also positively impacted the economy, benefiting the rich and the poor, as well as entrepreneurs and farmers. Veterans were given land to farm and the requisite tools. The increase in the number of magistrates and senators was a sensible improvement to the empire's understaffed leadership structure.

Caesar had grand plans for the empire. During his last year, in addition to building projects in Rome, he discussed infrastructure projects for roads, canals, ports and clearing land in Italy and beyond. He also planned to establish a national library and to codify Roman law. He reformed the calendar, because the existing one was increasingly off-balance with the sun and the seasons.

The way Caesar dealt with Egypt significantly contributed to the empire's prosperity. Egypt was the last of Alexander the Great's successor states that Rome had not yet conquered. Rich in corn, ships and manpower, Egypt was a critical supply base for Rome. Alexandria, its capital with a magnificent library, was a source of inspiration and intellectual talent for the Romans. Many teachers and other higher professionals in Rome came from Alexandria. As long as this partnership endured, no one in Rome saw the need to integrate Egypt as a province. By the time Caesar arrived in Egypt, the demand for food in the bustling city of Rome and the centre of power far outstripped the supply from Italy and nearby regions. Securing and stabilising Egypt, hence, was strategically important for Caesar when he found the country engulfed in a civil war in 48. Caesar decided to accept Cleopatra's offer of an alliance instead of annexing Egypt as another province. Doing so allowed Caesar to access Egypt's resources without leaving a mighty power base to a Roman governor and potential competitor.

The value of Caesar's decisions is once more demonstrated by how Octavian-Augustus followed Caesar's lead. In addition to the measures implemented throughout the provinces, Augustus also refrained from turning Egypt into a province. Instead, he integrated the country as an imperial domain wholly owned by the emperor. He appointed a professional executive, the Egyptian prefect, to govern the country in his stead. Augustus could henceforth distribute Egypt's riches as he wished.

6.3 Caesar's Leadership Behaviours at the Top

Again, using the Global Executive Leadership Mirror (GELM®)'s framework, we will analyse Caesar's leadership competencies based on his behaviour. The final period of Caesar's career was full of dramatic events and, fortunately, rich in sources and records. This allows us to analyse Caesar's leadership more extensively than in previous chapters. Figure 6.3 summarises the evaluation of Caesar's leadership behaviours during this period, notably as a public official and government leader.

6.3.1 Leading Self

Emotional Intelligence remained a development need. Caesar asked the Senate to take responsibility for the government. As of November 49, Rome had yet again a fully staffed government with yearly elected magistrates. However, Caesar did not realise the psychological impact his behaviour and

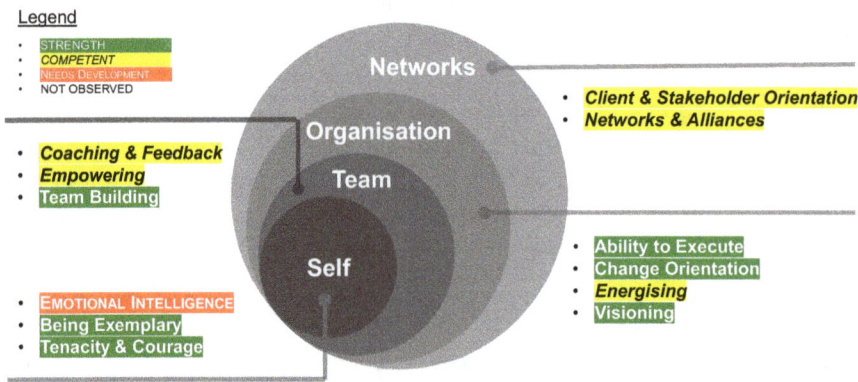

Fig. 6.3 Evaluation of Caesar's leadership behaviours during his final career stage. Author's adaptation: Based on GELM by KDVI

status had upon becoming dictator. Many among Caesar's generation still had active memories of the horrors borne from the combination of army general and dictatorship in a civil war. Such concentration of power stood in opposition to the ideology of the oligarchy, which had assumed power by toppling the autocracy; it had believed in shared leadership ever since. Furthermore, and errantly, Caesar expected the government to function as usual in his absence. To his dismay, the Senate and magistrates prudently avoided making decisions or proposing bills lest they displeased the person with the real power.

Caesar's relationship with the Roman government became a vicious circle of increasing disempowerment. Caesar empowered the Senate and magistrates, which led to ineffective government. Next, an impatient Caesar took power back. Then he tried to empower again. This back and forth continued until Caesar was nominated dictator for an unlimited time. Caesar's frequent and prolonged absences from Rome made it difficult to set clear objectives and expectations and give feedback. The Roman elite felt increasingly sidelined in this period of change and rapid decision-making by Caesar; they were also insecure about their future role in the Republic: Box 6.2.

Box 6.2 Missing Emotional Intelligence

One incident exemplifies how Caesar was unaware of how his behaviour could hurt others' feelings. In late 45, Caesar was finally able to start building his own forum, for which he had acquired the land years ago. While he was busy discussing the project with artisans and contractors, the Senate had met and agreed on a series of honours for Caesar. After the meeting, they decided to go together to Caesar to tell him the great news in person. Here is how Nicolaus of Damascus relates what happened next

(*Life of Augustus* 22; transl. C.M. Hall): 'In the meanwhile, up came a procession of Roman nobles, to confer the honours which had just been voted him by common consent. In the lead was the consul (the one who was Caesar's colleague at that time), and he carried the decree with him. In front of him were lictors, keeping the crowd back on either side. With the consul came the praetors, tribunes, quaestors, and all the other officials. Next came the Senate, in orderly formation, and then a multitude of enormous size--never so large. The dignity of the nobles was awe inspiring--they were entrusted with the rule of the whole empire, and yet looked with admiration on another as if he were still greater. Caesar was seated while they advanced and because he was conversing with men standing to one side, he did not turn his head toward the approaching procession or pay any attention to it, but continued to prosecute the business which he had on hand, until one of his friends, nearby, said, 'Look at these people coming up in front of you.' Then Caesar laid down his papers [and while remaining seated] turned around and listened to what they had come to say.' Caesar's behaviour was considered highly disrespectful and angered the senators. The incident embarrassed his friends and confirmed others' perception of Caesar as a future autocrat.

Another example shows that Caesar's Emotional Intelligence was still underdeveloped. He wrote a critical post-mortem of Cato the Younger, his career-long nemesis, as a reaction to several eulogies. When he wrote this anti-Cato piece, he was oblivious to his negative feelings and how they prompted him to react defensively. Equally, he was unaware of the impact it would have on those reading the pamphlet. Because he held absolute power as dictator in 45, his lashing out could be perceived as being uninterested in other opinions or possibly as autocratic behaviour. Furthermore, he was either unaware or too ambivalent towards the fact that a (top) leader is continuously in the spotlight. The truth is followers observe and interpret a leader's behaviour. Some of Caesar's actions (dictating letters while attending the games for the people) were perceived as arrogant.

The revolts towards the end of the war in Gaul and the end of the civil war in Spain are proof that Caesar's underdeveloped Emotional Intelligence, particularly towards groups, could put his career at risk. When seeking reasons for his assassination, it transpires that having arrived at the top, not having Emotional Intelligence could become a real career-stopper. The violent and public murder suggests broader feeling of dissatisfaction in the organisation. For example, did the tyrannicides, as they liked to call themselves, do it for the reasons they formally communicated, namely that Caesar was turning the Republic into a monarchy? Or was it simply a putsch by ambitious politicians? Oddly, the perpetrators did not have a day-after plan, indicating it was not a power grab. Instead, they seemed to have assumed that governance would continue much the same way, just without a dictator. Or, perhaps they believed in a return to the status quo before the civil war. Interestingly, the 60-odd conspirators were a mixed cohort of Caesareans and former Pompeiians.

Nicolaus of Damascus, a Greek contemporary scholar, wrote the following in his biography of Augustus (19. Translated by C.M. Hall): Box 6.3.

Box 6.3 Why Caesar was Assassinated According to Nicolaus of Damascus

'There were various reasons which affected each and all of them [the assassins] and impelled them to lay hands on the man [Caesar]. Some hoped to become leaders in his stead once he was removed from power; others were angered by what had happened to them in the war and embittered over the loss of their relatives, property, or state offices. They concealed the fact that they were angry and made the pretence of something seemlier, claiming to be displeased at the rule of a single man and to strive for a republican form of government. Different people had different reasons, all brought together by whatever pretext they happened upon.'

David Epstein carefully analysed the twenty conspirators, whom we know by name. He found that some indeed had a personal grudge against Caesar, as Nicolaus of Damascus tells us. These individuals were bound together by a common feeling of being unfairly treated, disempowered or ignored: powerful negative motivators indeed. Nicolaus's assessment corresponds to my experience as an executive coach. Motivations are multi-dimensional. Yet for most, the reason that often tips the balance, particularly for a far-reaching decision, tends to be personal, individualistic and often egotistic. Regarding Rome, killing the 'tyrant' became the umbrella purpose to which each person could subscribe.

Nicolaus of Damascus once more proves to be a fine analyst of group dynamics. This is showcased when he describes the group think and the mutual radicalisation among the tyrannicides (19. Translated by C.M. Hall):

> Every one of them put forward his own particular pretext for the matter in hand, and as a result of his own complaints, each lent a ready ear to the accusations of the others. They all confirmed each other in their conspiracy. They furnished as surety to one another the grievances which they held severally in private against him.

While the noble purpose of a 'greater good' and 'saving the Republic' was undoubtedly present, it was not the primary motivation for what happened on the Ides of March. Caesar's downfall was not a case of 'the establishment strikes back'. Instead, it was an aggregate of personal grievances, frustrated ambitions and feelings of disempowerment among a radicalised fringe of the establishment. Caesar's failure to understand these feelings among his followers, and his ignorance of how his own emotions and behaviour could affect others, ultimately undermined his career. He mistakenly believed that displaying no hard feelings towards former adversaries and offering material compensation would be sufficient to secure a committed following.

In the civil war's early days, Caesar wrote to Cicero, communicating that he was okay with the people he had pardoned taking up arms against him again. His vision aligned with his values, for Caesar wanted to stay true to himself. During these last 5 years of Caesar's career, he was Exemplary also in doing what he said he would do. This mainly concerns his leniency towards adversaries who were Roman citizens. Largely, he followed through on his commitments, limiting the loss of life and property during the civil war, even to the point of antagonising supporters who had been loyal from the beginning. Some found it unfair that former adversaries received similar honours; thus, they sided with the conspirators. Caesar dealt with political setbacks swiftly, such as Antony being unable to maintain peace in Rome or the Senate being unwilling to reach decisions. Instead, his focus lay in tenaciously pursuing the three strategies of this vision.

6.3.2 Leading Teams

All this leads to important questions. For instance, how open was Caesar to Feedback, and did he invite it? What feedback did he receive, and how did he interpret it? It is worth noting that Caesar lacked a person, internally or externally, to support him in his development as a leader. He never benefited from a supervisor who actively contributed to cultivating these important strengths and skills. Neither did Caesar have an Aristotle, who coached Alexander the Great.

Caesar was not closed to feedback. Several people, notably intellectuals like Cicero and Sallust, gave him advice in public speeches, memos and private letters. Caesar did in fact listen to their recommendations, largely because his measures to ensure a sustainable future for Rome and the empire aligned with their feedback. Regarding inviting feedback, we have two letters from Caesar in March 49. In one, he thanks his assistants Balbus and Oppius for their positive feedback regarding his plans and invites them to offer even more advice. In the other, he encourages Cicero to advise him. Yet Caesar also missed key opportunities, for example, in December 45, when he attended a dinner party at Cicero's. To the latter's frustration, who had been looking forward to the occasion, many things were discussed—but not politics and current affairs. However, perhaps Caesar just wanted to have a good time that night. Cicero recounts another disconcerting instance in several letters to his correspondent, Atticus, in May 45. Cicero had drafted a letter with political advice. Balbo and Oppius, who handled Caesar's correspondence, revised and commented on Cicero's letter, suggesting considerable changes so that the document would find favour with Caesar. This shows that the two staffers had actually become gatekeepers. We don't know what instructions they received from Caesar, if any, or what leeway they used to manage messages to Caesar. But one thing is certain: they obstructed unfiltered feedback.

What about receiving spontaneous feedback? Speaking truth to power is always complicated. Many will have been careful when sharing their thoughts with Caesar. However, followers often assume that upward feedback is unnecessary, as management scholar Kelly See and her colleagues demonstrated. When someone becomes a manager, subordinates tend to be reticent: they assume this person has been put in that position for a reason and, therefore, is less in need of feedback. In addition, the more confident the manager appears, the lower is the perceived need for subordinates' advice. This happened with Caesar, too. From the same correspondence between Atticus and Cicero in May 45, one can see that Balbus and Oppius not only suggested a rewrite but also let it be understood that Cicero had said nothing that Caesar hadn't already known.

Now take Caesar in this final stage of his career: he was someone who had reached the top because of continued success. What's more, Caesar was known to have luck on his side. In Roman times, people believed the gods favoured such a person. Thus, why would someone like that need feedback? Add to that Caesar's continuous signals of confidence. He never was known to show doubt. All this is to say that Caesar likely received little spontaneous feedback from his underlings. Sometimes he even was vexed about certain comments (Box 6.4).

> **Box 6.4 Caesar Gets Defensive**
>
> Caesar sometimes reacted defensively to feedback, for example his response to the eulogies of the late Cato written by Cicero and others, mentioned earlier. Cato had always taken the moral high ground and ideologically was Caesar's staunchest opponent. There was also personal enmity between the two. It took Caesar a year to write his anti-Cato. Perhaps he did not feel the need to have done so earlier or maybe he just didn't have the time. Either way, he obviously wrote it out of vexation, contrary to his policy of displaying no hard feelings towards adversaries. Caesar had won; Cato was dead. So, what was the point? Caesar wrote the pamphlet after the battle of Munda. Psychologically, the final uprising in Spain had taken a toll. He hadn't seen it coming, so he must have doubted himself, something that often makes leaders defensive. He had fought so hard, not only militarily but also personally, to end the civil war swiftly. He had attempted to pacify society and politicians by being generous and magnanimous to all soldiers and commanders who had fought on the other side. Thinking that the civil war was over, now the very people he had pardoned were revolting. Moreover, he had barely escaped after arguably the most hard-won battle of the civil war. He lashed out in anger. Meanwhile, the authors of Cato's eulogies in 46, also believing the war was over, saw them as a contribution to post-war conciliation. This was just like Caesar allowing Pompey's statues to be re-erected. Caesar's defensiveness simply did not court feedback to the mighty dictator.

Did Caesar interpret the feedback he received correctly? There are indications that he may not have. The Senate and magistrates bestowed upon Caesar honour after honour. Some he refused as a kind of humble brag and others because they seemed too regal. The great Cicero complimented him for his clemency in his speeches. Be that as it may, as Nicolaus of Damascus wrote,

Caesar took this feedback at face value, meaning that he interpreted it as genuine and positive feedback that he was doing the right thing. (Nicolaus believed Caesar was too naïve because he had been abroad too long.) Like with the anti-Cato piece, Caesar didn't realise that feedback contains essential information about the feedback-giver, too: in this case, honours to curry favour, people outbidding each other to get Caesar's attention and sorry attempts at showing agency. Finally, it seems that the feedback Caesar received and invited was mainly on the 'what', that is, his plans and decisions. We have no indication that he also received feedback on the 'how', namely, how to motivate his followers and manage resistance. He especially was missing the latter kind of feedback. Suffice it to say that Caesar did not see any red flags that could have prevented him from getting (quite literally) stabbed in the back.

Caesar spent little time on Coaching and Feedback to others, which explains why his subordinates were less successful during the civil war than in Gaul. There were two notable exceptions, though (Boxes 6.5 and 6.6). The first was Cleopatra, who ascended the throne when she was 18.

> **Box 6.5 Talent Development: Cleopatra**
>
> The senior civil servants of Egypt's public administration, who disliked reporting to a woman, ousted Cleopatra soon after becoming queen. Cleopatra's behaviour (dressing and acting like a male Pharaoh) only fuelled this bias. After Caesar had restored her to the throne, Cleopatra led her country successfully until well after Caesar's death. Her leadership was never again internally challenged. Whether she had sought Caesar's advice or whether Caesar had coached her, we can't know. What we do know for sure is that Cleopatra fundamentally changed her communication during her second stint as Egypt's leader. Caesar set Cleopatra up for success because he was acutely aware that her difference put her at risk of facing another misogynist putsch. Caesar propped up Cleopatra's power base with a few legions and suggested that she marry her younger brother. That way, at least nominally, she would conform to the tradition of women not ruling autonomously. Before Caesar, Cleopatra's acting like a man had cost her the throne. Later, she took it back by leveraging her difference, using ruse rather than violence to secure a meeting with Caesar. After working with him, her visual representations on coins and reliefs show her no longer as a male Pharaoh but in female dress or as a mother; in short, as an authentic female leader.

Cleopatra's remarkable improvement in communication and image-building could have been in part due to Caesar's deft guidance. Although much junior to Caesar, Cleopatra may well have asked for Caesar's support, considering that she had both the intelligence and the agency to do so. If that were the case, Caesar must have responded positively to her request. Caesar's

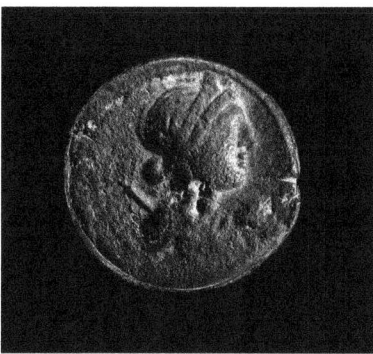

Fig. 6.4 Egyptian coin showing Queen Cleopatra holding the baby, Caesarion, she had with Caesar. © The Trustees of the British Museum. Reprinted under licence

emphasis on talent is also evidenced by his low opinion of Ptolemy, Cleopatra's younger brother and main competitor. Oddly, Caesar did not help her network effectively or build a positive reputation with stakeholders. She visited Rome twice on official business as Rome's new strategic partner. She was doubly exotic for the senators: a woman leader and a foreigner. Being Caesar's lover and mother of his son raised eyebrows in Rome's conservative salons. Unaware of all this, she thus committed several faux pas and left with a dented reputation. Moreover, Caesar failed to prevent this because of his own blind spots in Emotional Intelligence regarding the elite's collective mindset. Cleopatra (Fig. 6.4) became a highly successful leader after she crossed paths with Caesar, but, ultimately, her damaged reputation caught up with her. In the end, Octavian-Augustus ruthlessly exploited it to cause her downfall.

Box 6.6 Talent Development: Octavian

The second case concerns Octavian, Caesar's adoptive son and heir, who would later become Emperor Augustus. Like Cleopatra, Octavian spent much time in Caesar's company. According to Nicolaus of Damascus, he was an astute influencer. He interceded with Caesar on behalf of people in his network and found the right timing and tone to persuade Caesar. Nicolaus mentions that Caesar wanted Octavian to have the experience of staging theatrical productions, a clear development action. Given Caesar's track record as a popular leader, Caesar thought this to be good leadership training.

Caesar also invited Octavian along on his final campaign in Spain in 46/45 as another learning experience. Octavian was 17, which was then considered an adult. Ill, he missed Caesar's departure but joined him later. With a small party, he was shipwrecked in Spain and had to cross enemy terrain. Caesar was impressed. Nicolaus of Damascus records what happened next: Caesar gave Octavian positive feedback for succeeding and being the first from Rome to arrive in Spain. Then Caesar debriefed Octavian and was pleased with what he

> heard. Caesar found Octavian perceptive and intelligent. Moreover, he liked that Octavian was concise and to the point (and no doubt recognised himself in this trait). Travelling back together, Caesar further commended Octavian for being accompanied by ambitious and capable friends and working on building a good reputation at home. Interestingly, Caesar purposefully did not tell Octavian he would make him his heir. For Caesar, growing up in wealth was not propitious to developing the correct values. Such withholding reminds us that Caesar, too, had to work his way up from humble means.

Why, exactly, did Caesar do so well in developing Cleopatra and Octavian, and but not feel the need to do so with others? His laissez-faire attitude towards Marc Antony's and Curio's development, two other high potentials he identified, had been a mistake. So later, when he met Cleopatra and Octavian, he knew he had to start cultivating junior talent. Simultaneously, knowing both to be assertive, he knew they would be proactive in getting him to share his knowledge. In contrast, Antony and Curio seemed too self-confident to do so. Caesar counted on the *cursus honorum*, Rome's structured system of promotions and provincial and military assignments, which were supposed to raise the best to the top. After all, it had served him well, both personally and professionally. For the same reason, Caesar did not see the need to develop a succession plan; as he saw it, the system would take care of it. As a leader, Caesar was a passive developer and coached only those who asked for it. This explains why Caesar's empowerment was only partially successful. It also elucidates why several of his assassins were unhappy about their career development.

In the previous chapter we saw that—as a general—Caesar empowered others. Yet because he failed to develop his subordinates, he often had to disempower them and take control. In this chapter, we see a similar pattern of Empowerment in Caesar's organisational leadership. Let's now look at some of his most influential direct reports. In 48, Caesar was away in the field. He had left Rome to be governed by his consul-colleague Servilius Isauricus, a man with a standard career who did not stand out as an excellent leader. Under the circumstances, the job was too big for him, and he had difficulty keeping peace in Rome. Afterwards, Isauricus became governor of the province of Asia, where he did well. In late 48, Caesar was nominated dictator, with Marc Antony as his number two. This was a substantial promotion, as he had yet to retain the praetorship. While away in the East, Caesar left matters in Rome to Marc Antony. This, again, proved to be injudicious. Caesar had to return to Rome in August 47 to personally deal with the unrest in Rome and the army.

After Caesar conquered Spain in 49, he left Quintus Cassius Longinus in charge as provincial governor. He had served in Spain as quaestor a few years before, which is probably why Caesar chose him, but his performance was a disaster. He failed so badly that in 46, Pompey's sons could rally the Spaniards to revolt against Caesar. There were a few exceptions to this pattern (Box 6.7). One was Cleopatra, for sure, who ruled Egypt successfully for 18 years after Caesar had restored her to the throne.

> **Box 6.7 Empowerment: Lepidus**
>
> Another was Marcus Aemilius Lepidus. Ten years younger, he came from a noble family like Caesar. Politically, his family stood against Sulla, again like Caesar. Additionally, throughout his entire career, he supported Caesar. Thus, Caesar wanted him on his side. But there was more. In 52, he played a critical role in quelling political turmoil in Rome as an interrex. In 49, he was praetor and the highest-ranking magistrate who did not join Pompey. This position gave him the authority to manage affairs in Rome in Caesar's absence. At the end of the year, it was he who officially proposed to make Caesar dictator. Caesar sent him off to govern the province of Nearer Spain during 48 and 47. There, he impressed Caesar by peacefully preventing a violent conflict between Cassius Longinus and his army commander in the neighbouring province. Once back, Lepidus became Caesar's deputy in Rome, replacing Marc Antony. He was a better choice to manage the city administration while Caesar was away. Lepidus was not a military man but was more astute in government affairs. He was influential in securing deals in the background. He later became the junior partner in the second triumvirate with Antony and Octavian until these two finally fell out with each other. Lacking military capability, he could not play a significant role in the subsequent civil war and soon retired from public life.

> **Box 6.8 Empowerment: Balbus**
>
> Whereas many people lost out by being conquered by the Romans through death, destruction, enslavement, pillage and taxation, Lucius Cornelius Balbus belonged to the winners. He was an Iberian of considerable wealth and standing. He supported Pompey during his military campaign in Spain in 72, and Pompey rewarded him with Roman citizenship. Ten years later, in 61, still in Spain, Balbus served under Caesar as *praefectus fabrum*, chief engineer. Caesar employed him in the same role in his conquest of Gaul. Balbus, well-connected with both Pompey and Caesar, apparently played a central role in building the triumvirate coalition between his patrons and Crassus. Balbus was wealthy enough to climb the social ranks in Rome and become an eques. Caesar sent him back to Rome to represent his interests there, a position he filled successfully, together with Oppius, until Caesar's death. We know from Cicero that in 46, Balbus built houses in Rome as an investment or as part of Caesar's economic stimulus scheme.

Caesar employed some individuals such as Balbus (Box 6.8) and Oppius outside the formal Roman public administrative system. Caesar, Balbus and Oppius had much history, and they have been mentioned in previous chapters. Caius Oppius, an eques and possibly a banker, managed Caesar's affairs in Rome from 54 when Caesar was in Gaul. With Cicero's assistance, he bought land in Rome for Caesar's Forum, and he facilitated a loan from Caesar to Cicero.

Balbus and Oppius acted as efficient go-betweens, handling Caesar's private correspondence, distributing his public letters and advocating for Caesar's interests in individual discussions. For example, immediately after Caesar crossed the Rubicon, the two men started corresponding with Cicero and others to persuade them to support Caesar. After Caesar's death, they seamlessly found new employment with Caesar's successor, Octavian.

Capable as they were, one must wonder whether these two outsiders, the chief engineer of Caesar's army and Caesar's private banker, were competent enough to develop into representatives who could constructively mediate between the top leader and the rest of the organisation. Balbus spent many years being loyal to Caesar. But it was on the side of Caesar, the general, not Caesar, the politician. The two claimed to be in regular correspondence with Caesar. Yet we have no indication that their boss helped either to develop the competencies necessary for their new roles. If anything, this dynamic resulted in Caesar receiving filtered feedback, which likely contributed to Caesar remaining blind to the undercurrents of discontent in the organisation. This example shows that Caesar, as leaders often do, took collaborators he trusted and cherished along with him from one job to another. That can work well, provided these individuals develop—with the help of their boss—in tandem with the leader. If not, they may continue operating in a way suited to a previous context. Marshall Goldsmith's famous words, 'What got you here, won't get you there', can also apply to team members.

Caesar knew how to identify and select talented individuals for his Team Building. He was anything but snobbish about background. To get launched on the *cursus honorum*, one must have a certain social standing and personal wealth. It was Caesar who put a stronger emphasis on merit as a criterion. Thus, he was ahead of his time regarding diversity and inclusion. Balbus, thanks to his rise under Caesar, was the first person who was not a Roman citizen by birth and foreign-born to attain consul in 40. Caesar dismissed criticism for having made other such 'barbarians' senators. In his view, it rewarded people who served him well and showed an appreciation of their qualities.

Cleopatra was made queen despite Caesar having grown up in a society that shunned women from office. The public entertainment he offered to the inhabitants of Rome to celebrate his victories included stage plays in each ward of the city. Notably, actors performed these plays in several languages, as Suetonius remarks in his biography of Caesar: an act of inclusivity in this multicultural metropolis. On the battlefield, talent was concentrated with Pompey, whose officers won more victories than Caesar's. If it hadn't been for Caesar's personal involvement on the battlefield, the Pompeiians would have undoubtedly won the war. Pompey's talent pool for government officials was also filled with more experienced (ex-)magistrates. Given the equally disappointing performance of some of Caesar's direct reports in government, it appears Caesar drew the short straw regarding talent when the war started. Having lost key people, it took him a while before finding equally qualified replacements like Cleopatra and Octavian. Being open to diverse talent gave Caesar a competitive edge over his opponents.

6.3.3 Leading the Organisation

As a dictator, Caesar had formal authority to speed up decision-making and execution. And speeding things up is exactly what he did. He achieved an enormous amount during his short periods in Rome. Caesar's experience with the institutional establishment represented by the Senate was mixed at best. Generally, it was internally divided and its procedures were not conducive to coming to an agreement rapidly. Caesar was more effective in achieving his aims when working with the popular assembly and his army. Moreover, Caesar had hardly ever experienced that speedy decision-making and execution could have disadvantages. This simply reinforced his belief in the primacy of the executive over the Senate. Meanwhile, Caesar's followers pushed him towards decisiveness and taking charge. Once it was clear that he would emerge victorious, expectations to get the Republic back to functioning normally were openly expressed. Intellectuals like Cicero and Sallust did so publicly in speeches and in the memos and letters they sent to Caesar.

Caesar's vision was not only remarkable in its concise wording but also for not mentioning Rome, the capital and centre of political power. Having spent half his career in the provinces, Caesar saw that a re-balancing between the city and the empire was needed. Caesar's strategy was marked by a strong desire for continuity rather than disruption. Over time, the Romans had taken a pragmatic and incremental approach to governing their territory as it grew. All Caesar did for Italy, the provinces and the empire was, as such, not invented by him but instead had its precedents. Therefore, largely, Caesar's programme made sense to everyone. Rather than be cancelled, his measures were expanded and built upon after he died. He laid the groundwork, for example, for Augustus to construct the Roman Empire. However, the scale and the speed with which he introduced these changes were without precedent. Never before had a single leader implemented that many measures in so many different government areas; this was a testimony to his strong Change Orientation.

Caesar's way of Energising followers was to show no hard feelings towards adversaries and by conferring individual rewards in the form of promotions and jobs. Notably, he did not rely as much on actively using his vision of stability, peace and prosperity to inspire others. Communication was a critical success factor in getting changes implemented; he continued his 'embedded journalism' practice, which served him well during the Gallic War. He wrote a similar journal, intended for the stakeholders back home, during the civil war. However, this time, he had help from ghost writers. This proved an opportunity to highlight his achievements and explain his decisions and motives. For the rest, he had to rely on letters and intermediaries while on the road. As with today's email messages, this proved challenging. Even Cicero, who knew Caesar well, didn't know how to interpret Caesar's messages. Following the letter, mentioned earlier, in which Caesar asked for Cicero's advice, the latter asked several people, friends and Caesar's emissaries, what this was supposed to mean. In the end, he wrote to Caesar directly for clarification, but we do not have a record of Caesar's answer.

As a propagandist, Caesar had no equal. His triumphs—victory parades—were lavish and a tribute to his successes as a general. He decorated Rome with statues, temples and public buildings. He also erected a statue of Cleopatra. In Egypt, he and Cleopatra went on a 'road show on the Nile' to publicly display Cleopatra's newfound authority. Shortly before his death, after being nominated dictator for an unlimited time period, he became the first living Roman magistrate to have his portrait imprinted on a coin.

6.3.4 Leading Stakeholders and Networks

Any senior leader's challenge is to turn stakeholders into followers. Caesar managed that well regarding Rome's citizens in the way he responded to their needs. The same goes for the business elite, active in the private sector as traders, builders, tax collectors and suppliers to the Roman state and military. Caesar invested in infrastructure, provided stability in the provinces, maintained an army that required supplies and reformed credit flow and taxation. All of these provided plenty of business opportunity.

Caesar's relationships with states outside Italy, positioned at the fringe of the Roman empire, were as follows. From four kings, those in Africa (Bocchus), near Asia (Antipater and Mithridates) and Egypt (Cleopatra), he received active military support during the civil war. In return, they were rewarded and, as such, they continued their partnership with Rome. Three other kings in the same regions (Juba, Pharnaces and Ptolemy) turned against Caesar and were defeated. Shortly before his death, Caesar was busy making plans to start a war with Parthia in the Middle East. For the other borders of the empire, things were stable.

6.4 The End of a Career

In this book, we have reviewed the different stages of Caesar's rise to power. Now, we will examine how he fell from power. Before doing so, to be consistent, reviewing Caesar's brand and reputation is in order, as well as taking a final look through the lens of the leadership pipeline.

Leading an army into Rome to take power and becoming a dictator makes the comparison with Sulla obvious. Caesar was quite aware of the similarity and did his best to differentiate himself. In fact, he expressed this distinction between Sulla and himself repeatedly to his followers and stakeholders. He worked on his leadership brand, consistently emphasising leniency, generosity and delivering on promises as its main features. He held speeches before the Senate and the People whenever he was in Rome. While absent, he continued to use his practice of 'embedded journalism', which had served him so well during the war in Gaul. In March 49, he wrote a letter to his close collaborators, Balbus and Oppius, who forwarded a copy to Cicero so the letter could be widely spread among the Pompeiians and those anxiously staying behind in Italy. Referring to the bloodless takeover of the Pompeian army at Corfinium, Caesar writes that he wants to continue to act with leniency and work towards reconciliation with Pompey. In this way, he hoped to regain the goodwill of all and a lasting victory. Past Roman leaders had failed to maintain power by suppressing resistance through violence. The exception was Sulla, whom Caesar claimed explicitly that does not intend to imitate. Then Caesar says: 'Let this be a new way of winning, defending ourselves with mercy and generosity'(Cic. *Att.* 9.7C, authors' translation). Later, Caesar told the Romans that he had destroyed enemy generals' captured correspondence, which he left unread. Finally, he ordered the images and statues of his opponents (e.g. Pompey) to be put back in public spaces.

Back from Africa in 46 and believing the war over, Caesar thought he could now fully dedicate himself to governing. Caesar therefore decided that it was time to explain his motives and how he wished to exercise leadership. At that moment, Caesar addressed first the Senate and then the People (Dio Cassius recounts the speeches). Caesar proclaimed that contrary to Cinna, Marius and Sulla, 'I shall not be your despot, but your protector, not your tyrant but your leader' (43.17.2. Translation Loeb). His consistent behaviour of pardon and clemency towards former enemies should bear witness to that. Continuing, he says that he realises that with great power and fortune comes great responsibility, namely, to confer benefits on the people and use one's gifts and qualities wisely and with moderation. Only then can a leader gain trust and goodwill. He urges them to let bygones be bygones and start from scratch. What's more, Caesar—never short of a metaphor—describes the ideal relationship of a leader to his followers as being like a father towards his children. In this case, the senators and the citizens were his children. It is unlikely that the latter went down very well in the Senate. The senators could easily interpret it as disempowering the very institution that was supposed to act as a supervisory board. Among the People, however, Caesar succeeded in retaining a solid brand, authentic to his stance as a *popularis*.

Caesar was quite concerned about his public image (*existimatio*) and reputation (*dignitas*), both as a person and as a leader. At the beginning of the civil war, he asked his soldiers to protect both. Everyone in Rome thought highly of Caesar's ability to achieve results, although, regarding developing people, the perception was mixed among his direct followers. Even if Caesar was forgiving and extended career opportunities to former enemies, a sense of disempowerment, loss of social position and unfair treatment banded a group of individuals together to eliminate the leader. The picture differed for the people of Rome and the business community, not to mention Caesar's veterans and soldiers, for whom results were the most important thing. In their view, Caesar had delivered by creating jobs through construction projects, securing the food supply, organising games and festivities, distributing land, offering opportunities for those willing to emigrate to a new colony, stabilising the economy and expanding the empire. Baffled at first by the treacherous murder of Rome's dictator, citizens soon showed their disapproval of the act. In the events that followed, it became apparent that Caesar was immensely popular with the average Roman. This was the main reason the assassins had to flee Rome to save their skin.

So, how did Caesar master the sixth and final leadership passage to Enterprise Manager (Fig. 6.5)? From the perspective of the Leadership Pipeline, Caesar met four out of the five challenges: (1) he delivered results that ensured peace and reformed the state; (2) he developed a vision and set a clear direction; (3) his execution was fast and effective and aligned with his strategy; and (4) he looked at the empire as one entity. The one challenge he needed help with was the human side of the business, the Emotional Intelligence factor. This involves wielding power carefully. Although at this level, the leader's position of power is almost absolute, it is vital that one gets things done by commitment rather than mere compliance. In Caesar's case, this was all the more relevant since, as a dictator, he combined the roles of Chairman and CEO, to compare the Republic to a corporation. Caesar did reach out to the different groups and stakeholders who constituted the Republic to join him in his vision. At the same time, however, success depends on continual feedback so leaders can develop and adapt to overcome resistance. As a dictator, Caesar was more than an enterprise manager because even the Senate—his supervisory board whose advice he avowed to value—reported to him. In that context, he could only receive feedback from below. No other kind of feedback is more challenging to get.

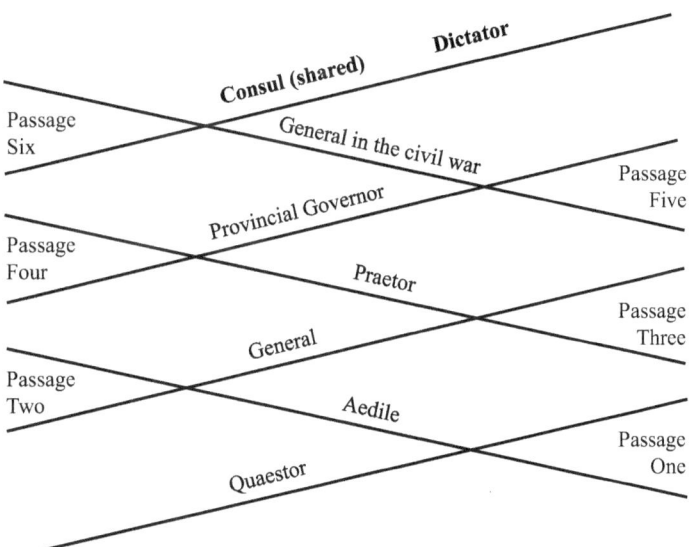

Fig. 6.5 Julius Caesar's final career passages in the Roman career system. Author's adaptation. Based on Charan, Drotter, Noel 2001

How could Caesar have prevented being stabbed in the back? Feelings of dissatisfaction with Caesar's leadership and concern for the future would have been present among a larger group within the Republic's upper echelons than the actual perpetrators and their personal gripes. As seen before, Caesar's skill at winning collective hearts and minds with a compelling and inspiring view of the future needed improvement. His communication was balanced towards listing his achievements rather than painting a positive picture of the future. His *Commentaries on the Civil War* recount results, mostly military ones, not plans or projects. In his speeches, he tended to refer to his outcomes as well. Thus, Caesar thought that his accomplishments and his decision-making would speak for themselves and that his past performance would predict future performance. (He did have a point, though: all of his decisions remained in force after his removal from office, some for centuries to come.)

Caesar towered over any other member of the elite. At the latest after the four triumphs he had celebrated in a row, he had become famous; everywhere he went he was recognised. Caesar felt comfortable in his situation. It is what he had always wanted: to merit a special status thanks to his achievements. Not as a king, but first among equals. Nevertheless, he was conscious of the fears that his power and influence could generate because of recent precedents of leaders who had abused both. He did once publicly refuse a crown that Marc Antony tried to place upon his head. Caesar told the Senate and the popular assembly that he had no intent of abusing power, but that was about all he said about his future plans. In the speech, mentioned earlier, that was given before the Senate in 46, he did explicitly say that he would be neither a despot nor a tyrant. It would have been helpful to have said it more often. Equally, he should have given an indication how long he intended to rule. He did call upon the Senate to draw a line under the past and start from scratch and work together. According to Dio, Caesar was thus able to shift their attitudes from apprehension to wait-and-see, but not much more.

To the delight of many a grammar school student, Caesar's language was clear and succinct. Therefore, for Caesar, his 'order in Italy, peace in the provinces and prosperity for the empire' did indeed encompass his whole vision. To him, what that meant must have been obvious. To his followers and his adversaries alike, less so. He rendered it difficult for them to grasp what would be in it for them. It would have helped if Caesar had expounded upon what he meant, particularly about the why and what would be the benefits for those who would follow him in his plan. Furthermore, he should have checked in with his audience to see whether they understood his message in the way he had intended.

Finally, of the twenty known assassins (Fig. 6.6), only a few had any expatriate experience and could have seen, like Caesar, that the Republic's future

Fig. 6.6 The assassination of Julius Caesar on the Ides of March 44 BC. Mural painting by William Holmes Sullivan (1836–1908), Royal Shakespeare Company Theatre, Stratford-upon-Avon. RSC Theatre Collection, image reference 11094. Reprinted under licence

lay beyond Rome. Some had participated in overseas campaigns as military officers. Only two, Brutus and Trebonius, had real government experience in a province. Trebonius, as we have seen, was removed from the job by Caesar and found it easier to blame Caesar than his own incompetence. What's more, Caesar failed to include the assassins and other dissatisfied or concerned members of the elite in his vision of empire. Without a convincing message from Caesar about what opportunities this vision could offer, an essential fringe of the elite could only envision what they stood to lose.

6.5 What Top Leaders Can Learn from the Final Chapter of Caesar's Career

Let there be no doubt: Caesar's achievements as a leader are overwhelming. He developed a clear vision and set out to implement it in the 5 years he headed the Roman Republic. Moreover, he did so while combining two huge jobs: commanding armies in a war that took place throughout the empire and governing a state that needed to be rebuilt after a civil war. Caesar was all over the place and, importantly, he was successful at both jobs. Any person with only a little less energy and of less quality would indeed have failed. It is all the more tragic that his career was cut short, a reality which merits some final reflections.

On the upside, as his position at the Republic's summit demanded, Caesar proved he could develop and implement a long-term vision. What's more, his vision drew on what he had learned during his career and benefited from input from followers and thought leaders. He laid the groundwork for his successor, who could construct an organisation (the Roman Empire), which endured for another 500 years and, in the form of Byzantium, another 1000 years after that. It is a tribute to the soundness of Caesar's vision. Caesar was a values-driven leader, a pillar of his strong leadership brand. His inclusiveness of diverse talent and ability to identify high potential people reinforced the leadership bench strength of the Republic.

Caesar's mixed results in delegation and his passive approach to leadership development contributed to the growing dissatisfaction among certain members of the elite. He put too much trust in the system, believing that his career path—self-development within the *cursus honorum*—would work equally well for other talented individuals. Caesar received only some of feedback he badly needed to improve his leadership on the job and pick up signals of disloyalty. Overusing his strengths—swift decision-making, drive towards execution, perseverance—led him to steamroll an influential fringe of his stakeholders and followers. Caesar had to rebuild the organisation designed to mobilise followers that had served him so well as consul and while he was in Gaul, and it took a while for it to become effective. Things improved, notably concerning the People, when Lepidus was placed in charge in Rome and when Caesar spent more time in the city. Caesar underestimated the importance of extending this organisation to win over the Senate, who never really became his enthusiastic followers. Tragically, Caesar remained unaware of what was going on below the surface and did not address fears, resistance and discontent.

The relationship between strengths and development needs changes once a leader arrives at the summit. Caesar had truly reached the pinnacle; arguably, there was no bigger or more prestigious job to hold in the Mediterranean world at the time. Whereas strengths are the motor for career progression, once at the top, a strength can, in some cases, and such was Caesar's, turn into a disadvantage. At the apex of an organisation, exerting leadership behaviours at the 'competent level' is enough. Otherwise, strengths risk being overused. Caesar overused his strengths to the extent that his development need in Emotional Intelligence deteriorated into a critical weakness. Blinded by success and unaware of the intangible, Caesar persisted in his action bias and did not adapt in time.

Julius Caesar did not revolutionise, at least not on purpose. Rather, he accelerated, which resulted in a revolution. He set in motion change processes that were not only all-encompassing but also incredibly fast. Before the establishment realised what was happening, a city-state run by an oligarchy had morphed into an empire-state run by a single, all-powerful leader supported by a professional army and civil service. It is not what Caesar had intended, but it is what he was remembered for. All his successors—the Roman emperors—called themselves 'Caesar'. Ultimately, his name became a synonym for the highest form of monarchy in the German (Kaiser) and Russian (Czar) languages.

Bibliography

Greek and Roman Sources

Appian, *Roman History. The Civil Wars*, Book I-II.
Caesar, G.J., *Commentaries on the the Civil War, the Alexandrian War, the African War and the Spanish War.*
Cicero, M. T., *Letters to Atticus; Letters to His Friends; Orations.*
Dio, L. C., *Roman History*. Book 41-45.
Nicolaus of Damascus, *Life of August.*
Plutarch, *Lives of Antony, Brutus, Cato the Younger, Caesar, Pompey.*
Sallustius Crispus, G., *Letters to Caesar.*
Suetonius Tranquillus, G., *Life of Julius Caesar, Life of Augustus.*

Modern Works

Badian, E. (1983). *Publicans and Sinners: Private enterprise in the service of the roman republic*. Cornell University Press.
Benferhat, Y. (2017). Des hommes à tout faire dans l'entourage de César. *Dialogues d'histoire ancienne. Supplément, 17, Conseillers et ambassadeurs dans l'Antiquité* (pp. 373–385).
Charan, R., Drotter, S., & Noel, J. (2001). *The Leadership Pipeline. How to build the leadership powered company*. Jossey-Bass.
Connelly, B. S., & McAbee, S. T. (2024). Reputations at work: Origins and outcomes of shared person perceptions. *Annual Review of Organizational Psychology and Organizational Behavior, 11*(1), 251–278.
Crook, J. A., Lintott, A., Rawson, E. (Eds.) (1994). *The Cambridge ancient history* (2nd Edn, Volume IX). The last age of the Roman Republic, 146-43 B.C. Cambridge University Press.

Drogula, F. K. (2019). *Cato the younger. Life and death at the end of the Roman Republic*. Oxford University Press.

Epstein, D. F. (1987). Caesar's personal enemies on the ides of March. *Latomus*, 46(3), 566–570.

Ferrary, J.-L. (2017). *Le nouveau fragment des fastes de Privernum et le projet césarien d'organisation des pouvoirs en Occident à la veille de la guerre contre les Parthes, Comptes-rendus des séances de l année - Académie des inscriptions et belles-lettres*, 161e année, N. 4, 1561-1581.

Gelzer, M. (2008). *Caesar. Der Politiker und Staatsmann*. Franz Steiner Verlag.

Goldsmith, M. (2013). *What got you here won't get you there. How successful people become even more successful*. Profile Books.

Griffin, M. (Ed.). (2009). *A companion to Julius Caesar*. Wiley-Blackwell.

Gruen, E. S. (1995). *The last generation of the Roman Republic*. University of California Press.

Hölkeskamp, K.-J. (Ed.). (2009). *Eine politische Kultur (in) der Krise? Die "letzte Generation" der römischen Republik*. De Gruyter.

Hölkeskamp, K.-J. (2010). *Reconstructing the Roman Republic: An ancient political culture and modern research*. Princeton University Press.

KDVI, https://kdvi.com/tools/

Meier, C. (1997). *Caesar*. DTV.

Morstein-Marx, R. (2021). *Julius Caesar and the Roman people*. Cambridge University Press.

Morstein-Marx, R. (Accepted/In press). Paper on the *Privernum fasti*. In: Matijevic, K., Raja, R., Rupke, J. (Eds.), *Caesar's Visions and Impact on the Roman Empire: Revisiting the Archaeological and Historical Record for the 40s BC*, Turnhout: Brepols Publishers.

Pauli, A. F. (1958). Letters of Caesar and Cicero to each other. *The Classical World*, 51(5 (Feb)), 128–132.

Pina Polo, F. (2011). *The consul at Rome: The civil functions of the consuls in the Roman Republic*. Cambridge University Press.

Richardson, J. S. (1996). *The Romans in Spain*. Blackwell.

See, K. E., Morrison, E. W., Rothman, N. B., & Soll, J. B. (2011). The detrimental effects of power on confidence, advice taking, and accuracy. *Organizational Behavior and Human Decision Processes, 116*, 272–285.

Strassler, R. B., Raaflaub, K. A. (Eds) (2018). *The landmark Julius Caesar*. Webessays. www.landmarkcaesar.com, accessed 26/01/2023. Pantheon Books.

Syme, R. (1939). *The Roman revolution*. Oxford University Press.

Vanderbroeck, P. (2012). Crises: Ancient and modern. Understanding an ancient Roman crisis can help us move beyond our own. *Management and Organizational History, 7*(2), 113–131.

Vanderbroeck, P. (2014). *Leadership strategies for women: Lessons from four queens on leadership and career development*. Springer.

Yavetz, Z. (1983). *Julius Caesar and his public image*. Cornell University Press.

7

Becoming a Leader: Caesar's Leadership Development

Caesar's leadership evolved significantly over his career, demonstrating his growth from a determined young leader to a complex figure at the pinnacle of power. This chapter reviews how Caesar's leadership developed over time with the help of the Global Executive Leadership Mirror (GELM®) framework. Figure 7.1 and the overview below detail how Caesar's leadership behaviours evolved throughout his career and summarise the previous chapters' evaluations. The chapter ends by reflecting on what contributed to and hindered this development.

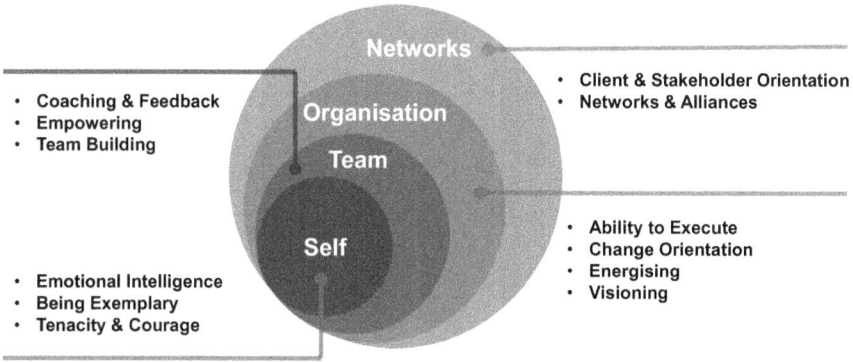

Fig. 7.1 The twelve key leadership behaviours. © KDVI. Reprinted with permission by KDVI

© The Author(s), under exclusive license to Springer Nature Switzerland AG 2025
P. Vanderbroeck, *Lead Like Julius Caesar*, https://doi.org/10.1007/978-3-031-83224-6_7

7.1 Leading Self

7.1.1 Emotional Intelligence

Early and mid-career, Caesar was competent enough in Emotional Intelligence not to be held back. He sometimes used it effectively, and sometimes he didn't. Caesar's typical pattern, that is, displaying strong Emotional Intelligence towards individuals but less so towards elite groups, was already noticeable during the first half of his career. By the time Caesar reached the senior management level of the Republic, the praetorship, he realised he needed to find a way to influence the senatorial majority to progress professionally. As a praetor, he had little success in getting the bills of his political allies accepted, and just before, he had suffered defeat in the debate over the Catilinarian conspirators. When he became consul, the need to win over the Senate collectively became critical. Caesar thus developed a strategy to compensate for his weakness by establishing an organisation to mobilise followers. While in Gaul, he continued to employ this approach effectively vis-à-vis politics in Rome with the help of his allies in Rome, notably Clodius, Crassus, Pompey and Cicero. However, Caesar did not take a similar approach to influence the tribes and their leaders in Gaul. He failed to anticipate the great revolt, which he overcame with incredible difficulty.

Having lost his influencing organisation in Rome and with his level of Emotional Intelligence needing development, he failed to fully grasp the mood among both his followers and the senators in Rome. Civil war seemed the only option for Caesar to resolve his differences with the senatorial majority. Towards the end of this conflict, Caesar again failed to sense the psychological undercurrent in a large group, this time in Spain; this was another setback that almost cost him his victory in the entire war. The third time around resulted in the Ides of March because he had failed to sufficiently develop Emotional Intelligence when it came to elite groups or to rebuild his influencing organisation in Rome. A case in point was when someone had to tap Caesar on his shoulder to become aware of the huge procession of dignitaries who had arrived to honour him. Emotional Intelligence, therefore, was the one skill that Caesar had the most difficulty mastering. At the height of his power, it had truly become a critical weakness.

7.1.2 Being Exemplary

Strong values, notably clemency, marked Caesar's early career. He consistently applied this value to his adversaries throughout his professional life, even in the face of political and operational challenges. He was loyal to his political and family ties. He developed a political philosophy based on executive leaders serving the interests of the People. He expended much effort to deliver on his promises. Being Exemplary was a strength during all of Caesar's career. He acted in line with his values, even at the cost of negative consequences for him or his interests. Such fortitude made Caesar stand out as an authentic leader and significantly contributed to his brand as a leader.

7.1.3 Tenacity and Courage

From the outset, Caesar exhibited great courage on the battlefield and in asserting himself towards powerful people. His propensity for risk became a landmark of his leadership style. Tenaciously focused on success, he marked his career by ensuring that each setback was overcome by an extraordinary achievement that soon followed. His career ended while he was relentlessly pursuing his post-war vision for the Republic and the empire. Caesar's tenacity and attachment to his values were so strong that they created an uncompromising attitude. A little more flexibility would have helped him, in particular and essential instances, choose a less risky course of action. Two notable examples are when he stood up to Sulla, Caesar then being a young man, and before he crossed the Rubicon as a senior leader. But then again, risk was never a reason for Caesar to diverge from his path – quite the opposite.

7.2 Leading Teams

7.2.1 Coaching and Feedback

Coaching and Feedback was Caesar's second weakest skillset after Emotional Intelligence. Having to supervise his staff often from a distance made it challenging to display this capability at the required level, most notably as a general during the civil war. Consequently, specific individuals had not received what they needed in order to be up to the task Caesar had delegated to them. Regardless, Caesar could have more actively developed people reporting to him instead of leaving most of it to the career system of the *cursus honorum*.

At the end of his career, when he had the opportunity to have face time with those working for and alongside him, he successfully developed the high potential of both Cleopatra and Octavian-Augustus.

Regarding his own professional and personal development, Caesar was open to feedback from peers and subordinates. Yet, it often reached him filtered through people in his entourage. The advice he received was biased towards his actions; he thus missed getting feedback regarding his behaviour. As his power and confidence grew, he received less and less spontaneous feedback, and he seemed to be unaware that he had to actively seek it, particularly from people less powerful than himself. Sometimes, he reacted defensively to feedback, which did not help invite future feedback. Caesar seemed unaware that a leader needs to interpret advice skilfully and consider the feedback-giver's potential self-interest.

7.2.2 Empowering

Upon receiving a position with formal authority, Caesar immediately set out to empower others. This approach significantly contributed to his success, both as a magistrate and as a military leader in Gaul. During his long absence, he worked with peers and intermediaries to look after his interests in Rome. He also delegated specialist tasks to professionals working for him, which allowed him to manage the complexity of these responsibilities at a senior level. In battle, he occasionally entered the fray, sword in hand, not to micro-manage but to turn a critical situation around when his presence was needed. While his empowerment strategy was less effective during the civil war, it was still commendable. Caesar was generally tolerant of mistakes and failures, which reassured his team. However, his preference for prompt action sometimes made him impatient with others. This impatience, particularly as a dictator, when he wanted to effect changes as soon as possible, generated a cycle of empowerment and disempowerment that was frustrating for all concerned.

7.2.3 Team Building

During the middle stage of his career, when Caesar started and completed the *cursus honorum*, he had the opportunity to demonstrate his competencies in leading teams, and he developed his skills over time. By the time he was consul, he proved effective in bringing together the right people with the right skills and empowering them to adopt different roles in an organisation designed to mobilise followers. Furthermore, Caesar demonstrated a particular eye and appreciation for diversity. Harvesting talent from layers just below the elite and new citizens became a distinguishing feature of his leadership. Being open to diverse talent and capabilities gave Caesar an edge over his opponents and competitors for the rest of his career. For example, Caesar started his career after Pompey and on the wrong side of Sulla. By the year 50, just before the final showdown, Caesar had matched Pompey's achievements. Meanwhile, such followers, thanking their career opportunities to Caesar, saw their interests as best served if their leader stayed in power; it was they who pushed Caesar into taking an uncompromising attitude and ultimately crossing the Rubicon. When the civil war started, Caesar was missing several vital supporters in Rome and officers of his army, who had either recently left or died. He had to replace them with more junior and less talented individuals. During his final years, he was in the process of rebuilding a solid team of talented individuals.

7.3 Leading the Organisation

7.3.1 Ability to Execute

Caesar's results orientation and particularly his speed of execution were his strengths throughout his entire career. Mainly, he achieved a lot when in a position of complete and autonomous authority, namely as a general or a dictator. Skilful management was more difficult for him when he had to work with or through others, such as the Senate. He was more effective in securing agreement in the popular assembly. As a top achiever, Caesar believed that strong executive leadership was the most suited to achieving lasting progress.

7.3.2 Change Orientation

Caesar was not someone to be held back by boundaries to achieve change, often pushing and sometimes defying limits. Trusting his strong performance and luck, he tended to ask for forgiveness rather than permission from his superiors. He reaped laurels thanks to his propensity for risk-taking, including with his own life; he brought about change through his military strategy, legislation and state restructuring; he was notably innovative in his communication and propaganda for his cause; and he leveraged speeches, images, buildings, public shows and his writings and correspondence to significant effect. As for government transparency, he favoured it greatly. Overall, Change Orientation was a strength throughout his career.

7.3.3 Energising

Regarding Energising followers, Caesar climbed the ranks of the public career ladder by winning over the constituencies he needed to get elected. He motivated influential individuals to fund and endorse him. Caesar also successfully created a followership by offering tangible benefits that responded to concrete needs and the customary expectations for people of his standing. As a general at war, motivating troops was critical, particularly after a setback or when faced with demotivated soldiers. Furthermore, Caesar employed a compelling mixture of positive and negative feedback, reward and retribution, rational arguments and emotional appeals, clear expectations and confidence building. He demonstrated care, including for his staff's careers, and stuck to his commitments. Another way he energised those around him was by showing empathy and giving people a second chance. Energising followers was a strength of Caesar's during most of his career. Nevertheless, during his final years as a dictator, creating the same enthusiasm in the Senate for his leadership as he did with the People proved challenging. Because of a lack in Emotional Intelligence, he did not find a way to gain the buy-in of the entire Senate.

7.3.4 Visioning

Caesar displayed a long-term perspective in his proposals and bills as a senator and a magistrate. Sustainability was foremost in his mind when he proposed changes in Rome and throughout the empire. As a military leader, he developed and implemented strategies successfully by seeking opportunities, pushing boundaries and using the element of surprise. Caesar's vision for the post-civil-war Republic was indeed forward-looking. It considered recent major trends and developments in both Rome and the empire. His ideas covered political reform, organisational restructuring, economic stimulus, infrastructure, demographic measures and governance. He deftly translated this vision into strategies that created a long-lasting and positive impact on the Roman state. Caesar's Visioning was particularly strong when he was leading from a position as a public magistrate, notably as consul and dictator.

7.4 Leading Stakeholders and Networks

7.4.1 Clients and Stakeholders

From the early days of his career onwards, Caesar developed a positive relationship with the citizens of Rome's lower orders. These stakeholders determined the outcome of votes in the popular assembly on bills and the elections of junior magistrates. Politically, Caesar followed the path of his father's and his mother's families to serve the interests of the People. This group of citizens included the *equites*, the demographic socially below the senators and often wealthy business owners whose votes counted particularly weightily in elections for senior public offices. Every time Caesar held public office, he took decisive action or passed bills that served his stakeholders. What is more, he consistently delivered on his promises. His emphasis on communication via many means (writings, images, buildings and showcasing himself) and his innovative methods helped him build effective relationships. The closer Caesar progressed to the apex of the Republic, the more vital the Senate as a stakeholder became. However, it did prove challenging for Caesar to bring the Senate's senior and most influential members to his side.

7.4.2 Networks and Alliances

Caesar was an effective networker. He first leveraged his family contacts to protect him from Sulla's purges and to restore him to the establishment. Next, he started building his own relationships with essential individuals to support his political career. Making himself known as a person ready for leadership also gave him the visibility and notoriety needed to launch his career. While away in Gaul, he maintained his network through correspondence, giving gifts and inviting visitors to his winter quarters in northern Italy. Moreover, Caesar's alliance with Crassus and Pompey helped him reach the top and maintain a position of influence. This alliance, however, disintegrated after Crassus died and Caesar's fall-out with Pompey shortly thereafter. Finally, Caesar had to start the civil war with few top-tier allies. Although alone at the top in Rome, he nonetheless built positive relationships with some neighbouring kingdoms but found himself needing to fight against others.

7.5 How Did Caesar's Leadership Develop over Time?

As a young adult, Caesar showed that, in the words of leadership scholar Morgan McCall, he was a 'high flyer' gifted with the innate raw talent that, with the appropriate development, can be turned into the 'right stuff' that makes a successful leader.

In his early career and before taking on a formal leadership position, Caesar seized opportunities to put himself through the right experiences that would grow this talent into leadership skills and behaviours. These experiences involved taking up challenging assignments, overcoming hardships and learning from others. Learning from experience was critical for his leadership development. With his mother, Aurelia, in the driving seat, Caesar's family gave him a support network that permitted him to take risks and gain experiences. He therefore started the *cursus honorum* with a series of strengths, which propelled him to the consulate without delay in his thirties. He then used such experience to develop his competencies to a high level so that his 9 years in Gaul could be marked by great success. However, the two jobs he had to combine during the civil war proved more challenging. As a military leader, he failed to develop three essential behaviours (Emotional Intelligence, Coaching and Feedback, Networks and Alliances) to the required level. However, he had enough qualities to win in the end. In his role as dictator, he again managed to develop all behaviours and capabilities except one to at least the level of 'competent', which, as discussed at the end of the previous chapter, is quite enough once having reached the very top.

As recalled above, Caesar compensated for his weakness in Emotional Intelligence when he was consul by establishing an influencing organisation rather than improving this behaviour. For us, it is essential to recognise how he managed to achieve this by leveraging strengths, notably Team Building, Empowerment and Change Orientation. When Caesar lost his key allies who had helped him keep this organisation working smoothly while he was away, this compensation approach came to an end. Rather than develop his weaker behaviour, in this case his Emotional Intelligence, Caesar again relied on his strengths to compensate. To win the civil war, he notably deployed Tenacity and Courage, the Ability to Execute, Change Orientation and Energy.

Come to think of it, Caesar, next to leveraging strengths to compensate for weaknesses in a given situation, sometimes—consciously or unconsciously—shifted the circumstances to put him in a position where he could use his strengths. For example, he aimed for a win-lose outcome when negotiating with Ariovistus in Gaul. Getting to a win-win would have required Emotional Intelligence. In contrast, a win-lose would inevitably lead to armed conflict unless Ariovistus backed down. Since the latter had no intention to do so, Caesar could confidently bring his strengths to bear in the ensuing battle. By the same token, Caesar perhaps felt or knew that choosing an alternative course of action when his dealings with the Senate did not go his way would put him in a position of strength. Thinking that breaking off the discussions could change the situation in his favour may have enhanced his impatience. Despite the risk it always went well for Caesar, until that fateful month of March in 44, when he was so eager to start his war against Parthia that he was prepared to leave many things unfinished in Rome.

Receiving and interpreting feedback were the most important factors hindering Caesar's leadership development. He was not always proactive in inviting feedback, and he was unaware that his direct reports and less powerful individuals hesitated to offer advice. This was not only due to the difficulty of speaking truth to power but also because others perceived Caesar as not needing feedback. Caesar was oblivious to the importance of interpreting feedback and not taking it at face value. Interestingly, his emphasis on honouring his commitments blinded him to the self-interest embedded in the advice he received from his followers.

After having reviewed what Caesar did and how constructive that was—his behaviour—the final chapter will shed light on why he did it—his personality.

Bibliography

Greek and Roman Sources

Plutarch, *Life of Caesar*.
Suetonius Tranquillus, G., *Life of Julius Caesar*.

Modern Works

Guillén, L., & Florent-Treacy, E. (2011). Emotional intelligence and leadership effectiveness: The mediating influence of collaborative behaviors. *INSEAD Working Papers Collection, 23*, 1–28.
KDVI. https://kdvi.com/tools/
Kets de Vries, M. F. R., Vrignaud, P., & Florent-Treacy, E. (2004). The Global Leadership Life Inventory: Development and psychometric properties of a

360-degree feedback instrument. *International Journal of Human Resource Management, 15*(3 May), 475–492.

McCall, M. W., Jr. (1998). *High flyers. Developing the next generation of leaders.* Harvard University Press.

Morstein-Marx, R. (2021). *Julius Caesar and the Roman people.* Cambridge University Press.

See, K. E., Morrison, E. W., Rothman, N. B., & Soll, J. B. (2011). The detrimental effects of power on confidence, advice taking, and accuracy. *Organizational Behavior and Human Decision Processes, 116*, 272–285.

Vanderbroeck, P. (2012). Crises: Ancient and modern. Understanding an ancient Roman crisis can help us move beyond our own. *Management and Organizational History, 7*(2), 113–131.

8

Being a Leader: Caesar's Leadership Personality

To understand what motivated Caesar to do what he did as a leader, this chapter examines his motivational preferences. The Individual Directions Inventory™ (IDI™), developed by Management Research Group® (MRG®), the US-based publisher of psychometric assessments, will be used for this purpose. As an executive coach, I frequently use the IDI™. It is a powerful instrument for understanding what drives a leader to adopt certain behaviours and make particular choices. But first, an important caveat: what happens in this chapter is reverse engineering. It's likely to make leadership professionals cringe. As the author of this book and a leadership professional myself, I apologise in advance to my respected colleagues. The appropriate way of working with internal preferences in leadership development is to identify a person's motivations directly from that individual, for example, through a questionnaire like the IDI™. A leadership development professional then compares the results to the person's actual behaviour to ascertain to what extent their actions match their stated preferences. These insights can then lead to development objectives that help the person adjust their conduct where necessary to enact behaviours more conducive to the results they aspire to achieve as a leader.

Since we cannot question Caesar anymore, here, by way of experiment, we will reverse the process by starting with his behaviour to get a sense of his motivation as a leader. The more pronounced preferences are, and the less self-aware a leader is, the more a leader's behaviour is influenced by these underlying motivational preferences. Hence, this attempt at gauging what went on inside Caesar's brain starts with the assumption that his most typical and consistent behaviour will most likely reveal his inner motivations. Personality, and particularly preferences and motivations, can make or break a leader's career. Awareness of one's personality and how motivational preferences may affect one's behaviour are as critical to leadership development as competencies. Hence, a book that allows leaders to learn from Julius Caesar as a case study must include an analysis of what lies below the surface of behaviour.

The IDI™ provides 17 Directions organised into five clusters. The Directions indicate the actions an individual is drawn to take because they give emotional satisfaction. Simultaneously, they reveal what an individual avoids because it causes emotional dissatisfaction. Because humans tend to pursue what gives them energy and evade what they dislike, these Directions can affect individual behaviour. In such cases, a person may behave more or less in line with the Directions, depending on the situation. The more pronounced, or if you will, extreme, Directions are the more interesting because they tend to influence a person's behaviour the most. Less pronounced scores indicate that one's conduct is influenced by both the Direction and the context. In such cases, the individual may act either more in line with the Direction or less, depending on the circumstance. Strong orientations can result in leaders overdoing certain behaviours to the point of becoming ineffective. Furthermore, it may lead to avoiding too much emotionally unrewarding behaviour, even if it is the helpful or most strategic option. All this is because of the very human tendency to try to maximise emotional highs and minimise emotional lows. Self-observation and feedback can help leaders become aware of and prevent themselves from either over- or underdoing certain behaviours. In this way, leaders develop more effective behaviour.

The IDI™ gives precise scores from 5% to 99%, distributed over a five-point scale and ranging from Low to High. Not having such precision regarding Julius Caesar—for obvious reasons—the following personality profile uses a three-point scale only: Low, Mid-Range and High. The subsequent analysis concentrates on the Low and High scores, the most likely to explain behaviour. Definitions of the Directions together with an explication of Caesar's scores follow Table 8.1. Next, the assessment is taken further by evaluating how the interaction between extreme scores could have also affected his behaviour.

Table 8.1 Julius Caesar's motivational profile. Author's adaptation: Based on MRG®'s IDI™

Julius Caesar's Motivational Profile

Affiliating		LOW	MID-RANGE	HIGH
	Giving			●
	Receiving	●		
	Belonging		●	
	Expressing	●		

Attracting		LOW	MID-RANGE	HIGH
	Gaining Stature			●
	Entertaining		●	

Perceiving		LOW	MID-RANGE	HIGH
	Creating			●
	Interpreting		●	

Mastering		LOW	MID-RANGE	HIGH
	Excelling			●
	Enduring			●
	Structuring		●	

Challenging		LOW	MID-RANGE	HIGH
	Manoeuvring			●
	Winning			●
	Controlling			●

Maintaining		LOW	MID-RANGE	HIGH
	Stability		●	
	Independence			●
	Irreproachability			●

8.1 Affiliating

The first cluster, Affiliating, has four Directions, which indicate if and how a person gains satisfaction through having and building close connections with others.

8.1.1 Giving

Giving is about gaining satisfaction from relating to others by providing them with support, affection and empathy. Although Caesar's Giving always contained a component of 'tit-for-tat', compared to his peers he was generous towards his followers, notably his army and the plebs in Rome. Moreover, individuals could count on him for financial and other support. Amidst the war in Gaul, he willingly let capable officers return to Rome to take advantage of career opportunities in the *cursus honorum*. His clemency towards adversaries and enemies was not only a matter of values but also likely to have given him an emotional reward in the Direction of Giving. Based on these behaviours, Caesar, therefore, is expected to have scored high on Giving, which means he would have enjoyed supporting and caring for others and being generous with his time, energy and other resources.

8.1.2 Receiving

Receiving is the opposite of giving. It's about gaining satisfaction by receiving others' support, care and empathy. In his profile, Caesar has been scored low on Receiving, suggesting he would have preferred to be self-sufficient and avoid being obligated to others. Caesar thus garners this low score for two main reasons. First, he appears to have felt most comfortable on his own, not having to collaborate with colleagues. Secondly, receiving feedback was one of his greatest development needs, as discussed in the previous chapter.

8.1.3 Belonging

Belonging is about gaining satisfaction by participating in a group and cultivating connections through loyalty, cooperation and friendship. Caesar seems to have been in the middle of this Direction. On the one hand, he was loyal to his family and friends, and he enjoyed the army's camaraderie. On the other hand, he never pushed the triumvirate towards solidifying into a real team. Additionally, Caesar's collaboration with the Senate was usually a source of frustration. For him, membership in the Senate may have been a means to an end rather than a goal to belong to this illustrious body.

8.1.4 Expressing

Expressing is about gaining satisfaction from connecting with others through direct and spontaneous communication and frankly expressing emotions and needs. Caesar had no trouble communicating in different ways, but he was economical with emotional expression. He was careful and deliberate about to whom, when and why he showed his feelings, for example, in his speeches to his army, the Senate or the popular assembly. His writings, be it his war diaries or letters, also contain little personal emotion. At the cost of connecting with others, Caesar started corresponding with people across the city instead of meeting face-to-face. Not taking the initiative to meet with Pompey in person to avoid civil war also fits this pattern. Caesar did stage public manifestations of mourning for personal losses, which were genuine—but they were hardly spontaneous. Caesar tended to keep his inner life to himself; expressing his feelings may have drained his energy. On balance, Caesar earns a low score for Expressing.

8.2 Attracting

The Directions in the Attracting cluster indicate whether a person gets an emotional reward by attracting others' attention.

8.2.1 Gaining Stature

People who score high on this Direction get satisfaction from being rewarded by others for their competencies and achievements through gaining recognition, status and respect. Caesar definitely would have scored high here. He relished in the—quite literal—laurels he was awarded and the prominence and reputation he obtained in Roman society over time. He thoroughly enjoyed the triumphs he could celebrate. He only forwent his first triumph to safeguard his candidacy for the consulship. Caesar's reasons for crossing the Rubicon were complex, but protecting his honour, his *dignitas*, was among the most important. Caesar found Gaining Stature so rewarding that he failed to see others' hidden agenda behind the many honours they bestowed upon him as a dictator.

8.2.2 Entertaining

Those who test high on this Direction obtain gratification from garnering others' admiration and rising in visibility. They enjoy being the centre of attention and entertaining others. Whereas Caesar took pleasure in giving parties when he was younger, and to the point of living above his means, he did so to build a network. Nor was he known to draw all the attention to himself during such events. It is true that when he organised games and banquets for Rome's city dwellers, he ensured he gained political credit. However, he was only sometimes personally present to reap rewards such as applause. Similarly, later, when presiding over games, he received bad press for dealing with his correspondence rather than basking in the audience's admiration. Caesar therefore earns a middle score here.

8.3 Perceiving

The two Directions in this cluster gauge people's desire to gain fulfilment by using their intellects in a creative and/or rational way.

8.3.1 Creating

A strong Direction towards Creating denotes receiving an emotional reward from being involved in innovative or unconventional pursuits and producing imaginative, original or creative ideas. This was likely how Caesar's mind worked. He was most of all innovative and unconventional in terms of his military strategies, in which he often did the new and unexpected. Moreover, the way he employed technology, logistics and manoeuvring in his campaigns was frequently novel. Whereas the designs and inventions had probably often originated from others, Caesar nevertheless valued and stimulated these approaches and allowed those he oversaw to develop ideas. He introduced innovations through his legislation, his state reforms and his communication. Leveraging diversity in his talent management was also unprecedented.

8.3.2 Interpreting

A strong Direction towards Interpreting connotes receiving an emotional reward from thinking rationally, logically and analytically. Caesar was a quick thinker, using data and logic to make decisions swiftly. Yet he was also drawn to using his intuition, and the risks he took were not always calculated. Therefore, he scored neither high nor low on Interpreting.

8.4 Mastering

Mastering is about how individuals prefer to interact with their environment and obtain results.

8.4.1 Excelling

A high score on Excelling underscores a preference for pursuing the highest levels of achievement in both quality and quantity. Such individuals enjoy constantly challenging themselves to push forward towards ambitious goals. They set high standards for their and others' performance. Caesar desired to be regarded as foremost among his peers. He also relished the meritocratic values of the Roman elite. Maintaining and growing his *dignitas*—honour based on achievement—were therefore prime motivators behind his choices, notably the risky ones. Caesar hated to underperform, indicating a strong orientation towards Excelling. After a setback or not having performed at the highest level, he exerted great energy to quickly erase the memory of this unfortunate experience by subsequently achieving excellence. Moreover, this allowed him to reap again the recognition (Gaining Stature) he equally craved.

8.4.2 Enduring

A high score on Enduring signifies getting satisfaction from reaching goals through persistence, endurance and stamina. Such individuals value demonstrating willpower. In this Direction, we can easily recognise Caesar, who truly never gave up. While marching with this army, he was willing to suffer hardships, even when his health suffered. Retirement and resting on his laurels were far from his mind. Although he was impatient, he did maintain a long-term perspective and had the stamina to push on relentlessly. Opting for a dictatorship of indefinite duration rather than fixed-term is a case in point.

8.4.3 Structuring

People who value organisation, efficiency and attention to detail to gain control over their environment score highly on Structuring. On the one hand, the laws Caesar passed were well-designed and covered several aspects and anticipated many contingencies. This is why many of the statutes stayed in force long after his assassination. Furthermore, his methodical approach to military tactics was vital to his success as a general. On the other hand, Caesar was flexible; he was not taken aback or thwarted when things did not go as planned. Thus, Caesar would find himself in between a high and low score on Structuring.

8.5 Challenging

The objective of Challenging is to acquire an emotional reward from overcoming obstacles by creating opportunities, engaging in competition and/or gaining control.

8.5.1 Manoeuvring

A strong Direction towards Manoeuvring means gaining satisfaction from leveraging opportunities. It includes creating options and being comfortable with risk and change. Clearly, this Direction fits Caesar's personality. A risktaker from an early age, he was always known to push and sometimes cross boundaries. Faced with the choice between standing for election or holding a triumph, for instance, he chose the avenue that was the least certain but gave him the most options.

8.5.2 Winning

When one has a pronounced Direction towards Winning, it reveals a competitive streak. People with high Winning scores tend to turn every interaction into a competition and—more importantly—they want to win. For this Direction, Caesar garners yet another high score. It may also well be the one he was most known for in his time and remains so today. His political career was a succession of must-win battles. Although he was willing to negotiate a peace agreement in the civil war, when he battled foreign enemies, he persisted until victorious. When working with Caesar, people for whom winning was less of a motivator may have perceived him as confrontational and quarrelsome. Caesar's Winning Direction was so extreme that he continued competing with Cato even after Cato had died.

8.5.3 Controlling

A prominent Controlling Direction accompanies those who enjoy being in charge and occupying a position of responsibility. They are comfortable with having power and authority over others. Caesar felt least at ease when he was not in a position of control. He found it challenging to share power, another notable feature of this Direction. This personality trait drove him to pursue a leadership career with a succession of positions of increasing authority. Caesar did delegate tasks, but when an underling did not meet expectations, his first reaction was to take over rather than develop the individual to the required level or find someone else to do the job.

8.6   Maintaining

The Maintaining Direction concerns how people prefer to preserve certain aspects of their life.

8.6.1 Stability

Enjoying keeping one's environment safe and predictable results in a high score for this Direction. Such individuals value reliability and consistency. When it comes to Caesar, however, one could say that he was quite comfortable with change. He certainly did not try to keep everything as is. Yet, there is some nuance here. For instance, the many changes Caesar introduced such as increasing the number of senators and magistrates were aimed at reinforcing and preserving the state and the society he loved and grew up in. All things considered, Caesar is expected to have had a mid-range score on Stability.

8.6.2 Independence

Valuing autonomy, self-reliance and freedom of choice results in a high score for this Direction, and it fits Caesar rather well. He found collaboration difficult and became quickly frustrated when things did not go his way. He was happiest when abroad, managing his provinces and leading his army with little interference from others. Just before his assassination, he was making haste to leave Rome and return to his zone of comfort, namely, commanding an army. No doubt, Caesar's preference for Independence contributed to giving his followers the impression that he needed little feedback.

8.6.3 Irreproachability

Having a desire to live by a personal code of conduct, and deriving great satisfaction from doing so, results in a high score for this Direction. Such individuals find it difficult to compromise on their principles and they hold to them firmly—even at the cost of not attaining their original objectives. Several examples point to Caesar having a high score for this Direction: standing up to Sulla by refusing to divorce Cornelia, his consistent clemency towards foes and adversaries, his constant pursuit of a political philosophy of serving the People and the importance he placed on adhering to his commitments.

8.7 Caesar's Motivational Pattern

If this reverse-engineered personality profile were to come close to Julius Caesar's inner world, then, on balance, it would look like this: in Caesar, we find a principled leader who enjoyed being generous while being self-reliant and seeking little support from others. He preferred to keep his feelings to himself. Furthermore, he was keen on being recognised and admired—an innovative leader who strove to be the best and was willing to work hard to get there. Caesar was highly competitive and leveraged opportunities. Finally, he preferred to be in charge.

To further understand Caesar, it is helpful to analyse how some of the highly scoring and low-scoring Directions interacted with each other. Caesar's willingness to give and forgive resulted in a loyal following and a strong leadership brand. His desire to push and cross boundaries, combined with his appetite for innovation, made him one of history's foremost agents of change. Caesar's achievements resulted from his relentless ambition to achieve, win and do whatever it takes. Overall, his personality traits supported a career that led him to the top of the organisation—the Roman Republic—he served throughout his lifetime.

Caesar's preference for innovation and his proclivity to seek opportunities stimulated him to leverage diversity in his talent management. But there is even more here. Caesar lived the experience of being the 'odd one out', making him a 'lonely leader' without role models to follow. To his peers in the Roman elite, Caesar was different: he was an aristocrat whose family lacked the means to live in a wealthy area of Rome. As for the children with whom he grew up, in this poor neighbourhood, they must also have perceived young Julius as different: he was the only upper-class kid they knew. This is why, for Caesar, social background was not a barrier when hiring talent. Later, Caesar was often mocked for a presumed same-sex relationship, which was perceived as 'unmanly' by Roman society. In his *Life of Caesar* (22), Suetonius recounts a particularly fascinating anecdote. As consul, Caesar received a sneer from some senators about this relationship, saying that he resembled a woman leader. Caesar retorted: 'So what? Queen Semiramis after all reigned in Syria, and the Amazons once ruled over a large part of Asia.' Twelve years later, at first opportunity, Caesar chose a woman leader—Cleopatra—over her brother to rule Egypt (*before* they fell in love, incidentally; Fig. 8.1).

Fig. 8.1 Busts of Caesar and Cleopatra (© Staatliche Museen zu Berlin, Antikensammlung/Johannes Laurentius; CC BY-SA 4.0, Inventarnummer: 1976.10. Reprinted under licence)

Caesar thought little of boundaries except when they infringed on his values, which he held very dear. He usually reacted ferociously when people betrayed his clemency. The cooperation among the triumvirs was limited to helping each other reach individual objectives. Why this group never developed into a real team with a joint purpose can also be explained by looking at Caesar's personality. Although he initiated this coalition, Caesar much preferred self-reliance and not receiving others' support. Furthermore, Caesar struggled to share responsibility and favoured being in charge himself. Finally, his competitiveness made him continuously compare himself to Crassus and Pompey and made him reluctant to strengthen his colleagues' power base.

Where, then, did Caesar's personality really get him into trouble? His principled approach made him eschew Sulla's order to divorce, and his emotional reserve prevented him from explaining why he refused to do so. Instead, Caesar simply walked away, thereby incurring Sulla's wrath. Self-reliant, comfortable with risk and happy to suffer hardships, he survived. But he also endured thanks to the protection he received from his mother and her family: support he must have accepted with some reluctance.

The motivational preferences of high Winning plus high Excelling made Caesar less inclined to compromise, which can be viewed as giving in or as settling for a less-than-optimal outcome. These characteristics were probably reinforced by Caesar's desire for self-reliance and autonomy. The combination of these Directions explains Caesar's difficulties cooperating with others in the Senate.

Garnering satisfaction from Giving and being Irreproachable regarding delivering on promises—combined with his desire for Excellence—could explain why adhering to the commitments he made to his followers was so important to him. This amalgam is likely what drove his decision to cross the Rubicon. Moreover, those working for him may have sensed that and told Caesar what he needed to hear to feel good about this consequential decision. Leadership decisions are seldom 100% rational or conscious.

Another example of his personality causing difficulties was his top-down approach as dictator, which made many senators feel disempowered. Errantly believing that his generosity, which paired so well with his value of clemency, was enough to satisfy these senators, he missed signals of discontent. In addition, the joy he manifestly received from being publicly recognised and admired made him unaware that others could misunderstand this behaviour and interpret as evidence that Caesar desired to become king. He found it difficult to get buy-in for the many changes he introduced from more conservative followers, less motivated by innovation and opportunity.

Finally, the combination of high Excelling and high Gaining Stature means that a leader gets energy from achieving at high levels while simultaneously looking to others to determine what high achievement is. In this way, the leader unconsciously hopes to achieve double emotional satisfaction with one achievement: excellent results and recognition. This pattern explains Caesar's surprise when people did not value his achievements as much as he had expected, to which his speech to the citizens of Hispalis after their revolt testifies. Secondly, *dignitas* was extremely important to Caesar and protecting it was a driving reason for crossing the Rubicon. Yet being recognised as having *dignitas* is about doing what others—the Republic—expect or ask of you, notably excelling in military achievements. Thirdly, equally important to Caesar was restoring the Julii to their former glory, an expectation most strongly held by his mother. Consequently, Caesar may have been less aware of what he really wanted to achieve for himself. Relentlessly performing to meet others' expectations can be mentally exhausting, making it challenging to feel truly happy at work.

Notably, we glimpse this very lack of joy in 45 BC, the year before Caesar's life and career ended violently. Let us look again at Caesar's emotional speech, which he delivered in Hispalis, having barely survived the battle of Munda, which is recorded on the final pages of his *Commentaries on the Spanish War*. Remember that Caesar expressed surprise, disappointment and frustration rather than anger at the locals for having revolted against him. In his mind, he had done so much for them and the province. He was right, of course, for Caesar's laws and organisation regarding the provinces would become one of the pillars of the Roman Empire. Yet the revolt defied what Caesar had expected to receive for his outstanding achievements: admiration.

Following this event, Caesar did not return to Rome with his usual haste, even if he had previously left the city in the middle of his legislative activities to rush to Spain. He did not sit still, though; he perfected the organisation of the provinces in Spain and Gaul as he passed through them on his way to Rome. Perhaps the major uprisings in Spain and, 7 years earlier, in Gaul made him think that he had not yet achieved the level of excellence in provincial government that he felt was expected of him. Perhaps he was exhausted after all his efforts and needed time to mull all this over. Had it been all worth it? Nonetheless, back in Rome after the summer, he went back to being his usual self. He churned out one law and reform after another while preparing for his next campaign. A victory over Parthia would grow the *dignitas* he never stopped striving for and surpass Alexander the Great, a conqueror whom Caesar considered a benchmark.

Bibliography

Greek and Roman Sources

Caesar, G. J., *Commentaries on the Spanish war*.
Plutarch. *Life Caesar*.
Suetonius Tranquillus, G., *Life of Julius Caesar*.

Modern Works

Kets de Vries, M. F. R. (1994). The leadership mystique. *Academy of Management Perspectives, 8*, 73–89.
Management Research Group. (n.d.). https://www.mrg.com/assessments/motivation/
Urnova, A. (2014). *Childhood story as a key to individual patterns of team behavior* [EMCCC thesis, INSEAD].
Vanderbroeck, P. (2010). Lonely leaders: And how organizations can help them. *The International Journal of Mentoring and Coaching, VIII*(1), 83–90.
Vanderbroeck, P. (2012). Crises: Ancient and modern. Understanding an ancient Roman crisis can help us move beyond our own. *Management & Organizational History, 7*(2), 113–131.
Vanderbroeck, P. (2014). *Leadership strategies for women: Lessons from four queens on leadership and career development*. Springer.

9

Conclusion

How to evaluate this most influential leader? Looking uniquely from an executive coaching perspective the following picture emerges: Julius Caesar's success as a leader resulted from his ability to develop his talents into effective leadership behaviours. Where he was less effective, he managed to compensate by leveraging his strengths—although at a certain point, this strategy ultimately failed him. For irrespective of Caesar's achievements and legacy, his career did not end well. That is because he failed to develop the one behaviour (Emotional Intelligence) that, once having reached the very top, really mattered. Rather, he continued to employ the approach that had served him well thus far: using strengths to compensate for weaknesses or changing the context to fit his strengths. Yet this very success may have made him over-confident and less open to feedback. Combined with his impatience for results, Caesar overused certain strengths, and to his detriment. More effective use of feedback could have warned him of this danger and prevented him from getting stabbed in the back.

Innate characteristics and significant experiences and influences during youth and formative years determine one's personality. Returning to Caesar's early life helps us understand the underlying dimensions that influenced his behaviour. For instance, Julius Caesar was born into a family on a mission. By marrying Gaius Sr, Aurelia signed up for that mission. Together, this power couple pursued the family project to restore the Julii to its entitled societal position. Their education and example imbued their children with the same ambition. After Gaius Sr passed away, Aurelia led the family on this same path until their only son could take over. Through marriage, Julius Caesar's elder sisters did the most they could to augment these efforts within the boundaries and restrictions of Rome's patriarchal society.

Young Julius lived through civil strife, which pitted neighbours, friends and family members against each other. The leaders on both sides of that war ordered the violence and cruelty that Caesar witnessed. Soon, he discovered and developed his propensity for risk and other motivators that would make him a truly unique individual. In Caesar's case, the expectations of his employer, that is, the Republic, and his 'shareholders', the People, and the expectations of his family merged into one: to reach *dignitas* through achievements that strengthened both the state and the empire and that would also reinstate the Julii at the apex of Roman society. These joint expectations become most palpable in 63 BC, when Caesar promises his tearful and apprehensive mother on their doorstep that he will return either as elected pontifex maximus or never at all. Indeed, it was clear to Caesar what the Republic, the People and his family expected of him. He identified with these expectations and made them his own. Still, it makes one wonder whether he ever thought about any personal expectations of his own.

Caesar's motivational pattern incited him to live a life of relentless activity, which left little time for self-reflection. If Caesar had had the opportunity in his 30s, 40s or even 50s to review his life story and realise how and why he had become the leader he was, he may have discovered one or two personal goals. If so, this could have imbued him with the same drive to pursue an objective besides those set by others. Who knows, it might have granted him a happier and less energy-consuming final career stage.

Being less overtly receptive to feedback and signalling that he was self-sufficient and did not need advice made it difficult for Caesar to become fully self-aware—which is critical for a leader's success. Importantly, it helps a leader make conscious choices to, in certain situations, adopt behaviours that may contradict one's preference or be emotionally dissatisfying, yet are more conducive to reaching a particular objective. Having a little more self-awareness could have helped Caesar become more conscious of others' agendas and realise that his conduct could be misinterpreted by and disenchant some important followers. In the end, self-awareness might have prevented the abrupt and violent end to Caesar's impressive and unparalleled career.

GPSR Compliance

The European Union's (EU) General Product Safety Regulation (GPSR) is a set of rules that requires consumer products to be safe and our obligations to ensure this.

If you have any concerns about our products, you can contact us on

ProductSafety@springernature.com

In case Publisher is established outside the EU, the EU authorized representative is:

Springer Nature Customer Service Center GmbH
Europaplatz 3
69115 Heidelberg, Germany

www.ingramcontent.com/pod-product-compliance
Lightning Source LLC
LaVergne TN
LVHW010340260326
834688LV00036B/800